Dr. Ngô Thế Vinh gives the reader a frightening picture of what dam construction in China is doing, and could do, to his beloved river."
> Aviva Imhof, *Campaigns Director, International Rivers, Berkeley, California*

The voice of the Southeast Asian people has been raised. To this effect, Dr. Ngô Thế Vinh has made no small contribution.
> Prof. Lê Xuân Khoa, *President emeritus, Southeast Asia Resource Action Center*

We need more people like you working to "Save the Mekong for our future generations" by helping to "Stop destructive developments for the Mekong's sustainability".
> Witoon Pempongsacharoen, *Publisher Watershed, People's Forum on Ecology, TERRA*

Thank you for your book "Mekong, The Occluding River." We applaud your great work.
> Michael Walsh, *President Mississippi River Commission*

In the last 15 years, Dr. Ngô Thế Vinh has intensely focused his attention on the Lancang-Mekong countries. He seeks to protect the cultural heritage and livelihood of the 65 million people living along the banks of this mighty river as well as the future of their children.
> Phạm Phan Long, *PE, Chairman, Viet Ecology Foundation*

In an apparent attempt to sound the alarm on the dangers facing the Mekong and the East Sea, Ngô Thế Vinh was first among the *"Friends of the Mekong Group"* to awaken public opinion to this immediate issue which undoubtedly will remain to be so for many decades to come.

Dr. Trần Ngươn Phiêu, *author of "Phan Văn Hùm –
A Biography and Accomplishment"*

Dr. Ngô Thế Vinh is deeply interested in measures that protect the eco-system of the Mekong. He never tires of drawing the attention of the Vietnamese as well as international public opinion to this issue. He does not live in Vietnam; nevertheless his heart and mind are inextricably anchored to the bed of his river

Prof. Võ Tòng Xuân,
Rector Emeritus, An Giang University, Vietnam

We are in the year 2010, the Mekong is drying up and its ecosystem gradually degraded. Those geological phenomena are no longer predictions but have become undisputed facts that sadly verify Ngô Thế Vinh's forewarnings. He is an author who lives with his time and yet sees well ahead of it.

Ánh Nguyệt, *former RFI Reporter*

I have in front of me a captivating and fascinating book written by Ngô Thế Vinh, not only because it is full of informative news supported by research materials, statistics, real persons and real events but also because it is written by a pen imbued with love of humanity, of life, and of country.

Nguyễn Xuân Hoàng,
author of "The Nonconformist"

Ngô Thế Vinh wrote *"The Nine Dragons Drained Dry, East Sea in Turmoil"* in the later part of the 20th century and then recently *"Mekong – The Occluding River"*. The writer is left with no other recourse than his prophetic vision.

*Phan Nhật Nam,
author of "On The War Trails"*

In my eyes, Ngô Thế Vinh is not merely a medical doctor, more than that, he is a *"pulse taker of rivers"* exploring for ways to mobilize public opinion to rally to the protection of the rivers' natural flow.

*Hoàng Khởi Phong,
author of "Men of One Hundred Yesteryears"*

When the reactions from the governments downstream turned muted, the voice raised by Ngô Thế Vinh and the *"Friends of the Mekong Group"* offers the most significant, objective forum [to discuss the issues pertaining to the Mekong] because it is free of any self-serving regional interests.

*Phạm Phú Minh, former editor 21st Century Magazine,
author of "Hanoi in My Eyes"*

I find, again, in *"Mekong - the Occluding River"*, a call for a socially and ecologically responsible management of the resources of the life-giving river. Dr. Ngô Thế Vinh is a physician, a writer, and most importantly a humanist.

*Prof. Đặng Văn Chất
UCLA and Charles Drew University, California
Editor, The Vietnamese Mayflowers of 1975*

This is an excellent book on the Mekong River, its ecology, the threat posed by dams and the economic, social, historical context of its influences on the lives of the people who lived in the basin of this great river

Dr. Nguyễn Đức Hiệp, *Senior scientist Department of Environment and Climate Change, NSW, Australia*

NGO THE VINH

MEKONG
THE OCCLUDING RIVER
The Tale of a River

iUniverse, Inc.
New York   Bloomington

Jacket photograph by Ngo The Vinh
The Dam of Manwan Hydropower Plant
漫 湾 电 广
Yunnan-China, 2002

MEKONG
THE OCCLUDING RIVER

To The Friends of The Mekong

Mekong
The Occluding River
Ngo The Vinh
Translated from the Vietnamese by
Nguyen Xuan Nhut & Thai Vinh Khiem
Art Cover by Khanh Truong

Copyright © 2010 Ngo The Vinh

Also by Ngo The Vinh
The Green Belt
The Battle of Saigon
The Nine Dragons Drained Dry /
East Sea in Turmoil

All rights reserved. No part of this book may be used or reproduced by any means, graphic, electronic, or mechanical, including photocopying, recording, taping or by any information storage retrieval system without the written permission of the publisher except in the case of brief quotations embodied in critical articles and reviews.

iUniverse books may be ordered through booksellers or by contacting:

iUniverse
1663 Liberty Drive
Bloomington, IN 47403
www.iuniverse.com
1-800-Authors (1-800-288-4677)

Because of the dynamic nature of the Internet, any Web addresses or links contained in this book may have changed since publication and may no longer be valid. The views expressed in this work are solely those of the author and do not necessarily reflect the views of the publisher, and the publisher hereby disclaims any responsibility for them.

ISBN: 978-1-4502-3936-3 (sc)
ISBN: 978-1-4502-3938-7 (dj)
ISBN: 978-1-4502-3937-0 (ebk)

Library of Congress Control Number: 2010909748

Printed in the United States of America
iUniverse rev. date: 07/01/2010

CONTENTS

Preface	1
Chapter one	
A Report from Yunnan	
Encounter With The Manwan Dam	5
Chapter two	
Laos_PDR.com	
Coming Out From Oblivion	51
Chapter three	
The Rise of The Phoenix	
Walking Through The Killing Fields	105
Chapter four	
From The Mỹ Thuận Bridge 2000	
to The Cần Thơ Bridge 2008	171
Chapter five	
Mekong - The Tale of a River	233
In Lieu of Epilogue	
The Mekong & Mississippi	
Sister-River Partnership	255
Advance Testimonials	271
Index	287

ABBREVIATIONS

ASEAN	Association of Southeast Asian Nations
BOOT	Built Own Operate Transfer
CNOOC	Chinese National Offshore Oil Corp
DEA	Drug Enforcement Agency
FCCC	Foreign Correspondents' Club of Cambodia
FEMA	Federal Emergency Management Agency
GMS	Greater Mekong Subregion
ICF	International Crane Foundation
IRN	International Rivers Network
IRRI	International Research Rice Institute
IUCN	International Union for Conservation of Nature
JICA	Japan International Cooperation Agency
MEREM	Mekong Resources Economic Management
MRC	Mekong River Commission
ODA	Official Development Assistance
UNDP	United Nations Development Plan
UNEP	United Nations Environment Programme
UNESCO	U.N. Educational Scientific & Cultural Org.
USAID	U.S. Agency for International Development
WCD	World Commission Dams
WHO	World Health Organization
WTO	World Trade Organization
WWF	World Wild Life Fund

PREFACE

"The Nine Dragons Drained Dry, East Sea in Turmoil" or "Cửu Long Cạn Dòng, Biển Đông Dậy Sóng," a non-fiction book, was published in 2000 to be followed one year later by a second edition. The book is now out of print. Between those years, the author made a number of on-the-scene fieldtrips to places ranging from Yunnan, China, in the north, to Laos, Thailand, Cambodia and the Mekong Delta of Vietnam in the south.

From the vivid collection of travel notes and pictures compiled during his travels in the region, the author wrote this book "Mekong - The Occluding River" or "Mekong Dòng Sông Nghẽn Mạch".

The book adheres to a geographical rather than chronological order. It begins at the upper reaches of the Mekong River and ends at its southernmost tip. Very early on, the author had intended to journey to Tibet, the birthplace of the Mekong, with other than sightseeing purpose in mind. Since Tibet had been relegated to the status of an autonomous region of China, such a trip became no longer feasible due to objective circumstances as well as political sensitivities.

From the data on hand, the author concluded that the degradation of the Mekong is the direct result of destructive

2 MEKONG THE OCCLUDING RIVER

exploitations that brought about a chain reaction of harmful phenomena such as ecological devastation, depletion of natural resources, and environmental pollution. All those disastrous outcomes are taking place sooner and at a more alarming rate than expected. A case in point is the Mekong Delta: a series of gigantic hydroelectric dams built in the upper Mekong caused this river to become increasingly polluted and drained dry. Furthermore, the ensuing drop in its fresh water level gave rise to the intrusion of salt water from the East Sea. As a result, her fluvial food harvests, plentiful only three decades ago, are now negligible.

Then, just two days prior to the New Year of 2007, an earthshaking event stunned all the countries of Southeast Asia as well as the environmentalists. On December 29, 2006 the China News Agency announced that the Beijing government had successfully completed via the Mekong two shipments totaling 300 tons of oil from the port of Chiang Rai in northern Thailand to a port city in Yunnan Province.

Bypassing the straits of Malacca, this new route will serve as a strategic waterway to transport crude oil from the Middle East to feed the industrial cities of Southwestern China. Should any of those tankers be involved in an accident resulting in a large oil spill, the ecological effects on the Mekong would be catastrophic. For this reason, the introduction of that new route is viewed as another fatal blow to the survival of the Mekong - the first being a series of gigantic hydroelectric dams known as the Mekong Cascades in the province of Yunnan. These dams are creating havoc in the lives of the sixty million people who reside in the Lower Mekong Basin.

To this day, there exists no feasible solution to save the Mekong as long as the nations that lie along its banks persist in a free for all exploitation of her resources to serve their own short-term interests while at the same time remaining totally oblivious to the nefarious chain reaction impacts they visit upon their neighbors - Not to mention the long run threat they pose to the very existence of the Mekong herself.

The worst offender among them is none other than China. So far, this country situated at the northernmost part of the Mekong is the only one that has built three gigantic hydroelectric dams across the main current of the Mekong. According to plan, eleven more remain to be built to complete the projected number of dams in the Mekong Cascades. The other countries did not behave any better. The Thai government is contemplating the implementation of two ambitious and costly projects that will significantly divert the waters of four tributaries from the Mekong. With its dream of becoming the "Kuwait of hydropower of Southeast Asia" Laos is building "pocket" hydroelectric dams on its many small rivers to produce electricity for export as well as domestic consumption. Vietnam has constructed the Yali hydroelectric dams on the Sesan River. The regrettable thing is that many of the rivers in those countries are tributaries that feed their waters to the Mekong's main current.

To save the Mekong, we call upon all the nations that benefit from the life-giving water of this river to show a common concern for and observe the "Spirit of the Mekong" in the implementation of all their exploitation and development projects.

To achieve this end, there must be a concerted and sustained commitment to cooperate from all interested parties.

NGÔ THẾ VINH, M.D.
Mekong Delta August, 2006
California January, 2010

A REPORT FROM YUNNAN ENCOUNTER WITH THE MANWAN DAM

"Every body lives downstream"
(World Water Day 03-22-1999)

Nowadays, taking a trip to China is no longer the hurdle it once was. It gets even better if you are part of a guided tour with a predetermined itinerary. To enter China for personal reasons, however, is another story. The recently introduced "Renovation" policy did not negate the fact that the country still remains basically a totalitarian and police state highly suspicious of newspersons, writers or any professions dealing with public communication including missionary work.

Therefore, even though the purpose of my fieldtrip is to study the upper Mekong and the dams of Yunnan, the best course of action for me is to declare tourism as the purpose of my travel and the profession definitely not newsman. In addition, I am also fully aware that if one has to write down the details of one's journey, it is preferable to leave out the sensitive name of "Tibet" altogether.

Once a tourist arrives in China, the first obstacle he or she encounters is the language barrier. Four months prior to departure my friend, Dr. Trần Huy Bích, introduced me to Mr. Trương Khánh Tạo who lived in the state of Oklahoma. Mr. Tạo in turn put in a good word for me with his close comrade-in-arms from the revolutionary years, Mr. Hoàng Cương, who has been stranded in Kunming since 1946. Having lived in China for more than half a century, he speaks Chinese fluently and expressed his willingness to help me upon my arrival in September. However, as my departure time drew near I learned that due to personal reasons Mr. Cương had to leave for Vietnam and would not be able to meet me in Yunnan as planned. Since the idea of changing my work schedule at the hospital looked rather daunting to me, I decided to go ahead with the trip while at the same time trying to reassure myself with the thought that once over there I could always "play it by ear". With the same happy go lucky frame of mind I also proceeded with my journey to Laos and Cambodia as intended.

Before leaving, I was deeply moved by the news that Mr. Trương Khánh Tạo had passed away. On a personal note, I would like to dedicate this writing about my sojourn in Yunnan to Mr. Tạo and his family in his memory.

KUNMING TODAY

After an uneventful flight, the China Southern airliner departing from Los Angeles landed in Guangzhou, one of the large and modern cities in Southern China. From there, I boarded another plane, destination Kunming, the capital of Yunnan Province. China is a gigantic land in many senses. Yunnan, one of the provinces of China, covers an area of 394,000 km^2 (larger than Vietnam's 340,000 km^2) and has 35 million inhabitants (approximately less than half of Vietnam's population).

A bird view of Kunming from the airplane window showed

that it resembled any big city in the West.

No where could be found the image of a Kunming depicted as "a remote, sleepy Oriental town" by the legendary American Air Force general Claire Chennault of the "Flying Tigers" who was stationed there during the Second World War.

You must be a former resident of Kunming to appreciate upon your return how extensive and complete a transformation the city has gone through:

"Kunming, our home, fifty years ago and now are two totally different cities. Gone are the old houses and narrow streets. In their place now stand huge buildings and wide boulevards with separate lanes for pedestrians and bicyclists. Large overpasses arch over the streets. Underneath are tunnels for pedestrians to cross the streets and shop at the stores along their walls.

"It could be said that the Kunming of half a century ago was razed to the ground to make room for a western style city. On my first day back, unable to reestablish contact with an old friend, I was at a loss trying to recognize the familiar places of the past. The climate in Kunming is moderate - neither too hot nor too cold all year round. The words Tam once uttered still resound in my ears: 'If I can choose a place to live when I retire it'd be Kunming not Đà Lạt.'"

That's how Mr. Trương Khánh Tạo felt on his return to Kunming.

To help the reader better understand the gist of the above quotation, a short elaboration here seems in order: Tam, whose full name is Nguyễn Tường Tam was born in Hải Dương, North Vietnam (1905-1963). He is also known by his pen name Nhất Linh. In his early years, he worked as the editor of the newspapers Phong Hóa and Ngày Nay. By founding the Tự Lực Văn Đoàn or Self-Reliance Literary Movement, he left an indelible mark in the cultural life of Vietnam. His three brothers Nguyễn Tường

Long / pen name: Hoàng Đạo, Nguyễn Tường Lân / pen name: Thạch Lam and Nguyễn Tường Bách / pen name: Viễn Sơn were also gifted writers. This Movement played a major role in the popularization of the Quốc Ngữ, the present day romanized alphabet of Vietnam. In addition to his literary works, Tam also was actively involved in politics. In 1963 he committed suicide in protest against the government of South Vietnam.

The city of Đà Lạt Tam referred to is the capital of Lâm Đồng Province, the home of 32 ethnic minorities in Vietnam. Located at 1,500 meters above sea level on the Lang Biang Plateau of Central Vietnam, it is blessed with a temperate climate. Its beautiful landscape is generously endowed with lakes, waterfalls and lush vegetation. Originally built for the French, its Swiss charm and abundance of flowers, especially roses and orchids, only add to its reputation as a favorite vacation place for many.

Wu, a 28 years old robust young man, was the first Yunnanese I came in contact with. A driver by profession, he earned his living by picking up travelers at the airport. Speaking fluent English he gave the impression of being a knowledgeable person. He took us to the Kunming Holiday Inn, a 4 star-242 room hotel, built according to American standards. At this hotel I expected to be spared an immediate confrontation with the language barrier and also find a driver working for a travel agency who can speak some English.

On the way from the airport Wu confided in us that the rapid transformation of Kunming only occurred during the last decade. "Since the day of the abundant supply of electricity from the Manwan Dam."

"At an altitude of 2,000 meters above sea level, instead of an old, dusty, and garbage strewn Kunming you have right before your eyes a different city" He added.

Driving inside the city on the way to the hotel, if you disregard the army of bicyclists, you would feel like being in any modern American city. The streets were wide and beautifully decorated with colorful wreaths of flowers. The cleanliness of the streets was utterly amazing.

With a touch of pride in his voice Wu explained: "The people of Kunming realize that this is their city. They love it and want to keep it clean and beautiful."

The challenge of clothing and feeding 1.2 billion souls seemed to me a thing of the past. That was the impression I had during my stay in Kunming. Not a single beggar in sight. Here and there in the streets, healthy looking sanitation workers wearing work uniforms still swept with brooms and picked up every strand of trash with pincers the traditional way. In the following days, I witnessed the same scene of sanitation workers sweeping the highways very far away from the cities and keeping them shining clean.

After a few exchanges with Wu on the way, I came to the very quick decision to use him and his Mitsubishi for the length of my stay in Kunming.

In the afternoon of the first day, Wu took us sightseeing the provincial capital, including the rare street corners of Old Kunming which have survived with their ancient houses topped by curved roofs covered with moss – the unmistakable signs of the passing of time. Purportedly those houses were kept standing there as a living contrast between tradition and modernization.

A visit to the Yunnan University revealed to me that it had not changed much from the picture Hứa Bảo Liên painted in her family autobiography *"Nguyễn Tường Bách and I"*: "This is the largest university in the province. It occupies an entire big hill covered by tall, colossal pine trees. Squirrels jump from one tree branch to another at the speed of flying arrows. To reach the campus one has to climb 99 stone steps. On the school premise are erected graceful and sturdy structures with walls built uniquely with red bricks."

On the day I came, the fast-footed squirrels were still around. They appeared utterly impervious to the turbulent years of the revolution in Vietnam over half a century ago or to the perilous days its famous children with names like Nhất Linh Nguyễn Tường Tam, Hoàng Đạo Nguyễn Tường Long, Viễn Sơn Nguyễn Tường Bách had to endure.

Alas! The integrity of the buildings on the Yunnan University campus itself was under siege. Before our very own eyes ancient houses hundreds of years old were being demolished brick by brick to make room for modern buildings.

The time I planned for the trip was limited yet my objective was crystal clear: to go to the head source of the Lancang Jiang, the Chinese name for the upper Mekong. I probed and probed to find out whether Wu or his connections could be of any help for me to achieve that goal.

Through our conversations I learned that Wu, a Han, graduated from a four-year college. He is married and the couple has a young child. A former mathematics teacher, he earned a modest salary. When the Chinese government introduced its "Open Door Policy" Wu quit his job to work as a taxi driver. Thanks to his command of English, he also acted as a tour guide and his income grew six folds to about US$ 600 a month. It allowed him to buy a house on installments and go from renter to owner. He expected to pay his house off twenty years down the road.

Self confident, Wu expressed his views forcefully on the politics and social issues of China. To name a few: Taiwan categorically is a province of China. That's it. No further discussions needed. Mao Tse Tung still deserves respect. The Chinese people owe a debt of gratitude to Dang Xiao Ping because he engineered an era of development and prosperity for the country. What about Jiang

Zemin? Just so so. He's too soft especially toward the Americans. It made the Chinese people angry. For example: He let an American plane land on the Hainan Island instead of ordering it shot down. On the other hand it gave China the opportunity to learn more about the aerial intelligence gathering technology of the Americans. The Hainan Island incident Wu mentioned took place on April 1, 2001 over the East Sea resulting in an international crisis between the US and China. A U.S. Navy EP-3 signal reconnaissance aircraft collided with a People's Liberation Army Navy J-8 jet fighter causing the death of the Chinese pilot while the EP-3 was forced to make an emergency landing on Hainan. The American crew of 24 was detained, interrogated and released 10 days later after the US issued a "letter of the two 'sorry'" to the Chinese government. The plane was then disassembled and returned three months later.

My naiveté did not go so far as to believe that taxi drivers and tour guides had no connections with the secret service. Consequently, I only asked harmless questions while trying my best to stay clear from all serious discussions.

That night, Wu took us to a restaurant famous for a simple dish called *"Across-the-bridge noodles"*. We were served a bowl of steaming hot broth covered with a thick layer of fat. All that we needed to do was to dump in some noodle, thin slices of meat, a teaspoon of red pepper and we were set. It's like a hot pot dish minus the pot. The meal was hot in its fullest sense!

The waitresses were Han. However, they were all dressed in the bright and colorful costumes of the Yi tribe. Visitors to Yunnan who made their acquaintance with this dish were unfailingly told the romantic anecdote behind its origin.

During the Quing Dynasty, a poor student was determined to pass the mandarin examination at the capital. To that end, he left his family and moved to a small island in the middle of a lake to devote himself to his studies. Every day his young wife had to cross a long bamboo bridge to bring him his meals. By the time she arrived the food had unavoidably turned cold. One day she inadvertently found out that if she covered the soup with a thick layer of fat it would stay hot until the time she saw her husband.

Although the dish was claimed to be "super delicious" we found it impossible to follow Wu's example and gulp down a jumbo size bowl of animal fat to bring the dinner to a grand finale. Greasy, steaming hot, spicy hot are the defining characteristics of the dishes from Yunnan.

On our first night in Yunnan, from the Holiday Inn hotel, we could see the city of Kunming sparkling below us. Naturally it was lit by the power from the Manwan Hydroelectric Dam, the first in a series of 14 to be built in steps along the Upper Mekong. Present day Kunming stood as a symbol of the development in Yunnan. What price the people in the Mekong Delta and the nations lying downstream must pay for it still remains an unanswered question.

SHILIN STONE FOREST

Driving along the 126 kilometers of Expressway 320 in the southeastern direction we could see endless verdant orchards and occasional small brooks and streams. Along the roadsides, all kinds of fruits freshly cut with leaves and branches still connected to the stems were on display for sale to the tourists. To name a few: mangosteens, pears, peaches, persimmons... Yunnan is reputed for its fruits. Peaches from Yunnan are sought after for their aroma and sweetness. I had never before set my eyes till now on such beautiful and big pears (bowl size) with skins so smooth and green. They would make exceptional gifts from Yunnan. Sadly, they were banned from import into the United States. Wu mentioned that the soil of the Yunnan plateau is suitable for growing fruits but not grains. Consequently good rice had to be imported from Thailand.

The railroad connecting Kunming to Hanoi-Haiphong built during the French time (1904-1910) has been replaced by a modern one. The expressway was constantly crowded in both directions with big trucks named Dong Feng or East Wind that were manufactured in China. From the capital city of Kunming going east you would be heading toward Shanghai. A system of eight lane freeways was being constructed to meet the transportation needs of the economic expansion in Kunming. At intervals along the route, you could stop for gas at stations owned by Petro China boasting 20 to 30 pumps each. Who can tell how many oil barrels supplied to those stations came from the archipelago of Paracels and Spratlys? Who can tell with certainty whether China has actually exploited the oil in that archipelago? Two giant companies named China Telecom and China Mobile vied with each other to supply the much-in-demand cellular phones for the 1.2 billion strong Chinese market.

We can safely assert that the Stone Forest, Himalayan chains and the high plateau of Tibet share a common birthday. Of the three, Tibet represents a case of special interest to us. It is the cradle of all the major rivers that serve as the lifeline of Asia - Among them the Mekong. In other words, those three regions have the same geological history. Approximately 300 million years ago, two pre-continental landmasses collided creating a tremendous pressure that pushed northward and formed the spectacular topography now known as the Himalayan chains and Central Asia. The Stone Forest covers an area of 80 hectares and is claimed to be a natural wonder of Yunnan. It was originally a seabed that was lifted up. Since then the seawater had completely receded leaving behind limestone mountain ranges. With the passing of time, water and wind erosion sculptured them into peculiar and bizarre looking peaks or crisscrossing crevasses. As a result, instead of a forest of green trees we have a dense forest of "stone trees" in all shape and form giving free rein to the imagination of the Yunnanese who came up with creative and romantic names for them: pool of swords, small elephant, immortal mushroom...

Yunnan, the land of anecdotes – When visiting the Stone Forest, one could not fail to hear the story of a handsome man named Ahei who ventured into the Stone Forest to rescue the beautiful Ashima being held captive there. Alas! A wicked sorcerer conjured up a torrential rain to sweep Ahei out of the cave. Thus Ashima and Ahei became separated forever. Nevertheless her soul always returned to the Stone Forest in the form of echoes that resounded throughout the place. Should one enter the Stone Forest alone, one would be lost in this labyrinth with little hope of finding the way out.

During this season of the year, the majority of the visitors were Chinese. With a more affluent life style came the need to travel and visit an immense land of countless beautiful landscapes without having to apply for visas as it would be the case if one visited a foreign country. Groups of twenty each thronged behind young female tour guides holding flags in different colors for easy recognition. Our group only consisted of three. Wu was so familiar with the roads and ways of the Stone Forest that he could read it like an open book.

The area around the Stone Forest was teeming with Han coeds wearing heavy make-ups and the vibrantly dyed costumes of the Yi minority. They were ever ready to pose or serve as guides for the tourists.

A high level of commercialization could easily be observed

at all tourism sites from the ancient temples of Angkor at Siem Reap to the Shilin Stone Forest in Yunnan. Every night a high-tech "sound and light" show was performed by the Lotus pond outside the Stone Forest. It was done in a grand scale using laser lights to relate the tale of Ashima. Though we were told it was a highly popular attraction, we did not have the time to spare for the show that night.

On the way back to Kunming the same day, I teased Wu with the remark that, being a guide, how could he forget to bring along a red flag. I also did not forget to ask if he knew the song "The East is Red"? Without waiting to be coaxed, Wu started to sing in a very spirited and warm voice. The image of the Red Guards came back to life in our mind even though Wu was not born at that time yet.

After a trial period of two days, Wu proved to be a resourceful and equally reliable individual. I inquired once more with him about the Manwan Dam, the supply source of electricity for the provincial city of Kunming. The only information Wu could come up with was that it is located about 500 kilometers south of Kunming midway to Jinghong. The road leading to the place was mountainous with several sections in disrepair but still drivable if there was no rain or storm.

Considering that his Mitsubishi had only four cylinders and more than 100,000 miles on the odometer, I urged Wu to rent for us a Jeep-like vehicle suitable for mountainous terrains. In a voice full of confidence he replied that though his car was old it ran better than the new ones and could easily negotiate the round-trip to Manwan so long as we had enough gas and oil.

That was enough to convince me to embark on the trip to Manwan the very next morning.

THE FIRST DAM – THE HISTORIC DAM

16 MEKONG THE OCCLUDING RIVER

Manwan (Sino-Vietnamese name: Mạn Loan), the first hydroelectric dam in Yunnan, was located right at the mid point of the Langcang Jiang. It had an output of 1,500 Megawatt and was the first hydroelectric dam being operated as a joint venture between the central and local governments. Its construction costs exceeded US$ 1 billion or 3.8 billion yuans.

It must be said that the Manwan Dam played a crucial role in the electrification, industrialization and urbanization of the entire Southwest of China. Thanks to it, this region could catch up with or even rival the prosperous cities in the East and Northeast.

Even though the plan to build the dam dated back to the 1970's, a lack of fund forced the official ground breaking ceremony to be delayed until May of 1986. The water diversion efforts were completed in October of the following year. The dam reaches 99 meters in height and sits astride the river between two mountain ranges running parallel to its banks. As for the sidewalls they are 35 stories high. The first unit went into operation on June 30, 1993 and two years later; on June 28, 1995; the remaining five units followed suit as called for in the first phase of the project.

At this point, it would be advisable to recall a noteworthy event that was reported in the middle of 1993 and had since become the subject of much discussion. At the time, a sudden drop in the water level was registered downstream of the Mekong. It did not happen during the dry season either. Only then did the people find out that the building of the Manwan Dam had come to an end and the process of diverting the waters of the Mekong into its reservoirs had begun. The Chinese government did not find it necessary to advise the countries lying south of its border of its actions. The Manwan Dam alone requires the retention of up to 20% of the water flow in the main current of the Mekong that meanders through Yunnan.

In the aftermath of that event, people began to voice their

concern about the impacts caused by the dams of the Mekong Cascades in Yunnan. A total lack of information on the part of the Chinese government only served to feed on those concerns.

The design and construction of the first dam at Manwan was acclaimed to be "a historic achievement" by the Yunnan Provincial Electric Power Bureau. It introduced this institution to the Mekong's enormous potentials for hydroelectricity generation and the exceptional suitability for the building of other mammoth, high yield hydroelectric generators with extra-high voltage distribution grids.

The construction of additional hydroelectric dams in the Mekong Cascades would give further impetus to the social and economic development of not only Yunnan Province but also facilitate the implementation of the strategy of "transferring and distributing electricity from Yunnan to the other provinces in China".

As soon as the Manwan Project came to fruition, the top management of the installation set this guideline for the entire workforce at the dam: "work hard, make concerted efforts, be strict, meticulous and realistic, and strive for a first class enterprise. It has overcome various difficulties, difficult circumstances, more equipment defects, less experience and other difficulties so as to realize the three historic leaps, thus scoring great successes in building an enterprise that is advanced both materially and culturally and ideologically." [sic]. [Source: From a pamphlet issued by Manwan Hydropower Plant of Yunnan Province (Manwan Town, Yunxian County, Yunnan Province)]

In December of 1996, the Party Committee and government of Yunnan awarded the title "Civilized Unit at Provincial Level" to the Manwan Dam. At the same time the dam was also named "Vanguard Unit" by the Yunnan Provincial Electric Power Bureau for five straight years. In April of 1998, the State Power

Corporation of China designated it as "One of the National 400 Best Advanced Units in afforestation". Then in March of 1999, the same State Power Corporation went a step further and recognized Manwan as a "Creating First Class Enterprise". This was a rare honor considering that for several consecutive years, as a major hydroelectric installation, Manwan has satisfactorily met all operation standards while operating solely with domestically made equipments.

Faced with the new opportunities and challenges of the 21st century, the Manwan Hydropower Plant will strive to attain the international standards for modernization and automation prevalent at the other hydroelectric units in the world in order to meet the demand for energy of the future.

Our third day in Yunnan was truly a memorable one! In the early morning we departed from Kunming by car for a 500 km ride to visit a desolate area in the South that even our driver cum tour guide confessed he never set foot in before.

Bidding goodbye to Kunming we headed west on the new expressway connecting Kunming to the ancient citadel of Dali. This expressway was a gift from the central government to the people of Yunnan on the occasion of the Kunming's 1999 World Horticultural Exhibition. It was quite modern, complete with signs in English and a tunnel built under the mountains measuring almost 4 kilometers long. It could compare favorably with any of its American counterparts. Using this expressway one could reduce the driving time between Kunming and Dali from 12 to 4 or 5 hours. Along this scenic route, we drove pass mountains and valleys covered with verdant foliage and flanked by villages with houses boasting thick red brick walls and gray curved roofs or the occasional elevated dome of a Muslim mosque. The provinces of Yunnan and Xinjiang are traditionally populated by a large number of Muslims called Hui by the Han Chinese.

Those descendants of the invading Mongols in the 13th century are at the root of frequent uprisings and thus viewed as a threat to the national security of China. According to Wu, the Hui are gifted tradesmen. Benefiting from their tax-exempt status, they enjoyed a rather comfortable standard of living.

Good road called for fast driving. Therefore, it was no surprise that less than half way into our trip we witnessed at least three car accidents including a fatal one. It involved a large East Wind truck leaving blood splattered marks and a multitude of shattered glass on the road.

The drivers of those trucks were usually very young - in their early twenties. They passed each other at breakneck speed, heedless of the traffic tickets or even the suspensions of driver licenses that might be waiting for them at the police roadblocks further down the road.

After having traveled more than 150 kilometer of the 500 kilometers long trip on the 320 expressway in the direction of Dali, our driver turned into national route 214 heading south toward the Manwan Dam. At that point I was able to figure out the codes used to name the highways in Yunnan. The number "3" of expressway 320 indicated an East West axis while the number "2" of national route 214 referred to a North South one. The same applied to the letters on the license plates: the letter "A" showed that the car was from Kunming, "L" Dali, "K" Jinghong, and "J" Simao.

In the opposite direction, a bus covered with red dust bearing the "K" license plate of Jinghong was taking an overload of passengers to Dali. If everything went well it would be another day and night before they reached their destination.

On the ride to the south we had to stop at every three-way intersection to ask for directions. Some of the local people had never heard of the name "Manwan". Those who did might not know about its location. Wu spoke the local dialect well. Besides, he was patient, so eventually we were able to find our way. The car passed by villages and paddies covered with golden ripe rice stalks. Nowadays, each family could own a private lot of land. Depending on how hard they sweated they could afford a new house, a refrigerator, a TV set and so on.

Here school children were dressed in comfortable clothes while their counterparts in the Mekong Delta were going bare foot. Looking at a boy or a girl, one cannot help but wonder whether he or she is the "only child of the family" as called for by the official family planning policy. For ages, the Chinese prefer to have many children. Aware of Wu's family situation I asked him what would happen if his wife decided to have a second child. "That's unthinkable! And if you do, you'll have to pay a very dear price for it!" Wu replied. In a society of 1.2 billion souls, the enforcement of the population control policy of one child per family for the sake of economic development is not an easy task unless you are dealing with a totalitarian state. You could still see now and then children wearing red scarves around their necks albeit carrying "Mickey Mouse" backpacks on their shoulders. Wu explained that those were students who had outstanding grades or politically correct background. "What we are witnessing now in Vietnam is probably only a second-rate copy of the Chinese original except that it's twenty years behind". One could not fail to recall the statement made by Mr. Lê Khả Phiêu, the Secretary General of the Vietnamese Communist Party: *"If China succeeds in its reforms, we'll succeed, if China fails, we fail"* (FEER 06/22/2000). [sic] This amazing statement made quite a few Vietnamese frown in disbelief and shame.

As midday drew to a close, we had covered more than half of the way. So far we had enjoyed a relatively smooth ride. Now came the fun part. It's time for the car to climb the pass. A narrow one-lane road stretched out to the far horizon ahead of us. It was all going up the hill and down the ravine over and over again like riding in a roller coaster. The traffic was not heavy but it moved in both directions. This road was narrow and tortuous similar to the one between Vang Vieng and Luang Prabang in Laos.

Though the road was narrow, the daredevil drivers invariably drove in the middle of the way as if they owned it mindless of the oncoming traffic. Whenever two cars faced each other, it was then only a question of near misses. The faint of heart who can't resist looking down the ravine, would soon find it hard to stomach the seemingly unending trip.

Wu had a good grip on the wheel. Each time a risky situation arose he would murmur: "Safety first" as if to reassure himself and his passengers. Although confident in Wu's driving skill I was still reminded that safety is a two-way proposition. It involved both our car and the others. Could it be that after having survived the many years of fighting during the Vietnam War I would end up lifeless in a ravine due to an East Wind. I am referring here to the heavy-duty Dong Feng trucks that plied the roads and ways of Yunnan.

Dark clouds covered the sky. It was raining hard ahead of us. Our vehicle had to slow down to a crawl at a section of the road strewn with loose rocks. That was when we really felt for Wu's car. It was built for city driving not mountain climbing where its tires had to go over rocks with sharp edges or deep potholes, running the risk of hitting the road with its undercarriage. Probably Wu himself did not expect to drive on roads in such bad condition. He boasted of having been in worse situations and of taking French or German tourists in the same car on ten-day journeys from Kunming to Lhasa, the capital of Tibet. Young, self-confident, optimistic – Could he represent, before our eyes, the living symbol of the future of China?

What's more, the fuel tank was running almost empty with the gas needle nearing the "E" mark. Wu brushed all our warnings aside with the assertion that we still had enough gas to go a long way yet. At the altitude of 2,500 meters the tiny car still managed to wind its way up the slope. "We are not driving on flat land. Climbing up the car would consume more gas" I warned Wu. Not trying to appear obstinate Wu took a rosy approach to the situation with this explanation: "But on the way down it would consume less". An understandable way of reasoning for a former teacher of mathematics which is a science based on pure logic and not always relevant to real life. However it was Wu who was proven right at the end. The car did make it haltingly to a small gas station where we were charged a hefty sum of money for the reassurance of having a full tank to drive on.

Like a "no man's land", the thick and luxuriant green color of the rain forest covering the mountain slopes loomed large before us. It then became apparent to us why only a few people knew the location of the Manwan Dam. The high voltage cables dangling from gigantic electric poles signaled to us that we were approaching the dam. A glance at the odometer gave us a rough estimate we were 40 to 50 kilometers from our destination and could expect some rough ride ahead.

We drove by a small waterfall rushing down from a high mountain slope. Tiny white water mist sprinkled the road just enough to render it wet. From our vantage point looking down at the valley below we could see cradled between the long arms of two mountain ranges the huge reservoir lake of the Manwan Dam sparkling under the bright sunlight. We were still too far away to make out the contours of the dam.

We passed a mountain village then started to coast down a narrow road leading into a valley. Once more Wu had to stop for directions and was told we were heading the right way. Though hidden by the bushes, the sound of running water betrayed the existence of a nearby river. Finally the river made its appearance. Looking upstream we could recognize the silhouette of the dam.

One last bridge to cross before we could reach the left bank and actually enter the construction site of the Manwan Hydroelectric dam. A boundary marker at the head of the bridge greeted us with the inscription: "YUNXIAN – MANWANZHEN" (Yunxian District – Manwan City).

Small houses, a few grocery shops and restaurants bordered the road.

A guard station stood at the gate. On its wall hung an imposing plate engraved with two glistening lines of scripts in Chinese and English: "YUNNAN MANWAN POWER GENERATING Co. Ltd". Once inside, we were greeted by the nearest large and multi-storied public office building. Further back, we could distinguish the structure of a mess hall and the workers' residential quarters that consisted of three to four story buildings going up the hillsides. There was also a guesthouse used as a hotel for the visitors. Wu's resourcefulness made us feel at home in this strange place. He did not encounter any problems booking for us two rooms on the fourth floor of the hotel. The back window of our room offered a panoramic view of a stretch of the Mekong.

At that time we did not have any idea how long we were going to stay there. Even though our bodies felt sore after the long trip, I still asked Wu to take us on a tour of the place. In the warm colors of the sunset, the light was hardly ideal for photographic endeavors. However, this was the only occasion for me to take pictures of the dam. Before my departure from the United States I could not imagine the day I would set foot in this place! We drove along the right bank. It must be around 4 or 5 o'clock in the afternoon. The area was rather deserted probably because the workers were still in the middle of a break. I did not want to miss this opportunity and it took me no time to use up two rolls of film to photograph the landmarks of Manwan.

Standing on a high bank with the water flowing below I tried my best to come as close as possible to the foot of the dam. My friend and fellow traveler always acted as a "safety brake" for me. He did not want me to linger even a minute longer at a location which was definitely not designated as a "tourism spot" to take so many pictures.

I fully understood that regardless of its "open door" policy China still remained at the core a "totalitarian" state. Limitations on matters of information and communication including picture taking made up the staple features of the official policy. Nevertheless its enforcement varied with the time, place and officials involved - Not to mention the luck of the newsperson himself.

Officially, no pictures were allowed of military installations, harbors, airports, rail stations and also bridges at strategic locations. The Manwan Hydroelectric Dam that supplied electricity to the entire Yunnan Province and was defended by the armed forces undoubtedly must fall within the classification of strategic military installations.

This fact did not escape me. Nevertheless, those hydroelectric dams and bridges over the Mekong constituted the very focus of my trip. Consequently, I traveled light to save room for two cameras and a good supply of high-speed rolls of film. Moreover, I did not forget to pack in my luggage a good dose of optimism mixed with some mental preparations to ready myself for the worst. I might return empty handed or even worse like falling victim to fabricated accusations and finding myself implicated in precarious situations. Once I finished taking those two rolls of film I felt I had done enough for my first hours with the Manwan

Dam.

SUNSET ON THE MEKONG

Back at the hotel we were shown the way to the employee mess hall for dinner. This communal eating facility was clean and roomy. Engineers and workers of all kinds looked young. They all rubbed shoulders at the tables. It was from the differences in their facial features that helped us guess the types of work they do. A man entered the mess hall holding a big white enameled bowl in his hand. The eyeglasses he wore added an air of intelligence to his young face.

The metallic enameled bowl used to contain the meal gave me a flashback to the more than three long years I endured in the reeducation camps - or more precisely concentration camps - in my homeland. Overwhelmed by the memory, I asked Wu to take us to any small restaurant downtown. We ended up at a place with no business sign and furnished with a few tables and chairs.

Unexpectedly, a pleasant surprise awaited us there: from the rear of the restaurant we could look down on the sandy bank and water of the Mekong. The river still flowed but with a whimper. It had run out of breath after being held stagnant in the reservoir before being run through the giant 675 ton turbines of the Manwan Dam. Exhausted the current could no longer whip up the roaring waves of the good old days.

On the other bank we could see mountains covered by the dense green foliage of the jungle. The sun had set behind the mountaintop.

Another sunset on the Mekong! That day we tasted for the first time the local dishes of the Yunnan high plateau: sautéed mushrooms, grilled bamboo shoots, fried bee nests and naturally one could not forget fresh fish caught from the Mekong.

FROM MANWAN TO THE PARTY COMMITTEE OF KUNMING

Things appeared calm on the surface but I did not feel at ease staying any longer in the Manwan area. I decided to leave early the following morning. In his over zealousness Wu came up with the idea of booking us on a visit inside the generators' room because he had heard that there were guided tours of that nature.

We took our breakfast at a small place located in front of the installation. The Arabic handwriting on the business sign was a telltale indication that the owner was a Hui, a Muslim.

After breakfast, Wu led us to the Administrative Office of Manwan. When the head of the office learned that we were foreigners, she asked us to wait for her to report to her superiors. About ten minutes later, a lady in a short blouse with austere demeanors that I took to be from the Organization Office, a seemingly benign name for the Security Office, made her appearance. She engaged in a lengthy discussion with Wu and informed him that the tours he had in mind were reserved for the local people. Since this was the first time that foreign nationals were involved, she would need to obtain the final approval from the Party Committee. Truly Wu had placed me in an intractable situation since it was quite unwise for us to get ourselves enmeshed with such burdensome bureaucracy. The moment the lady stepped out of the room I sounded retreat and told Wu that we should drop the idea of the tour because I did not think we had enough time. However, both of us were kept willy-nilly waiting there. We found ourselves between a rock and a hard place. I tried to keep a straight face but deep down I felt like having an army of ants crawling in my stomach. All the while I had to prepare myself for the eventuality I might have to fend off endless questions that might come my way.

Time seemed to drag on at an excruciatingly slow pace.

Finally the lady from the Organization Office returned. This time she was very courteous and talked to me directly using Wu as interpreter. I was advised that the Manwan Committee did not turn down my request but if I had a valid reason for the visit I should address it to the Party Committee of Kunming Electric Power Section. Strange as it might seem, the rejection brought great relief to my soul. Thanks to that red tape, that cumbersome bureaucracy, I was free to leave Manwan with no further ado. In my mind I did not entertain the slightest intention of returning to Manwan any day soon to seek an official authorization from the Kunming Party Committee.

WITH THE CORMORANTS ON THE ERHAI LAKE

We left Manwan by car and arrived at the ancient citadel of Dali in the late afternoon. Dali was often referred to as the small Katmandu of Yunnan. It is a land of many beautiful landscapes and historical sites where more than one million Bai, the heirs to a culture reaching back over three thousand years, lived. In the 7th century the state of Nanzhao rose to preeminence and grew powerful enough to defeat the T'ang Dynasty troops in the following century. Going into the tenth century Nanzhao became known as the kingdom of Dali and was made an integral part of China along with the entire region of Yunnan during the Mongol Yuan rule four centuries later.

Still standing there to be admired were ancient buildings like the 9th century Three Pagodas (Dali San Ta) and the old stone houses bordering the tortuous cobblestone roads. Actually the real ancient Dali Citadel only existed in name. Its original formidable stone walls and gates have fallen in total ruins. A replica model was erected in its place. The inside of the new walls housed jewelry and souvenir stores to cater to the tourists. Strolling from the North to the South Gate of the ancient citadel along the narrow tile-covered alleys lined with restaurants and café internet shops, we mingled with throngs of tourists led by their Han guides. These ladies wore the same type of makeup used by airline stewardesses but their colorful attires were those of the Bai minority.

To the West of Dali lie multiple mountain ranges and to the East Erhai Lake. This is the second largest lake in Yunnan and its fresh water feeds into the Mekong through a tributary named Xi'er. Considered a "fairy land" by the Bai, this lake is very deep and holds more than forty varieties of fish. Most famous among them is the "bow fish". A carp like fish, it has the ability to hold its tail in its mouth before releasing it and spring up high above the water. Yunnan is located deep inland but the Yunnanese like to use words with marine connotations to name their big lakes. A pouring rain fell on Dali all night long until the following morning. Finally the sun showed up. The weather was good enough to call for half a day of fishing with cormorants on the Erhai Lake.

Our car gingerly made its way on a stone path between two paddies to reach a small fishing village on the west bank of Erhai Lake where we met a well tanned Bai fisherman in his late fifties. He lived with a flock of about twenty well domesticated cormorants.

At the approach of the visitors the birds were set free from their cages. They joyfully frolicked at our feet stretching their legs and wings. Instead of using rings the man took out a bundle of bamboo strips to tie them deftly in swift movements of the hands around the birds' necks – just tight enough to prevent the fowls from swallowing the big fish they caught. Then he signaled the birds to jump into the water and swim alongside the boat toward the center of the lake.

Around the edges of the lake the polluted water was thick

with weeds and mosses. We were not surprised to see drainage pipes from the city dump their waste water into the rice paddies and from there directly into the lake. Only near the center of the lake would the water become clearer. The birds and their master worked with each other in rhythmic coordination like a well choreographed troupe of dancers.

It was quite a strange scene to watch waves and waves of the birds flop their wings then dive into the water in unison at the short and sharp commands of their master. After a while they emerged. Those with a bulging throat above the string's knot were the ones that caught big fish. The fisherman quietly approached the birds then pried open their beaks to retrieve the preys. Two carps measuring about half the size of a palm of the hand made up the catch of the day.

The flock was a friendly bunch. They playfully jumped aboard ship, perched on the oars or hands of the visitors. Amidst that lovely natural environment host, visitors and birds really entered into a true communion with each other. In a show of friendship, the Bai host offered me a cigarette. It was the first time in more than thirty years that I accepted a cigarette and enjoyed smoking that aromatic tobacco from Yunnan on the Erhai Lake.

"Almost eight centuries ago (1278) Marco Polo traveling on the Southern Silk Road visited this place and noted that the fishes of Erhai Lake ranked 'the best in the world'. Afterward Marco Polo crossed the Mekong in Western Yunnan to leave China".

Six centuries later, in 1868 the French exploration group led by Doudart de Lagrée and Francis Garnier left Saigon to sail up the Mekong on a perilous expedition lasting two full years. Eventually Francis Garnier was able to reach Erhai Lake to the east of the ancient citadel of Dali. When the local sultan, the Muslim monarch, refused to grant him an audience, he was left with no other alternative but to depart immediately from Dali.

More than 130 years after Francis Garnier, we came to the beautiful but extremely precarious ecology of lake Erhai probably during its final moments. Its increasingly polluted water flowed into the big Xi'er affluent to find its final destination in the main current of the Mekong.

Oral tradition has it that every year around April the Pla Beuk fish gather at the deep pool of Luang Prabang to the north of Vientiane. There, they compete to select those among them that would continue to swim upstream for over 2,000 kilometers to Erhai Lake and spawn their eggs. The ones who fail the contest would stay behind and become prey to the fishermen of the Chiang Khong village on that Pla Beuk fish festival.

Pla Beuk (Pangasianodon gigas) is a giant variety of catfish unique to the Mekong. They can measure up to three meters in length and weigh over 300 kilograms. The Thai and Laotian fishermen living along the banks of the Mekong believe they are sacred fish that will bring them luck during the fishing season. For the last ten years, dating back to the day the construction of the Manwan Dam was completed in 1993, not a single Pla Beuk made it past this bottleneck to Erhai Lake to spawn.

After smoking their cigarettes both host and visitor were elated. In high spirit, the old fisherman announced he would sing for us a very old love song of the Bai. Though I did not understand the lyrics I could still appreciate the enchanting melody of the song. According to Wu, the song relates the romantic and passionate love of a young Bai couple who was rowing on Erhai Lake amidst the beautiful scenery, under the blue sky, by the high mountains, on the immense water…Each note in the song echoed the throbbing of their hearts. Though approaching his sixties this tanned, skinny and austere looking man sang with all his soul as if he was trying to relive the first love of his youth. The cormorants still swam close to the boat. A few jumped on board to perch and strain their necks in an apparent attempt to follow attentively the musical rendition of their master.

I inquired with the fisherman about the catch of the cormorants. He replied that he had been pursuing his profession for at least four decades and as far back as ten years ago he was still doing fine. However it is a different story of late. The catch grew meager and meager. The cormorants still brought in some money but his family gets by mostly thanks to the money from the tourists.

Before bidding farewell to Dali, we paid a visit to the Mekong River Culture and Art Center on Wen Xian street. The place was in fact nothing more than a motel surrounded by orchards and fishponds. It was an exaggeration to call it a cultural center of the Mekong. Besides the tens of rooms being offered for rent, there were only a few classes for drawing, calligraphy, music and Tai Chi. Several crudely done oil paintings and unfinished sculptures that hardly qualified as art works made up the exhibition. The writings and poems on display were not published works for the general public. Except for its name this place has nothing to do with the Mekong. It does not warrant a trip half around the world to come for a visit.

NETS OVER THE MEKONG

There were no flights for the next two days between Dali and Jinghong, so we decided to return to Kunming by land. Once there, we bade farewell to Wu and took one of the daily flights to Jinghong, the capital city of the autonomous region named Xishuangbanna. A number of ethnic groups but mainly Dai lived in the region. It is viewed as a "mini kingdom of Thailand" in the People's Republic of China.

Apart from his ability to translate, Wu did not know much more than us about this autonomous region to the south. Without Wu we would have had to fend for ourselves in a completely new and unfamiliar environment.

In Jinghong we left the Banna Airport for the Xishuangbanna Sightseeing Hotel. Though rated a three star hotel, the staff only spoke Chinese and we had to wait until the afternoon to see the lady manager who probably came from Hong Kong to help us contact a travel agency.

At the other end of the line Oliver picked up the telephone. He spoke English like a Chinese American. Half an hour later he showed up in our hotel room to work out with us an itinerary for the next three days. On the first day we would use a motorboat to go upstream to the future location of the Jinghong Dam and visit a minority group. The following day, we planned to drive to the hydroelectric dams on the Liusha tributary, the river port of Simao and possibly go on a net fishing excursion on the Mekong. The main objective of our stay in Jinghong was to study the ecology of the Mekong and visit the construction site of the future dam. On the last day we would go to Simao, the uppermost reachable riverine port in Yunnan Province.

It was an itinerary unlike any Tour Route Oliver had organized for his customers in the past. Naturally there was a price to pay for such service. Our guide is a 22 year old man of the Yi minority with the peculiar name of "Potato". The Yi do not use last names so his parents called him "Potato". A name he really likes. He is a minority - A very bright one. Potato worked to save money to attend the university in Kunming. Every night he went to the library to read books and newspapers. At the stroke of midnight he listened to the VOA or BBC broadcasts to study English. A day spent with him invariably turned into an exciting one. There are always new things to be learned. On the second day while we were traveling on the river, Potato turned to me and asked if I knew of another name for the Mekong? Without waiting for a reply, he gleefully answered his own question: *"Danube of the*

East". He found it out the previous night at the library.

After Kunming, another surprise awaited us in the city of Jinghong. It was only during the last five years (since 1998) that the old Jinghong was razed to the ground to make room for a brand new city complete with multi-story hotels, grocery stores, not to omit libraries and bookstores, asphalted wide streets lined with green trees and as usual a large group of Chinese Han coming from all parts of the country. In the following year (1999) The Shanghai Bridge and Road Construction Company put the final touch to the construction of the splendid Jinghong Bridge that looked like a dancing peacock with spread out wings. The bridge served as an important link in the transportation network of the Greater Mekong Subregion. An old bridge built by the Soviet in 1977, a second-class technological structure, is now only suitable for pedestrian and bicycle use.

In the early morning when the sun was still asleep, a motorboat was already waiting for us on the Mekong near the Jinghong Bridge.

Only three weeks ago, a torrential rain in Yunnan had caused flooding and the death of twelve persons. At the same time, my friend from Nong Khai, a town in the northeast of Thailand, right across from Vientiane informed me by email: "evacuating due to the flood – the Mekong's water level rose to the edge of the road running along the river banks because for a whole week roaring water had been rushing down from Yunnan. Police cars crisscrossed the city sounding the alarm. Many shop owners stacked sand bags around the entrances to their stores or moved their goods to Udon Thani to seek refuge from the flood."

The water had now subsided. Small and large rocks started to poke their heads out of the water along the riversides. Though the river was deep, to navigate it safely, one must be familiar with the route or risk having the boat collide with submerged rocks and break apart. Our motorboat moved north against the current toward the site of the future Jinghong Dam. The water of the river wore the red color of alluvium deposits. The current ran swift, causing areas of whirlpools to form. High mountains ran parallel to the riverbanks. Try as we did, we could not detect the faintest trace of the rainforests. Instead we only saw the boundless lush green foliage of the rubber plantations. Fast growing industrial trees like rubber and eucalyptus were planted to take the place of the eradicated rainforests.

This reforestation effort was supposed to substitute one kind of forest for another. What it actually did was to transform the area where a natural forest once grew into an industrial monoculture tree plantation. The idea for the planting of industrial trees originated in Thailand. It was then duplicated in Yunnan, China. From there it quickly spread to Laos, Cambodia and Vietnam. In reality it is universally acknowledged now that these plantations of industrial trees could not in any way or manner replace the original forests because this unnatural ecology system also turns the water and land into a sterile, non-productive environment for the indigenous population.

Lumps of dried grass and plastic bags of all colors hanging on the branches of tall trees indicated to us that at one time the water level must have been at least 3 to 4 meters higher. Those plastic bags in various stages of disintegration bore the living proof that the Mekong was being used as a sewage system for industrial waste and domestic garbage. Its current continued to flow swiftly along sparsely populated high mountains. The stiff gorges it snaked through formed ideal topography for the building of many additional hydroelectric dams. The Jinghong Dam project dated back to the time of the Manwan Dam and its construction was scheduled for 2005. Considering the countless benefits the dams would bring about and regardless of the point in time, sooner or later China will gradually complete the construction of the series of dams of the Mekong Cascades on the Mekong. No power on earth could stop them. That is a certainty.

It was right in the middle of the high water season that a young Japanese lady named Mika undertook a journey of 4 days and 4 nights on board a big cargo ship with a crew of five male strangers to brave the Mekong current from North Thailand to Jinghong. This pretty and slightly built lady might look like a high school student but she actually held a doctorate degree and taught at the Centre for Southeast Asian Studies of a university in England. Undoubtedly she must hail from an intrepid stock to dare embark on such a dangerous and difficult journey. Freighters are not allowed to carry passengers. However, through the good office of an acquaintance she was accepted on board as a relative of a crewmember. At checkpoints, all of the five men were more than eager to volunteer themselves as her husband. They had to work hard on the freighter and were separated from their families for months at a stretch. Mika came to them as a fresh breeze and yet she felt safe because, without fail, they took it upon themselves to take her under their protective wings.

We first met Mika at a market meet of the Akai minority who came all decked out in their colorful traditional attires. They belonged to the Hani group. For them the market meet was not only a place to exchange goods but also an occasion to establish social contacts. The territory inhabited by the Akai encompassed the autonomous region of Xishuangbanna in addition to Northern Thailand, and Laos. Mika came to this place to conduct a research on the topic of "Transnational Migration of the Ethnic Minority Akai". For these people national boundaries only exist as virtual borders. We had a lot to exchange with each other because we nurtured a common concern for minority peoples. We all concluded that the Montagnards of the Central Highlands in

Vietnam would represent an interesting topic for Mika to study in the future.

That day Mika joined us on a research trip on the Mekong. The current gushed forward swiftly forming whirlpools and foaming at the crest of the waves around the reefs. Amazingly Mika started to show real fear. She could not imagine that after having undergone a voyage of four days and nights on this turbulent river she must once more sail against its tormented current.

It was not until then that we could follow with our own eyes the large cargo ships sail past us from Simao all the way to Northern Thailand and Laos then down to Vientiane. In April, 2001 China signed an accord for fluvial transportation on the Mekong with three nations: Laos, Myanmar, and Thailand. The accord called for the dredging of the riverbed; the use of mines and explosives to destroy the rock formations at the whirlpools, waterfalls, and the small islets in the current to widen the passageway and make it passable to the big ships with 500-700 tonnages. Ships could then navigate from Simao (Yunnan) down to Chiang Khong, Chiang Sean (Thailand) and straight to Vientiane, the capital of Laos. All the while, Cambodia and Vietnam, the two countries that lie at the southernmost part of the river and have to suffer from the direct consequences caused by that accord were unceremoniously brushed aside. It is too early to gauge the severity of those consequences. Nonetheless, one thing is certain: The natural rate of flow of the current will inevitably be disturbed entailing chain reaction effects on the ecological system of the Mekong. The blushing sun began to make its appearance on the top of the high mountain still shrouded by an early mist. Straining against the strong current, our boat had to slow down noticeably. Still, we were able to stop at all the reefs where the nets were set during the previous night.

In total twelve nets were placed along the banks of the river at the spots which were close to the future site of the Jinghong Dam. We did manage to pull up each and everyone of them with our own hands. There was fish in all of them. Albeit small ones. Smaller than those caught in the Vientiane River of Laos or the Tonle Sap Lake near Phnom Penh. We did find some of the nets heavy to pull up. However it was not because the catch was big but rather because the nets got caught in the reefs. In a word, the catch for that day was poor.

Even if we disregarded the disappearance of the rare and valuable fish like the Pla Beuk and Irrawady dolphins, my mind was still incessantly haunted by this troubling question: "where have the other big and familiar fish of the Mekong gone?" Being a die-hard optimist, I maintain that it is still too early to assert that they have all gone the way of the dinosaurs.

THE WAY TO SIMAO

Situated 165 kilometers from Jinghong to the northeast, Simao serves as a gateway to the Xishuangbanna autonomous region in the south. This mountain route is narrow but rather easy to use.

Potato was able to hire for us a Han driver in her early twenties and sporting a short haircut. She was an expert driver who knew the way too well to deign slowing down even when entering a curve. Our car zoomed past green mountains, through valleys, along rivers and rivulets.

Midway on that one-lane route we came to a checkpoint set up by youthful Red Army soldiers on a mountain pass. They were disciplined and polite in sharp contrast to the extreme coldness and vigilance of their faces. They reminded me of the Red Army soldiers clutching their rifles on the Paracels Islands that used to belong to Vietnam 28 years ago.

The TV broadcasts run by the Chinese government always

set aside a channel to show the military might and prowess of mainland China.

We all had to get off the car for them to check every single page of the passports. Though we were bearers of American passports, Potato introduced us as Vietnamese and Mika as Japanese on account of her Japanese passport. They asked for the permission to search our car from front to rear because we were on a road coming from the wild frontier town of Ruili which was located midway between southwest China and Myanmar. Unknowingly we were traveling on a favorite artery frequented by smugglers to transport opium from the Golden Triangle into Yunnan. Only God knows what would happen to us if those soldiers came upon just a trace of drug in the car. To our great relief they waived us off after finding nothing more compromising than several cardboard boxes of dried food in the trunk our lady driver's vehicle.

Finally we arrived at the town of Simao renowned for its teas from Yunnan. Simao sat astride two historical routes: the Southern Silk Road, a trade route dating back to Marco Polo's time if not all the way to Ancient Rome, and the Tea-Horse Road frequented by horse caravans transporting tea to Sichuan and even Tibet. A new 910 kilometer long highway named the Yunnan-Myanmar Freeway was being built to connect Kunming to Ruili. It was an important link in the transportation network serving the port city of Simao on the bank of the Mekong River. The port itself was located almost 80 kilometers away from the city proper. It was getting late and the road was in bad condition so we decided to return to Jinghong after paying a short visit to Simao's main streets and savoring a few sips of the famous Pu'er tea. Back to Jinghong we had to stay an extra day there and spend most of the night at the airport because a huge storm was approaching the city.

DIAN LAKE – KUNMING AND THE RED RIVER

A succession of small and large lakes runs all the way to Hekou at the northern frontier of Vietnam and form the unique topography of the Yunnan plateau. Dian is the largest lake to the south of Kunming. Marco Polo visited the place on his trip to the capital city of Kunming in the 13th century and described it as "a lake hundreds of lis long where the fishing is abundant". The lake measures 40 kilometers long and covers an area of 300 km^2 about half the size of the island nation of Singapore. It is sandwiched between mountain ranges to the west and lakes to the east. The land here is flat. There used to be a fishermen enclave in the area. Unfortunately pollution from the industrial zones on the lake's southeast bank had almost killed off the fish population and brought the local fishing activities to a halt. The government found itself powerless when faced with the intractable problems caused by industrial waste water coupled with the ever-increasing pollution of Dian Lake. At one time Wu told us of a daring plan by the Yunnan government to construct an aqueduct at the cost of 2 billion yuans to dump the waste water of Dian Lake into the Red River and have this water run through Vietnam and ending in the East Sea. Afterwards the waters from the Yang-tze will be used to replenish the emptied lake.

At this point in time we were still unable to verify whether there is any grain of truth to this imaginative but nefarious plan of the "project engineers of the great Han". How could anything be verified when plans are always kept under strict secrecy by the Chinese authorities? For sure Wu, the former high school teacher, does not possess an imagination rich enough to invent such a story. Using the Red River as a sewage pipe for Lake Dian? Can anyone imagine the calamitous consequences that would befall the millions of Vietnamese inhabitants of the Red River Delta whose very existence depends on the river's water? Who will be the concerned party willing to assume the role of a watchdog over this issue? How much does the Vietnamese government know about the possibility that the Yunnan authorities may adopt such a cavalier and irresponsible approach to come up with a "solution" to their ecological problems? It would not be right for me not to sound the alarm with all due reservation. The ball is now in the Hanoi government's court. It is incumbent on the government to try to shed some light on this issue. It is imperative that it conduct "investigations and verifications" to find out whether there exists any ground for concern. This task could be done with the cooperation of the domestic and foreign press corps as well as the ecology proponents or activists.

Should this turn out to be true - and I hope not - one could hardly anticipate how the Vietnamese who live in the Red River Delta will think and react. At the time, it seemed pointless for me to engage Wu in a discussion about the ecology. Besides, he is always extremely proud of the projects that bring prosperity to China, his country.

SOME PERSONAL NOTES

On our last day in Yunnan Wu insisted on taking his wife, young daughter and us to dinner at the Old House, a famous eatery about the size of a theater located next to the World Horti-Expo Garden. After more than two weeks of constant interaction the nature of our relationship had changed. It was no longer of a "business" character. Instead Wu and his family have accepted us as their friends. In his late twenties, Wu can look forward to a bright future in front of him. Wu is not his real name. I use that name to protect his safety and that of his dear ones. For the same reason, I prefer not to reveal the name of my close friend and fellow traveler in this chapter, "Report from

Yunnan." It goes without saying that we both shared memorable experiences during the entire trip - some really tense, and others more enjoyable, for sure. For the two of us, those are the days we are not about to forget any time soon.

That night, on the fourth floor of the Old House people celebrated big birthday parties complete with candle blowing. Hundreds of revelers stood up and sang the song "Happy Birthday To You" in English followed by a refrain in Chinese. In the eyes of optimists, this is a welcome sign of the "globalization" - to be understood as "Americanization" of China - while at the same time disregarding the "Sinicization" of America with its department stores from New York to San Francisco being flooded by the day with "made in China" goods.

ONLY ONE CHOICE: DEVELOPMENT

On the Boeing 777 that took off from Guangzhou, destination the United States, for no particular reason, an inconsequential picture suddenly came back to life in my mind: a huge billboard on the side of a peaceful country road in Yunnan. The road ran through the countryside between a village on one side and golden rice fields on the other. That billboard showed the picture of Dang Xiao Ping standing next to a slogan written in big letters: "ONLY ONE CHOICE: DEVELOPMENT". It was the unambiguous message Chairman Dang Xiao Ping wished to convey to his people. For him simple development is not enough. It must be development at a breakneck pace conjuring up the image of a China marching into the 21st Century as a super power.

For older generations of Chinese, the rapid development of China made its debut on the day President Nixon came knocking at the tightly shut "bamboo curtain" to meet with Chairman Mao and introduced a new era for China.

One has to witness with one's own eyes the extraordinary

change the entire backward southeast region of Yunnan went through to arrive at an accurate idea of its extent. The signs of development and construction are evident not only in the big cities but even in the "in-between" towns dotting the sides of the national highways. Lush green rice paddies basking under the sun, power lines reaching the most remote corners of the country could be seen everywhere one looks. Furthermore, one does not need to see a TV disc on a house's verandah to know that there is a TV set inside.

It could not be said that we were brainwashed or taken for a ride by the Chinese government because they only let us see what they wanted us to see. The simple reason is we did not travel using a tour route but freely chose the itineraries ourselves. My general impression is that from the cities to the countryside the Chinese people are well fed and well dressed. To provide the 1.2 billion Chinese with those basic necessities while at the same time implementing the nation's economic development is quite a feat in itself.

The reasons behind this remarkable achievement are:
- They possess the "gray matter" (Brain power)
- They have the high technology
- They have a studious, hard-working labor force
- They have the discipline (voluntary or not) of a totalitarian government
- They have pride and love for their country China.

Naturally, as is the case with any society, this country does not lack in deficiencies. Having gone through heart wrenching experiences that were drenched in blood and tears, the Chinese people of today are standing on their steady feet to march confidently toward the future.

Shifting the focus from China to Vietnam, a country smaller in size than Yunnan Province, which faces the threat of disintegration and the United States which is becoming increasingly isolated and losing its moral leadership role in the world in spite of its military might, we can fairly surmise that the 21st century belongs to the Chinese. At any given time, a people will have to espouse or be resigned to a destiny that befits their choice and their way of life.

Kunming – Manwan
Jinghong – Simao – Dali
September, 2002

Kunming: contrast between tradition and modernization

A quotation from Einstein in lieu of Mao Tse-Tung thought

Yunnan University: English as a second language

Shinlin Stone forest: a natural wonder of Yunnan

South Gate of the ancient citadel of Dali

The 9th century Dali San Ta (Three Pagodas)

Drawing Chinese characters, another step toward Sinicization

48 MEKONG THE OCCLUDING RIVER

Bai fisherman the with the cormorants on Erhai Lake

New "made in China" Jinghong bridge looking like a peacock with spread out wings

Old "made in Russia" Jinghong bridge - a second class technology construction

Manwan Dam: the first and historic dam in the Mekong Cascades

Yunxian District Manwan City: construction site of the Manwan Hydroelectric Dam

LAOS_PDR.COM
COMING OUT FROM OBLIVION

From being a "forgotten country" Laos strives to become the "Kuwait of hydro-power of Southeast Asia."

REOPENING THE LAOS FILE BEFORE DEPARTURE

Long known as the "forgotten country", Laos recently made a come back in the news, thanks to its Ecotours that attract more than 600,000 visitors to this land annually. However, it was the reports in the foreign news media concerning this nation's political events that brought it under the world political spotlight again. Naturally this resurgence of political attention must have come from the overseas media since freedom of the press or more precisely free press activities were non-existent in Laos. Both the French weekly, Le Rénovateur (Renovation), and English biweekly, Vientiane Times, were government run and primarily aimed at foreign readership.

We were in December. The weather at this time of the year (from November to March) is most propitious to visit Laos. After that, it will turn extremely hot and dry before giving way to the

Rainy Season. The good weather that greeted us did not preclude the forecast of disquieting political developments in view of the following breaking news:
- A series of bomb explosions from Vientiane to Pakse rocked the country. Vang Pao, a former Hmong general in the defunct Royal Lao Army, now living in exile, denied responsibility for those acts. (AFP 07/26/2000). During the Second World War, he fought the Japanese and was afterward recruited by the French to combat the Viet Minh. After the French's defeat in the First Indochina War, general Vang Pao served in the Royal Lao Army. As the Second Indochina War unfolded, he sided with the Americans and led the Hmong Secret Army trained and armed by the CIA in the fight against the Pathet Lao and North Vietnam's People Army. When the Pathet Lao gained the upper hand and seized power in 1975, Vang Pao fled to the United States. Recently, all eyes were turned on him again because of an alleged plot to overthrow the government of Laos in 2007.
- The armed uprising in the mountainous region of Muong Khoun, Laos was kept tightly under wrap (AFP 08/04/2000).
- Rumors that the Minister of Finance Mr. Khamsay, son of the Red prince Souvanouvong, had sought political asylum were denied by the Laotian government (AFP 08/05/2000).

Other news soon followed:
- Attacks along the Lao and Thai borders involving the flying of the Laotian Royal Family colors, disappearance of Lao American nationals on their way to Laos, burning of the market at Kilometer-52 on Route Nationale 13 to the north of Vientiane by the Hmong, convoys

transporting the Communist Vietnamese military going through the capital city of Vientiane.
- The American Secretary of State Madeleine Albright, categorically declared that the US Government did not support the resistance movement in Laos. At the same time, the American Embassy issued a travel advisory for the region north of Vientiane.
- Then a long article on the Internet about political upheavals in Laos pointing to troubling uncertainties.

Such were the time and place or the political setting of my journey to Mae Nam Khong (the Lao-Thai name for the Mekong). I did not enter Laos as a participant in a guided tour or as a tourist. For companionship, I carried with me a large volume of data covering the "two years and 24 days" of the Mekong Expedition undertaken by the French explorers Doudart de Lagrée and Francis Garnier more than a century ago (1866-1868).

In America, right after Thanksgiving, people were still busy with the festivities and preparations for Christmas and New Year celebrations. We were in 2001, the first year of the 21st century. One day before departure, my friend, a reporter and an old hand of Laos, cautioned me to be careful once I got there.

FROM BANGKOK TO VIENTIANE

Thailand was immersed in the election season. The Thai people might be divided in their politics but as far as their veneration of their monarch is concerned, they were of one heart and mind. The whole country was jubilantly celebrating the 72nd birthday of his Majesty King Bhumibol. The bodies of all the planes of the Royal Thai International Airlines were painted with the proclamation: "The King's 72nd Celebration", for all to see.

At two in the afternoon, our jetliner touched down at Bangkok's Don Muang International Airport which was operating in full swing as usual.

The following morning, a Boeing 707 of the Royal Thai International with its crew of beautiful stewardesses acclaimed to be "Smooth As Silk - First Time Every Time" brought me to Vientiane. The flight was fully booked with foreign tourists and Lao expatriates from the U.S. or Australia returning to their homeland for the first time after 25 years of absence. A mere hour later, I disembarked at the large and pleasant looking Wattay International Airport the Japanese finished building not long ago. No propaganda posters of the type *"Farmers, Workers, Soldiers Unite in The Defense of Socialism"* were in sight. Vientiane in the year 2000 was a far cry from the city depicted in the book "The Quiet American" Graham Greene authored in 1955.

In the 1930's, in order to improve the administrative system of Laos, the French protectorate rulers brought a large number of Vietnamese civil servants and their families to the country. Consequently, except for the old royal capital of Luang Prabang, the Vietnamese formed the majority of the populations of Vientiane, Savanakhet, Xieng Khouang, and Pakse. The Chinese made up the second largest immigrant groups.

The capital city of Vientiane had undergone some growth but managed to keep the charms of a small city with a vanishing number of French period villas hidden behind green trees. All that remained of the old Treasury Building were its four yellow walls and a roof standing in disrepair. They offered a sharp contrast with the majestic White House next door that served as the Presidential Palace of the Chairman of Laos.

However, on the green flat land of Vientiane. workers were busy with the construction of high-rises and buildings. Most noticeable among them were the 4-star, hundreds of rooms hotels overlooking the streets teeming with automobiles; Honda motorcycles; three-wheeled tuk-tuks; small cars; and taxis belonging to the Lavi company, a Lao Vietnamese joint venture.

With the rapid advent of "Renovation", like a sleeping beauty, Vientiane woke up from her slumber to greet the princes coming from Thailand.

The busiest place in town was the Nam Phou Circle where the water fountain only worked during the night. Tourists from the four corners of the world congregated here. The largest group came from France. The locals called those young hippies "Western backpackers" on account of the backpacks they carried on their shoulders.

MAE NAM KHONG – THE MOTHER RIVER THAT IS DRYING UP

We were in mid December. The Rainy Season just drew to a close and we were still a long way from April or May, the peak of the Dry Season. Yet the section of the Mekong running through Vientiane was reduced to a trickle exposing the sand bars and stones patches in the riverbed. From the third floor of the Lane Xang hotel on the left bank, Laotian side, I could see the green foliage of the corn and banana fields extending all the way to one third of the river bed where the water line of the small current began. In the middle of the water meandered a sand bed separating the Laotian left current from the Thai right. Such was the sad state the Mekong was reduced to these days.

Could this really be the almighty Mekong, the third largest river of Asia and the 11th in the world, the lifeline of the people of Laos, Cambodia as well as the millions of Vietnamese inhabitants of the Mekong Delta?

Nang Ouane was born and grew up in Vientiane. An educated and knowledgeable person she could speak Vietnamese, French and English besides her native tongue. She held the high position of expert at her bank and was among the rare intellectuals who chose to stay in the country when the Pathet Lao marched down from the caves of Sam Neua to take control of Vientiane. She led the normal life of a civil servant and saw her future in her seven sons and daughters who excelled at school. Four of them were studying abroad. The oldest daughter, a college graduate with a major in computer science from Australia, was the founder of the fast growing Internet network in Laos.

This morning, leaving home for work at the Bank of Foreign Commerce not far from Fa Ngum Street, Nang Ouane wore a skirt woven in the traditional style of the Laotian women. She possessed a beauty best described as quiet and gentle, a voice soft and sweet.

"The Mekong only started to dry up in the last six or seven years. Before that, the current that ran through Vientiane was always full. Naturally the water level varies with the Rainy or Dry season but the river had never exposed her bed like now. All the while the amount of rainfall remains unchanged."

She uttered those words in 1993, the year marking the completion of construction works on the 35 story high Manwan Dam. It was also the first in the series of 14 dams to be built in the Mekong Cascades in China. By itself, the Manwan Dam produces 1,500 MW - enough electricity to supply the entire region of Yunnan and Guizhou. At the time, a sudden drop in the water level was registered downstream of the Mekong. It did not happen during the Dry Season either. Only then did the people find out that China had begun the process of diverting the waters of the Mekong into the Manwan's reservoirs.

What would happen to the flow of the Lower Mekong when all the 14 dams (initially only 7 were planned for) of the Mekong Cascades are built during the first two decades of the 21st century? The waters contained in their reservoirs will not only be used to run the turbines but also to irrigate that immense arid region of China.

Thong Dien, the Vietnamese Lao taxi driver, told me: "I moved with my family from the "liberated zone" of Xieng Khouang to live in Vientiane since 1976. Our house was located near the river so I went there to play with my buddies daily. I clearly remember that in those days the water level of the Mekong was very high even during the Dry Season - around the time of the Pimay Tet. Needless to say one cannot imagine how fast the river flowed during the Rainy Season. But only for the last five or seven years or so did the river become that dry. We are only in November or December and the water level already is so low. The Dry and Rainy Seasons remain the same. I do not know where all the water has gone!"

Pointing down to the corn and vegetable fields along Fa Ngum street which ran parallel to the dry riverbed, Thong Dien continued:

"Those lands used to be under water. There was no room for planting much less building like now."

Looking at the direction Thong Dien pointed to, I could see several thatch huts hiding under clusters of banana trees. He added:

"The alluvium soil is very rich. Using them for planting vegetables, corn or even banana is just 'vô tư'".

My knowledge of the Vietnamese vocabulary - if not extensive - could not be considered poor either. Nevertheless, the way the Vietnamese Laotian taxi driver used the word "vô tư" sounded quite new to me. The term "vô tư" as defined in the dictionary bears a positive connotation. It means "to be impartial, neutral". Judging from the context Thong Dien used it in, I suspected that it must mean something very different. From now on Thong Dien to me would be known as the "Vô Tư" or "Easy Do" taxi driver.

The Laotians and even the Lao government seemed to remain

almost unperturbed to the fact that the Mekong is drying up before their eyes.

Throughout my stay in Laos, I had not heard anybody mention the existence of the dams in the Yunnan Cascades. Could a dying Mekong in one way or another continue to serve as the water source to the Tonle Sap and the Tiền Giang and Hậu Giang Rivers of the Mekong Delta in Vietnam?

In my mind I visualized a completely different river: a gigantic Tiền Giang overflowing with silt and at places stretching over 3 kilometers in width. For centuries this large river has embraced and nurtured hundreds of small or large islets like the Cù Lao Rồng, Cù Lao Phụng, Cù Lao Quy and Cù Lao Thới Sơn as well as watered the houses and orchards in the countryside of the western part of the Delta...

One of these days when the source of silt and fresh water stops flowing to give way to the onslaught of salt water, we will witness the sunset of the "Orchard Civilization" of the Delta. Then we will also behold this scene on the Mekong:

Sông kia giờ đã nên đồng
Bên làm nhà cửa bên trồng ngô khoai
Vẳng nghe tiếng ếch bên tai
Giật mình còn tưởng tiếng ai gọi đò... (Tú Xương)

The old river is long gone
It has turned into an open land
On one side people build homes
On the other corn and yams they plant.
Afar, a lonely frog is croaking
Startled I think somebody's calling
A boat for the traveler
To cross the long gone river...

The author of the above poem is Trần Tế Xương, alias Tú Xương. He was born in Vị Xuyên village, North Vietnam during the transitionary period when the Vietnamese society was moving from a feudal to a colonial system under the French. Though very intelligent, he repeatedly failed to pass the court's mandarin examinations. This fact probably explained why he was very good at writing satirical poems that endeared him to the people of the late 19th century. He died at the premature age of 37, poor but well loved.

FISH ON THE SECTION OF THE MAIN RIVER
Throughout my stay in Vientiane, I took advantage of the cool weather in the early mornings to take my daily walks along Fa Ngum Street that ran along the bank of the Mekong, a street layout somewhat similar to those in Saigon.

A new leaf was turned after the construction of the Mittaphap or Friendship Bridge (1994) during the "open door policy" era. One could no longer witness the frenzied sight of people boarding the ferries on the Laotian side with empty baskets and containers in their arms only to return later from the riverbank of Nong Khai in Thailand with loads of goods in tow.

Now only small fishing boats plied the river. I kept a close watch on them from the early morning until the time they went back to port and discovered to my utter disappointment that the fish they brought in was no bigger than the palm of a hand. Even then, the fishermen could not afford the luxury of returning the smaller ones to the river with the expectation of having a bigger catch in the days to come. The fish they caught represented the sole source of protein for their families on that day.

With a resigned air the old fisherman whispered: "The river continues to dry up and the harvest from the river grows scarcer and scarcer". The current still showed the red color of alluvium but its flow was reduced to a trickle. As a result, the river has ceased its normal activities like the building up or eroding of the riverbanks. Her only on-going activity was the non-stop baring of the riverbed along the banks. Incredibly that did not stop the authorities from bringing in bulldozers to build higher dikes. In so doing, did they really intend to suppress the last few breaths of fresh wind that still managed to blow from the current of an exhausted river that had lost almost all of its vigor and water?

THE NAM NGUM DAM THIRTY YEARS LATER

If the golden stupa of That Luong symbolizes Laos' historic past then the Nam Ngum Dam would represent the proud achievement of the Laotian people on their march toward progress and development. Pictures of the Nam Ngum Dam were shown on postcards, stamps, and 50 kip banknotes that were later withdrawn from circulation due to a galloping inflation.

It was the first dam to be built during the very early and stormy years of the Vietnam War with loans received from the World Bank and several other nations. The United States also provided additional funds to Laos to speed up the construction of the dam in order to ensure additional supply of electricity to the strategic air force base at Udon in the northeast region of Thailand which was at that time abuzz with activities.

In 1971, the first phase of the construction of the Nam Ngum Dam was completed marking a historical moment when the Laotian monarch, Savang Vathana, and the Thai King, Adubjadej Bhumidol, met on a ferry luxuriously decorated with garlands and lanterns in the middle of the current on the Mekong's main tributary. They came to "jointly press a button to start the flow of electricity and dollars going in opposite directions between the two nations of Laos and Thailand".

One must travel the full 420 kilometers of land route between Vientiane and Luang Prabang - including the 170 kilometers of mountain pass road along tall mountains and deep ravines - to have a fair grasp of the multifaceted makeup of Lao minority groups [Lao Lum (Lowland Lao), Lao Theung (Highland Lao), Lao Soung (Mountain Lao)] and realize how far out into the countryside the electricity from Nam Ngum reached. That is to say to the most remote and secluded areas or mountain hamlets.

In the implementation of its electrification program, the Lao government wisely sought to balance the need for gradual and harmonious development with the concern for the conservation of the ecological system. To a certain degree, it became irrefutable that this two-pronged strategy had enabled the Laotian government to use the electricity generated by the dams to bring civilization to their people and render their life better.

The well-informed and progressive Laotians who fully realize the potentials of their country's natural resources have no desire to keep their nation in the permanent status of a "museum exhibiting the artifacts of the stone and bronze ages" for the enjoyment of the tourists.

The reservoir of Nam Ngum Dam covers an area of more than 250 km² (1/3 larger than the island nation of Singapore). Its majestic beauty lies in the natural setting of the surrounding mountains and its hundreds of big or small islands. Large animals no longer roam around but monkeys, all kinds of birds and water snakes still populate the area.

We were held spell bound by the odd looking sight of myriads of tree tops, at times more than 50 meters tall, bristling out of the water. They were vestiges of a hastily submerged forest that was left untouched by logging. The trees not only tore up the fishing nets but also presented a collision risk to the boats navigating the lake.

The Thai lumber traders did not limit themselves to the destruction of the rainforests. They also hired divers to cut down the precious trees under the water of the lake with electric saws.

Those hired hands told of seeing submerged buffalo drawn carts and house frames belonging to the people in Na Bon village who had to abandon everything behind to flee from the rushing water. Made of good wood, those objects will survive for hundreds of years. Nevertheless they were sinking deeper and deeper as they were being buried under the deposits that were continually coming down from the mountains and islands. This unending natural process resulted in the gradual rising of the lake's bottom rendering it shallower as time goes by.

Nam Ngum was transformed into an attractive tourism spot with good restaurants and motorboats for water sports. On the south shore, Malaysian businessmen made plans for the construction of the Dan Savanh Nam Ngum Resort, a four-star 200-room hotel offering artificial beaches, golf courses and an Eco-Casino. Another form of prostitution of the term "ecology" by the business people! No wonder, a professor from Stanford University on a tour of the country was led to remark: "A day will come when the Laotian people will find themselves second class citizens in their own land".

The fish in the lake represented a source of revenue for the near 4,000 local fishermen. The annual catch came to 850,000 tons in the good old days. Unfortunately things have changed lately due to the new "search and destroy" fishing methods being introduced. This new way of fishing called for the catching of all fish regardless of their sizes as well as the adoption of any imaginable means to catch them be it air guns, electric currents or even dynamites.

To compensate for their losses, the people began to plant bananas trees on the islands: sweet-smelling and mouth-watering bananas in their bright golden skins being sold at a bargain not by the bunch but by the whole stem. In the early morning as the boats were leaving their berths to start a new day of fishing, others also set out from the islands to take their loads of bananas to the opposite shores.

Who could have imagined that since 1975, the "creative mind" of the Pathet Lao had led them to transform the two big islands in the lake into "reeducation camps" to incarcerate the social classes they considered "trash of capitalism": prostitutes, thieves, juvenile delinquents...Whether political prisoners were also included in this group, no one could tell but the poor victims themselves.

For our own safety, (with the words "Safety first" Wu uttered still fresh in my mind) instead of a wooden boat, we chose a flimsily built metallic diesel craft to venture into the lake bristling with the tops of hardwood trees. The ride reminded me of the battle the Vietnamese king and freedom fighter Ngô Quyền once fought against the Southern Han troops on the Bạch Đằng River.

General Ngô Quyền lived during the Southern Han's occupation of Giao Châu (ancient name for Vietnam) in the Red River Delta. In 938, he soundly defeated the Chinese at the famous battle on the Bạch Đằng River putting an end to one thousand years of Chinese domination that dated back to 111 B.C. Afterward, Ngô Quyền ascended the throne and became the first ruler of an independent Vietnam.

Tenoi Laxami, our Laotian captain and also boat owner was gentle looking like his compatriots. In his early thirties, he was not born yet when the Japanese engineers came to carry out the initial studies for the construction of the Nam Ngum Dam. He did not come from the Na Bon village so did not know about the hamlets which lay deep under the lake's water. Nevertheless, he is quite familiar with the dam's area of his early childhood. Very much so!

Considering my newly acquired and rudimentary knowledge

of the Lao language commonly displayed by a tourist, I was fortunate to benefit from the excellent translation service of Thong Dien, my Vietnamese Lao driver. Once the language barrier behind us, I was able to share with him and Laxami my views concerning the building of the Nam Ngum Dam.

At nine o'clock in the morning the west bank of the lake was still shrouded by a dense layer of fog. At this time of the day; probably the Western backpackers, those night owls, were still enjoying their sleep. The Nam Ngum Restaurant just opened its doors for business. Sabaidee! The Lao waitresses with their pitch black hair rolled up into chignons revealing their ivory white necks had reported to work. Some were already busily going about their tasks like setting the kettles on the stove to boil water...

Thong Dien ordered a *"Kafeh hawn"* or "hot coffee with milk". As for me it would be *"Kafeh dam baw sai nam tan"* or "black coffee without sugar". The baguettes bread and "café au lait" or "coffee with milk" introduced by the French have proved very popular with the people of the three countries formerly known as French Indochina.

A two story white pavilion was built right in the middle of the lake to let the tourists admire the panoramic view of the dam and take pictures.

"That pavilion used to be a three story structure which was recently reduced to two due to the rising water level." Laxami remarked.

It suddenly dawned on me that for the last 30 years (since 1971) the bottom of the lake has been rising on account of the deposits coming down from the mountains and the need to store more water for the planned increase in the output of the Nam Ngum Dam from 30 to 150 MW.

Lurking at a distance were fishing boats. The fishermen have set out to work since early dawn. Laxami commented: "The daily catch is getting meager and meager. Several years ago, princess Maha Chakri Sirindhorn of Thailand came to attend a ceremony freeing more than a hundred Pla Bleuks into the lake. So far no Laotian fisherman has been able to catch a single one of these Pla Beuks yet."

I was glad to be reminded by Laxami that the Pla Beuks, those rare giant catfish unique to the Mekong, were being bred through artificial insemination by the Thai scientists to save them from extinction.

Those Pla Beuks of the deep currents and mighty flows are born well equipped for their annual swim of thousands of miles to spawn their eggs in the Upper Mekong. How many of them would survive if condemned to live in the confinement of a reservoir?

Our vessel reduced speed as it approached a small boat owned by an old fisherman couple. A dozen of frail looking fish about the size of the palm of a hand lied belly up inside the boat. Laxami ventured that the fish would fetch about 7,000 Kip at the market. Less than one US dollar but enough to pay for the daily food of the couple which consisted of a pot of glutinous rice and a condiment of salt, hot pepper and preserved fish called Padaek.

"It is rumored that in a few months the government will issue a ban on fishing with small mesh nets and electrical shocks in order to preserve the fish population of the lake."

There still exists a huge gap between the enactment of a law and its implementation in Laos. To name a few: ban on opium, laws governing deforestation and fish preservation in the lakes...

In Laxami's mind anything that deals with the Nam Ngum Lake must have a history, an anecdote behind it. Pointing to a long mountain range covered with dark green trees running along the right bank Laxami intoned:

"That's Pu Mut – the dark mountain. So called because it looks constantly dark even on a bright sunny day. It serves as a weather forecast station to the fishermen on the lake. Winds and storms always visit the mountain first, long before they spread to the lake."

Laxami went on:

" On windy days, the waves could surge to a height of more than one meter – enough to capsize small boats. A short time ago, a Vietnamese fisherman named Trần lost his wife and child in such an event. Heart broken he left for Vientiane but occasionally returns to visit the lake."

Leaving the Dark Mountain behind, our boat passed small and large islands bearing romantic names like Pu Padang Nang Non (the sleeping young beauty), Pu Kao Nang (mountain of the nine ladies), Pu Eng (the curved mountain), and Pu Huot (the mountain of the glutinous rice pot)...

Guests at the Xantiphap / Peace Inn could stay in wooden bungalows built on the island. It was largely frequented by tourists who preferred to spend the night in seclusion amidst the immensity of the lake.

Laxami could not come up with romantic names for the two reeducation camps on the islands: Don Thao (island of the lad) and Don Nang (island of the lady). – A more appropriate name for those infamous camps manned by security forces would be "Lao Sodom."

"I heard that officials of the former renegade regime were also detained there?" I inquired.

Growing up in the Plain of Jars "revolution", "renegade regime"...were every day's words for Thong Dien. For his part, Laxami replied in a very compassionate voice: "Renegade nor not, if you are a good person it shouldn't make any difference!"

It was quite difficult for me to accept the thought that a gentle people like the Laotians could abolish their monarchy by sending their king, queen and crown prince to die in the caves of a reeducation camp in Sam Neua.

Talking about the Nam Ngum Dam, thirty years have gone by and I was wondering what the Laotian people thought of it.

As usual, Laxami was straightforward and fair in his assessment:

"There could be no joy in seeing the villagers of Na Bon lose their houses, rice paddies and ancestral lands. On the other hand, the people in the region do benefit from the amenities of electricity, the fish in the lake, and the money from the tourists. In addition, from our daily contacts with them, we can also keep abreast of progress and civilization."

But Laxami was also fully aware that sooner or later the lake will dry up on account of the deposits coming down from the mountains. He could not hide his fear when he confided in us:

"The older generations warned us that the building of the dam may offend the spirits and one of these days there would be retribution from them."

Laxami was alluding to a prediction in Lao mythology that an earthquake and ensuing great flood will devastate the villages and sweep away the inhabitants of the region.

Whether one believes it or not, reservoir triggered seismicity still remains a scientifically proven possibility.

FROM THE NAM NGUM DAM TO THE ELECTRIFICATION OF LAOS

According to the statistics compiled by Électricité du Laos (EDL), as we stand at the threshold of the 21st century, 19 of the country's 121 districts are still deprived of electricity. Those are the remote and inaccessible villages located close to the borders. Life of the villagers in those areas is still plunged in darkness because electricity remains unavailable to them even though Laos is a power-exporting nation.

Laos is a mountainous land. In addition to the mighty Mekong and its tributaries, this country is also endowed with a large number of smaller rivers. Consequently, EDL had envisioned the building of "Pocket" hydroelectric dams on them to bring the benefits of electricity to the people.

Since 1975 the government of Laos has been operating three hydroelectric dams: Nam Ngum, 30MW, in Vientiane Province; Nam Dong, 1MW, in Luang Prabang; and Selabam, 2MW, in Champassak. Those power sources were for the most part earmarked to satisfy the needs of the big cities.

The Laotian government relied on foreign loans to expand the capacity of the existing hydroelectric dams as well as build two new ones. As of the year 2000, EDL operated five hydroelectric dams with a combined total output of 270 MW. The outputs of the Nam Ngum and Selabam Dams were raised from 30 MW and 2 MW to 150 MW and 5 MW respectively. As for the Nam Dong Dam, its output of 1 MW remained unchanged. Two new hydroelectric dams were added to the list: Sexet with an output of 45 MW in the province of Savannakhet and the Nam Leuk Dam with 60 MW in Bolikhamsay. The country still maintained two thermoelectric plants running on gasoline: one in Vientiane with an 8 MW output and the other in Luang Prabang with 1 MW.

It goes without saying that Laos also had other power generating plants like Houay Ho, 150 MW; Nam Theun Hinboun, 210 MW…Those were either foreign owned or joint ventures with foreign partners under the BOOT (Build-Own-Operate-Transfer) formula.

In the last years, Laos has been exporting electricity to the neighboring countries of Thailand and Vietnam. However it had to import 163 million KWH to provide electricity to the isolated regions along its borders where the topography of the land does not favor the installation of high-voltage cables for power distribution. As an illustration: The electricity used in Sam Neua came from the hydroelectric dam of Hòa Bình in Vietnam. In a country known as "the Kuwait of hydropower of Southeast Asia", the Laotian people are still encouraged to conserve electricity for export.

160 KILOMETERS BY ROAD TO VANG VIENG

Bidding farewell to the Nam Ngum Dam we traveled on road number 5 to get to Route Nationale 13. Along the riverbanks a lush green canopy of foliage stretched to the distant horizon. On the sides of the road, with money sent home from overseas, people built new brick houses here and there to replace their old stilt abodes.

Pointing to the water buffaloes swimming to the other side of the river Thong Dien wondered:

"How could those really fat water buffaloes float in the water? When I was a buffalo boy I let them swim across the river with "vô tư" (without any qualms)..."

At this point in time the term "vô tư" bore another meaning - that of an adverb. A Vietnamese proverb says: *"Đi một ngày đàng học một sàng khôn"*. Its equivalent in English would be something like "A day spent traveling, a basketful of learning". My Vietnamese vocabulary has certainly been enriched while on this trip to Laos.

A very familiar scene we encountered on the way to Vang Vieng was the sight of beautiful young Laotian girls riding Honda motorcycles in their skirts instead of jeans. Occasionally, we would meet a tractor taking a full load of passengers to the market. This innovative means of transportation was similar to the one we saw in Yunnan.

Pigs, chickens, ducks, geese and even turkeys with their bright red cockscombs were allowed to run free on the roads. Thong

Dien commented:

"The cows and buffaloes here are fat and healthy. They do not have to work hard. Like the Laotian people they lead a leisurely life. Hay and grass are plentiful. They just eat "vô tư" (at their leisure)."

If the baguette bread and coffee with condensed milk are vestiges of the French influence; then turkeys, the offspring of those who survived the Thanksgiving meals at Kilometer Six (the American base called Six Clicks City), represent the only positive legacy the Americans left behind in contrast to the countless number of unexploded bombs they dropped all over the Laotian landscape.

On a sunny day and on a windy mountain pass road, we occasionally drove pass pretty young Hmong girls. In spite of their youth they already became mothers and carried their babies in a cloth band on their back. In this harsh environment, if they survived past their fifth year, those undernourished youngsters would in no time turn into formidable jungle fighters. During the Vietnam War, those under aged, fearless guns served in the CIA supported Hmong forces commanded by general Vang Pao. Not a few of them had valiantly rushed forward to serve as cannon fodders to be at the end abandoned by the Americans. Their story was dramatically related in the book entitled "Tragic Mountains" by Jane Hamilton-Merritt.

At the foot of a mountain, several Laotian farmers were driving tractors to turn the furrows on a paddy strewn with uprooted rice stubbles. The hydroelectric dams paved the way for the electrification of the country which in turn ushered in the first phase of industrialization characterized by the building of cement plants, Pepsi Cola and Lao Beer (quite sought after) factories. Next came the mechanization of agriculture, the latest phase of development in Laos.

Nestled between the east bank of the Nam Xong River and the massive mountain ranges looking like a fortress wall to the west, this small highland city of Vang Vieng had been turned into an attractive tourism spot to a growing number of visitors. The majority of the local inhabitants came from the Hmong and Yao minority groups. During the Vietnam War, it was a well known military base with a STOL (Short Takeoff and Landing) runway. The CIA gave it the code name Lima Site 6 and conducted its active secret war in Laos from there. The airstrip, now deserted and littered with empty gas tanks, still lies at its usual spot.

This was the time of the year when tourists flocked to Vang Vieng. They came to climb the mountains, visit the Tham Cheng Cave, bathe in the streams, swim in the river, go boating, even smoke opium which was sold freely at a bargain in the Hmong villages.

It is no longer a rare occurrence to see hippie type Laotian girls going out with Western backpackers. The inexpensive guesthouses charging one US dollar a night mushroomed around the market place. Nonetheless, luxury accommodations like the Vang Vieng Resort with English style bungalows catering to the businessmen from China, Taiwan, Hong Kong and Singapore also abounded. Business was brisk and the hotel owners were laughing contentedly on their way to the bank.

A stream with water as clear as crystal flowed leisurely from the foot of a stone mountain. An ideal place for you to soak yourself in and relax! At a distance, the Nam Xong River looked ever blue and sparkling in the sunlight. Laos is about one third the size of Texas. Destructive deforestation, extensive hydroelectric exploitation and the projected annual influx of almost one million tourists in the coming decade will rapidly turn the once pristine streams, rivers, mountains and natural ecology of Laos into a thing of the past. Like in Vietnam, future generations of Laos will have to pay a very dear price for its Đổi Mới as far as ecology is concerned.

Like in Vientiane and Luang Prabang, even the Internet Cafés in this small town of Vang Vieng were constantly packed with foreign customers. As a rule, the young and dynamic Laotian managers of those shops could speak English.

Tim, the American from San Francisco, who was introduced to me as a writer and a part-time worker in an Internet Café, told me in these exact words:

"It's quite amazing to think that only two years ago, the Internet was still illegal. But now it is free to open everywhere."

The prices charged by an Internet shop for going online were quite reasonable. They were cheaper than in the United States. Handsome postcards, stamps, on-site mailboxes and T-Shirts printed with the phrase "Laos_PDR.com" were on display for the ready use of the customers. To top it all, the coffee was free.

From now on the People Democratic Republic of Laos has an address in the virtual world to enter the 21st century: The Century of "Globalization".

LUANG PRABANG – THE OLD ROYAL ROUTE

Heading north from Kasi, we took Route Nationale 13 and drove on a steep, narrow and winding mountain pass road for more than 170 kilometers - Long enough for us to view all the landscapes of high mountains and deep ravines the road had to offer.

In the early 1940's, the French started the construction of this road to connect Vientiane with the old capital city of Luang Prabang and named it the Old Royal Route. During the First Indochina War, it fell into total disrepair and was restored to usable condition by the Americans in the 1960's. After 1975, sections of the road again became unusable.

It was not until 1996, after much effort and hard work on the part of the Vietnamese, that the road became drivable again. This assistance from Vietnam also came at the cost of about twenty lives at the hands of armed insurgents. Work related casualties were not included in this figure.

Nowadays, provided that everything goes fine, driving time between Vientiane and Luang Prabang is reduced from three to one day only.

On the same Route Nationale 13, the Chinese corps of engineers were busy building the section of the route linking Luang Prabang with Kunming. The concept of "leopard spots" fit perfectly well in the case of Laos. This country received aids coming from different nations but the major contributors were Vietnam, China, and Japan. To assess the fierceness of the competition for influence those two neighboring countries were engaged in against each other in Laos, one only needs to look at the scale of the huge Palace of Culture built by the Chinese in the center of Vientiane. As for the Vietnamese, they spent US$ 4 million in non-refundable money to erect the Kaysone Phomvihane Memorial Museum at "Kilometer 6".

Probably it would be worthwhile for the readers to stop here and take a side trip to a location named "Kilometer 6" also known as "Six Clicks City" during the Vietnam War. It was a special enclave set aside for the Americans with all the amenities they were accustomed to like bungalows, housing units, schools, swimming pools, tennis courts, movie houses, restaurants, bars, not to omit steam houses. As expected, within the confines of forbidding barbed wires were to be found the offices of USAID dispensing aids, the US Embassy acting as a center of power, and the CIA bureau directing the secret war in Laos. The country, as noted by Bernard Fall, was no longer looked upon as a geographical, ethnic or social entity but rather merely as a political convenience.

After the Americans left in 1975, this complex was turned into the general headquarters of chairman Kaysone Phomvihane until the day he passed away in 1992. Now it serves as a museum. Souvanouvong, the Red prince, might be a better known public figure but the person behind the scene who actually called the shots in the organization of the Communist Party was Kaysone Phomvihane. A 1942 graduate of the Hanoi Law School in Vietnam, he led the Pathet Lao with a masterful hand for more than four decades until the reunification of Laos in 1975. On December 13, 2000 - the inauguration of the museum bearing his name - the weekly Le Rénovateur proclaimed him *"The Soldier of the People that the Laotians will never forget"*.

The national route built by the Vietnamese was up to standards but there was no way to vouch for the safety of the people traveling on it. Personnel working for the United Nations and foreign NGO's were advised to avoid using it because at some sections of the way they could run the risk of being robbed or even killed.

Not long ago, a curfew was imposed in Luang Prabang because an enraged Hmong officer went on a rampage killing policemen, government officials, and Vietnamese construction workers in an ambush.

There were understandably many theories concerning such an event. To the outsiders it looked like a sign of the growing strength of the anti-communist movement of which the Hmongs were the main proponents. The government, on the other hand, attempted to explain it away by claiming that this was simply an individual case of a discharged officer who became discontented with his meager pension. The authorities in Vientiane put yet another spin on the situation by blaming the "bad guys" for the whole thing. No matter what face you put on the incident, the fact remained that there was bloodshed - including the blood of Vietnamese. Though that Hmong officer was eventually caught and sent to an unnamed reeducation camp, sporadic attacks on that route continued to be reported. According to some quarters of the public, it appeared that the instigators were Hmong fighters formerly armed and supported by the CIA during the Vietnam War.

Traveling on that Old Royal Route one must always be prepared for the unpredictable. One's heart is sure to skip a few beats when one gets stopped in the middle of a mountain pass road by a group of soldiers with skin burned black by the sun. They looked even more menacing with their disparate uniforms and brandished AK47 assault rifles or shotgun carbines. What do they want? Asking for cigarettes? Exacting a bribe? Or something worse? No matter what they might do to you, a cover up could be easily arranged in the form of a simulated accident to make it look like your car has gone off the cliff. Whether someone would find out about it is also hard to say.

Our car continued to coast down the road effortlessly. As it approached a curve with a huge stone blocking our sight, out of the blue several militiamen with AK47s and M16 automatic rifles slung on their shoulders appeared in front of us and waved for us to stop. With a big grin on his face, Mr. "Vô Tư", our driver, waved back then floored the gas pedal to speed away. Dead silence ensued. Not a single shot was heard. What would be the right course of action when facing such a situation? We could never get a clear answer to the question. My own inclination was to attribute everything to luck.

As if talking from experience, "old hand" Mr. "Vô Tư" explained: "I forgot to buy cigarettes before we left. Even if I stopped I would not have anything to give those guys."

Clearly Mr. "Vô Tư" only wanted to reassure me that it was a simple case of those armed guys asking for cigarettes. Let's assume that it was so. However, I had no intention of becoming a second Bernard Fall meeting my maker, not on the "Street Without Joy" in Vietnam, but on this Old Royal Route in Laos during peace time.

On our arrival in Luang Prabang, I learned that it was imprudent for us to drive on the mountain pass road at sunset when we could be easily detected by the lights of our car. Drawing from that experience we left very early on the return trip. Lo and behold, this time our car had to move down the mountainside at a snail speed with all lights turned on because a thick fog had reduced our visibility to no more than three meters ahead.

If the security situation were good, the Old Royal Route would prove to be an extremely picturesque scenic route, rivaling the Hải Vân pass between Đà Nẵng and Huế in Vietnam that Paul Theroux ranked number one in the world. This American novelist and travel writer is best known for his book "The Great Railway Bazaar" in which he told about a trip he made by train. Born in 1941, he joined the Peace Corps and taught at different universities. He currently lives in Hawaii.

VISIT LAOS – YEAR 2000

Laos is a land a large number of ethnic groups choose to call home. Besides a long history rich in culture and arts, Mother Nature has adorned her lovely landscapes with numerous mountains, streams and above all the mighty Mekong, her lifeline.

Ecotour proved to be an increasingly attractive business activity that needs to be developed into an industry to serve as a springboard for Laos' economic growth. In November of 1986, the Fourth Party Congress adopted a resolution to shelve the old "closed door policy" ushering in the dawn of a new economic era. The resolution stated: "Tourism represents a source of income and a factor of capital importance in the development of the nation. It ranks among the eight top development plans of the country." The National Tourism Authority of Laos is a member of the World Tourism Organization (WTO) and the Pacific Asia Tourism Association. It was established concurrently with the expansion of the nation's tourism infrastructures. Starting in the 1990's, a fund of more than US$ 180 million coming from the national budget and foreign entrepreneurs was set up to invest in the facilities that support tourism. More than 300 tour guides and tourism police officers have been trained. Of particular significance was the integration of tourism into the development plan being implemented in the Greater Mekong Subregion. It was reported that 5,500 hotel rooms were built and 11 ports opened to serve the tourists. Of these three could issue them visas on arrival.

In addition to the ancient city of Luang Prabang which was designated a World Heritage Site by UNESCO, the country is well endowed with scenic spots and historical vestiges. Tourists coming here could also enjoy boating tours on the Ou and Ngum rivers, or the highly popular cross jungle hiking trips at Sepien in Champassak Province.

Web pages advertising tourism in Laos had been introduced. Minority groups actively participated in the Year for Tourism in Laos by organizing traditional festivals with folk dances and colorful dresses: the Pimay water festival at the start of the year in Luang Prabang, the That Luong festival in Vientiane, the That Inhang festival in Savanakhet, the Wat Phou festival in Champassak and rocket festivals all across Laos…

Some impressive statistics about tourism in Laos:

In 1991 the number of tourists was recorded at a mere 37,000 bringing in US$ 2.25 million.

In 1999, that number grew almost 20 folds resulting in an inflow of approximately US$ 100 million - a significant source of foreign exchange to the Lao national budget that was perennially running in the red.

Going into the first decade of the 21st century, the number of tourists shows potentials for reaching the one million mark. If so, the attractiveness of Laos as "the land with the most pristine nature in Southeast Asia" would quickly lose its luster and turn into an empty slogan.

A PRIMITIVE HEALTH CARE SYSTEM IN LAOS

The imposing new building of the Health Department of Laos on Samsenthai Street and the profuse use of slogans could not obscure the fact that the nation's health system still remained at a very primitive state in spite of the 27 years of forward march by Socialism.

The infant mortality rate continued to be extremely high and the average life expectancy in Laos very low even when compared with those of the neighboring nations.

Mahosot, the main hospital in Vientiane, was outdated and poorly equipped. Sadly, no expected date of completion could be given for the Settathirat hospital which was being built and equipped by the Japanese. The hospitals at the district and provincial levels fared even worse. Patients stricken with contagious diseases like tuberculosis had to share rooms with those afflicted with digestive conditions without anybody even raising an eyebrow.

The country could count on only 1,800 doctors to care for a population of almost five million. Even then, a very limited number of them were trained abroad. After seven years of training, a doctor earned about US$ 150 per year. Just enough for him to spend on transportation if he was assigned to a hospital in a remote province or district. When they fell sick, foreign businesspersons, tourists or wealthy Laotians traveled to Thailand for treatment. A Thai hospital in the province of Udon 50 kilometers across from the Mitthaphap Bridge was superior to the hospital of the Mahosot University in Vientiane in every aspect.

Laos was striving to emulate Thailand in developing its tourism industry regardless of the cost: Going from Green Tourism (Ecotour) to Black Tourism (Opium and Sex tour). Venereal diseases were widespread in Laos with the number of HIV infected young Laotian girls in the countryside increasing by the day. The threat of an AIDS epidemic was real. Tourist manuals constantly reminded tourists to pack "condoms" with them before coming because those sold in Laos were made in Thailand and found to be sub-standard with a failure rate of more than 10 percent!

Due to inadequate means of detection, statistics concerning the spread of HIV did not reflect the real situation. According to a study done in 1993 when only 102,000 tourists per year were reported, already 0.8% of the blood donors were HIV infected. Going into 1999, with a six-fold increase in the number of tourists, including a considerable number of Western backpackers in search of opium and AIDS-free young Laotian girls, the spread of HIV could be expected to rise at an exponential rate.

The Infectious Diseases Department of the Mahosot hospital was sadly outdated and in dismal condition. A time worn sign still hung there with the French inscription: "Service des Maladies Infectieuses et Médecine Tropicale". Laos was undeniably ill prepared to cope with the HIV/AIDS epidemic that young Laotian girls contracted - compliments of the Western backpackers.

MUONG LUONG WORLD HISTORIC SITE

Chuông chiều ngân trong gió
Tháp núi ẩn màn sương
Lầu vua thu bóng nhỏ
Chùa bụt lạnh hơi sương (Vân Đài 1942)

In the wind linger the evening bell's chimes
Behind the veil of fog the mountaintop hides
In the upper chamber the king curls up for the night
In the pagoda the Buddha shivers with the mist.

In spite of the fact that UNESCO classified it as a World Heritage Site, the ancient capital of Luang Prabang (Muong Luong) was undergoing some very swift metamorphosis. Guesthouses and restaurants went up everywhere. Their menus were unfailingly accompanied by an English version and it did not surprise anybody when another popular joint added a Hebrew one.

We returned to pay a visit to the former Royal Palace on Phothisarat street. It had been converted into a National Museum with fewer and fewer things on display. Many of the gifts the world leaders presented to the king and formerly shown in the King's reception room had disappeared from sight. To name a few: a hunting rifle with an encrusted mother of pearl butt from Leonid Brezhnev, a tea set from Mao Tse Tung…Inquiries addressed to the guide were answered with a gentle smile. Only the mural done by the French artist Alex de Fontereau titled "A Day in Luang Prabang" painted in the Throne Hall was left intact because it could not be removed for sale.

Several 600 to 1,000 year old bronze drums found in the north of Laos were added to the exhibition. Right at the center of the face of the drum, was depicted a sun with radiating rays while representations of fish, flowers and birds were shown inside concentric bands around it. Frog figurines, symbols of the Rainy Season, were placed at intervals on the rim of the drums. The entire artwork offered a harmonious portrayal of "Life, Fertility and Prosperity".

Not far from the Royal Palace, to the north of Manthatoulat Street runs the Mekong. The Dry Season was still months away yet this river was already reduced to a shadow of itself. The vegetable lots on the riverbanks kept on expanding as the water level continued to drop. *"Life, Fertility and Prosperity"* one day will become distant memories and exist only on the face of the drums. Nobody paid any heed to the occluding river. As for me, I knew that several hundreds miles to the north of here, the Manwan Dam, Dachaosan Dam, the Jinghong Dam and the soon to come Xiaowan Mother-Dam...all of the eight mammoth dams in Yunnan had something to do with the lowering of the water level of the Mekong and preventing the silt from flowing downstream.

For thousands of year, the Mekong's current has been colored dark red by silt, that precious gift she receives from Mother Nature. Lately, this color has turned a shade paler.

OF WESTERN BACKPACKERS AND HENRI MOUHOT (1826 – 1861)

Nowadays, Henri Mouhot has become an unfamiliar name to most Laotians. Though he was the first Frenchman to set foot in the capital city of Luang Prabang, he earned his fame for being the person who "rediscovered" the ruins of Angkor.

Mouhot was not the first Westerner to come to Angkor but his name was inextricably associated with the monument thanks to his exceedingly captivating and fascinating travel notes which were published three years after his death. His works inspired many artists and writers of his time as in the case of Anna Leonowens who penned the novel "The English Governess at the Siamese Court" in 1870.

Born a Frenchman, Mouhot was received with indifference by his compatriots and had to seek the help of the British to finance his expeditions. He was both an explorer and a naturalist. During his explorations, he managed to collect rare species of insects. In December of 1860 Mouhot departed from Bangkok on a second journey to Laos. This time he traveled to the northeast of Thailand to visit the minority tribes known as the "Realms of the King of Fire" in the present day provinces of Korat and Loei. The indigenous inhabitants had never set their eyes on a Westerner before.

Youngsters in the north of Thailand and Laos soon became fond of that Westerner with a red beard and his faithful companion, a dog named Tin Tin. They would earnestly hunt for insects to give to Mouhot in exchange for bronze bracelets and cigarettes prompting him to observe: "It seems to me that those kids learned to smoke since the day they were weaned from their mother's milk".

It took Mouhot more than seven months of arduous travel to reach the capital city of Luang Prabang which was as charming as Geneva. There he was received warmly by king Tiantha.

"After waiting for ten days I have at length been presented to the king with great pomp. The reception room was a shed such as they build in our villages on fête-days, but larger and hung with every possible colour. His Majesty was enthroned at one end of the hall, lazily reclining on a divan, having on his right hand four guards squatting down, and each holding a sabre; behind were the princes all prostrated, and farther off the senators, with their back to the public and their face in the dust." [sic].

Using Luang Prabang as a staging base Mouhot led several

expeditions to explore and observe the distant jungles and mountainous regions. Unfortunately, he succumbed to forest fever (probably malignant malaria) three months later. He passed away at the young age of 35 leaving behind these last words in his diary: *"Have pity on me, Oh my God!"*. His remains were buried on the bank of the Nam Khan River, a tributary of the Mekong, while Tin Tin, his ever faithful dog, howled at the side of his shallow grave.

It was not until 1867, six years later, that the French Exploration Group reached Luang Prabang and located his grave. The head of the expedition, Doudart de Lagrée, erected for Mouhot his first tomb, one that he deemed befitting.

The Pha Nom hamlet is 5 kilometers away to the east of Luang Prabang. It consisted of more than 100 houses belonging to the Lu ethnic group from Yunnan. These people were famous for their woven fabrics that were offered as tribute to the royal court in the old days.

We followed a beaten road covered with red dirt. It was dusty and difficult to drive on since several sections of the road were under repair forcing us to take a detour. The travel guidebook indicated that the signs showing the direction had been taken down so in the end we had to solicit the help of two barefoot youngsters in the Pha Nom hamlet to lead us to Mouhot's tomb hidden under a dense foliage.

I let my mind wander back about 140 years in time when at this place the jungle was still dense and wild, and the current strong and rushing. I still could not imagine how lonely and courageous Mouhot must have been then.

The tidy and whitewashed tomb had already turned a mossy color. Two black, chipped and time worn tombstones (more than one hundred year old) read:

> Henri Mouhot 1826 – 1861
> Doudart de Lagrée built this tomb in 1867
> Pavie, consul of France in Luang Prabang, rebuilt it in 1887

During the last work in 1990, a new plaque made of white stone was added to the tomb. It came from Montbéliard, the birthplace of Mouhot, and bore the simple but meaningful engraved inscription:

> *La ville de Montbéliard fière de son enfant 1990)"*
> *(The town of Montbéliard, proud of her son 1990)*

Mouhot was a fine representative of the educated and bright generation of French youth of the 19th century. It was a period of forbearance and stoicism. They were the precursors of the French soldiers who imposed French rule in the three countries of Indochina.

Following in Mouhot's footsteps almost 140 years later, hordes of Western backpackers descended into Laos from Thailand, not to hunt for rare species of insects but for the thick sap oozing out from the opium plant. Quite a few of them never returned to their homeland.

THE BUDDHA CAVE OF PAK OU

Not long ago, in the absence of a land route, the only way to get to the hamlet of Pak Ou from Luang Prabang was by a two-hour motorboat ride upstream the Mekong. Pak Ou or "the mouth of the Ou River" is the juncture where its water clear and free of silt flows into the Mekong. At the other side of the river stands an imposing mountain. A ferry takes the travelers across.

Thanks to financial aids from Sweden, nowadays travelers can reach Pak Ou by a land route which runs through the hamlet of Shang Hay – very well known for making jars and distilling rice wine. One could expect the car ride to Pak Ou on the left bank of the Mekong to be smooth.

The "Pak Ou Caves" is the common name used for two Buddha caves: Tam Ting (the Lower Cave) and Tam Phum (the Upper Cave).

As unbelievable as it may seem, this place has caves large enough to house more than 4,000 statues of the Buddha of over 300 years old in all size and shape. It is equally extraordinary to think that the Laotian people had to row their boats in the thick of the night to hide them in those caves while their capital Luang Prabang was being invaded by foreign troops.

"The first illustrated description of the Buddha Cave of Pak Ou was found in the narration of the 1865-1867 exploration of the Mekong by Francis Garnier."

When monarchy was still in place, according to tradition, every year during the Pimay Tet the King visited the Buddha Cave then spent the night at the royal temple in the Pak Ou Hamlet. The people follow in his example and left Luang Prabang by boat in droves to go upstream the Mae Nam Khong to the Pak Ou cave on a pilgrimage. Once there, they used scented water to bathe the statues of Buddha. After climbing more than 200 steps I reached the Upper Cave. The place made me feel I had entered a completely different world. In the dim light of dusk, the humid and placid atmosphere was permeated with a light mossy scent. I felt as if time had come to a stand still.

From the inside of the cave looking out, I saw rows after rows of statues covered with the dust of time. They might show chips and cracks but placid and immovable remained the smile of the Buddha that appeared to radiate all the way to the Mekong below. The current of this river is still rich with silt even though it was inexorably drying up.

The Pak Ou cave is reputed to be a holy ground where you feel a natural urge to pray. "I am not a Buddhist but I burnt incense and brought a fresh bouquet to offer to the Buddha along with a fervent prayer that the Mekong will be safe and remain forever the lifeline of the people who live in the seven countries along its banks…"

However, as I stepped outside the cave, a quick glance at the alarmingly low water marks on the stone walls made me realize that my prayer will forever remain an "impossible dream".

The sand bars appeared sooner than usual. The people living in the region rushed to the place earlier than expected to prospect for gold.

A GLIMPSE OF THAILAND – AT THE OTHER END OF THE MITTAPHAP BRIDGE

This bridge was built in 1994 by the Australians to provide Laos with a door to the outside world. Travelers crossing the bridge into Laos from Thailand could obtain an entry visa just like the way it is done at Wattay International Airport. At the other end of the bridge they were greeted by a foreign exchange booth, a post office, and a duty free shop. A story has it that with the help from Singapore; a very simple Vietnamese Laotian lady, a former gold trader, founded the chain of duty free shops meeting international standards at all the entry points into Laos. She was at the time living in Pakse.

Standing on the bridge, I watched the current flow by leisurely below, a tiny section of the 4,661 kilometer long course of the Mekong stretching from Tibet to the East Sea. Looking at its water, I could visualize its historic depth. Its surface mirrored past and present civilizations including the Văn Hóa Miệt

Vườn, which - at barely 300 years old - is now facing the threat of extinction.

On the other side of the bridge lies Nong Khai, a small town located at the northernmost tip of the Isan plateau, formerly a dry and immense land surrounded by the Mekong. This seemingly natural frontier line was formerly part of Laos' territory that the French and British arbitrarily allocated to Thailand in 1941. Laotians made up one third of the population of Isan while the rest were Thais. They speak the same language and it becomes easily understandable why the entertainment shows and daily news reports on Thai television broadcasts are common staples to the wealthy families in Laos. We would be amiss if we fail to mention the presence of a significant number of Vietnamese expatriates who moved here for safety in the 1940's and 1950's as the resistance movements against the French spread to the three countries of Indochina.

Until the 1960's the Isan plateau was still an impoverished region. To deal with the growing intensity of the Vietnam War as well as to prevent communist infiltrations into Thailand, the Americans poured money into Isan to finance its development: expansion of modern highway networks, construction of four military strategic airports from which the jet planes took off on their bombing missions over North Vietnam, and the setting up of special teams to rescue the airmen should they be shot down. The U.S. also helped Thailand build hydroelectric dams on the Mekong tributaries like Nam Pond and Nam Pung to bring electricity to the countryside and improve the irrigation system resulting in an astronomical surge in agricultural production.

For ages, Nong Khai has always served as a gateway to Laos. It lost the charms of a little city on the riverbank the day the Mittaphap Bridge was constructed. Tourists who came by land disembark at this stop station before crossing the river into

Laos.

Convenient guesthouses and 4-star hotels crowded the place including the eight-story, 200-room luxurious Holidays Inn Mekong Royal on Jomanee road overlooking the Mekong River.

Nong Khai was caught up in the middle of an electoral frenzy. The streets were flooded with posters proclaiming the campaign slogans of the candidates. My Thai taxi driver with smiling eyes and a gentle voice commented: "We will vote for the richest candidates because they do not need money and are only out for fame. This way we can avoid corruption". I did not know since when the Thai people had become imbued with the American sense of practicality. This may explain why the Thai Rak Thai Party (TRT) meaning the "The Thai loves the Thai" of billionaire Thaksin Shinawatra won an easy victory clearing the way for him to form a new cabinet. Thaksin's education deserves some elaboration: a graduate of Houston University in Texas, he became the richest man in Thailand thanks to his dealings in electronics. He was hailed as the "high-tech mogul" by the American press.

Thaksin represents a new generation of leaders in the developing countries in their drive toward globalization – a synonym of "Americanization". Like him, the leaders of Taiwan, Chile, Mexico, and soon to join the club Thailand and the Philippines were all trained in the U.S. and holders of American doctorate degrees.

Thailand was the only country in Southeast Asia to escape the yoke of French or British colonial rule in the 19th century. Not only was it spared half a century of warfare, it also benefited greatly from the Vietnam War. This windfall continued on even after the war ended as Thailand became the main supplier of rice, food, fruits and vegetables to the two million Vietnamese expatriates who left their country. It must be said that the 1980's was the golden age of economic development for Thailand.

As usual, the Thai people living in the countryside only gain notice during election time. Each vote has its set price paid in bath, the currency of Thailand. If money did not do the work then violence could be the next option. Money and violence form an inseparable "Dangerous Duo" of the Thai political scene. The words uttered by a professor of political science reflect that state of affairs: "Why do you want to waste 30 million baths (more than half a million US Dollars) to buy a village chief when you can spend one tenth of that to buy the service of a hired gun to do the trick?"

To put the people at ease, the chief of staff of the Thai armed forces promised that: "there will not be a 'coup d'état' regardless of the election's results" [sic]. But who could forget that changing his mind at any time was also within the general's prerogatives.

The Military Events of 1932 marked a turning point in the political life of Thailand. On June 24 of that year, a clique of generals and civilians staged a coup d'état while the king was vacationing at a seaside resort. This episode is later known as the Revolution of 1932. It ended absolute monarchy rule and replaced it with a constitutional monarchy form of government similar to that of Great Britain. The king and the royal family merely kept to a ceremonial role. Then things changed drastically during the reign of king Bhumibol. The monarch is revered as an arbitrator, a "common denominator" standing head and shoulder above all for the people to rally around.

When the king embodies the foundation on which rest the unity and stability of society for over half a century, a big question mark inevitably arises: "Once king Bhumibol leaves the scene, who will step in his shoes to assume the duties of the throne when the crown prince is reputed to be a 'prodigal son', a poor reflection of his father?" Considering that the monarch is now 72 years old, it has become a matter of grave concern to every Thai. Some have turned their eyes to princess Chakri Sirindhorn who may ascend the throne as the first queen in the country's eventful history as Thailand crosses the threshold of the 21st century.

Coming to this frontier town I did not harbor much concern about the politics of Thailand. I went to a joint on the riverbank to seek the serenity of the Mekong. My mind was haunted by the image of the Pla Beuk / Pangasianodon gigas, those giant catfish weighing more than 300 kilograms. I could not help asking myself whether they were still swimming around the foot of Mitthaphap Bridge or not.

Pla Beuks have been around for thousands of years, long before they were mentioned in 1930 by the Western press. Furthermore, going back over half a century, the British explorer James McCarthy (1881-1893) in his book, "Surveying and Exploring in Siam", gave rich details about the Pla Beuk when he wrote: "…helping the fishermen pull aboard a Pla Beuk weighing 130 lbs, measuring 7 feet in length, and 4.2 feet in waist line. A fish without scales and teeth…" McCarthy also mentioned the eggs of the Pla Beuk and compared them to the sturgeons' caviars. They were very tasty and sought after. So much so that Laotian kings sent them as gifts to the courts at Hue and Bangkok.

I paid a visit to the marketplace of Nong Khai to have a look at the fish which were caught from the Mekong. The place was not much different from a Vietnamese market in colors and tropical fruits. I never saw so much dry tamarind in my life – lots and lots of crates and bamboo baskets overflowing with the fruit arranged into circles on the stalls. Quite a few of the merchants I met were Vietnamese but they avoided speaking in their own tongue. The Thai people do not look at the Vietnamese with a kind eye and consider them a security risk because of their past affiliations with the Communist Party of Thailand. In fact, Vietnamese revolutionaries like Phan Bội Châu, Hồ Chí Minh had at times sought refuge and carried out their struggle in this country while being hunted down by the French.

THE VIETNAMESE IN THAILAND

Hoàng Văn Hoan (1905-1991), personal friend of Hồ Chí Minh, was a founding member of the Indochinese Communist Party and a member of the Vietnam Worker's Party politburo. He served as ambassador to Beijing from 1950 to 1957 and acted as a crucial link between the Democratic Republic of Vietnam and China. After Hồ Chí Minh's death, Hoan lost much of his influence. He eventually defected and surfaced in Beijing in 1979.

According to Hoàng Văn Hoan 's book, "Giọt Nước Trong Biển Cả / A Water Drop in the Ocean", at the start of the resistance against the French in the mid 40's, the Vietnamese living in Thailand – coming mostly from Laos – numbered about 100,000. At first the Thai were well disposed toward the Vietnamese revolution. The people as well as their government not only accepted the presence of such a large number of Vietnamese on their land but also earnestly gave them assistance. Thailand became a safe haven and base of operation for the resistance against the French.

Though in exile, the Vietnamese expatriates found their lives so comfortable that they forgot they were living in a foreign land. So much so that they became subjective or arrogant in their thinking and careless or ostentatious in their behavior in total disregard for the customs and habits of the host country. They set up an agricultural cooperative and named it Việt Nam, organized fairs and festivals flying their flags all over the place while their militia walked around toting their guns in public...

The inevitable came in the 1950's when the local Thai people openly voiced their complaints. The country's newspapers owned by the new rightwing government also joined in and mounted a public campaign against the Vietnamese.

Willingness to help gave way to animosity. The end result: the Vietnamese were being ostracized. Though not forced to repatriate, they were forbidden to travel outside of their area of residence. While the Chinese met easy acceptance and assimilation into Thai society, the Vietnamese in Thailand found themselves for a time relegated to the status of second-class citizens.

The situation has improved somewhat lately when after more than half a century, the Thai government finally allowed the Vietnamese who were long time residents or born in the country to become naturalized citizens.

Most of the Vietnamese in Thailand are of the third generation and have lost touch with the real conditions of life in Vietnam. Nevertheless, they still identify with their homeland and the Communist regime in Hà Nội on account of the August Revolution and the Resistance Against the French of the old days. Older men of the first generation who are now in their eighties still hang pictures of Uncle Ho at an honored place in their homes.

At the fish market of Nong Khai I was overjoyed by the abundant display of fresh fish caught from the Mekong. On a fish stand, a big Papu fish weighing more than 50 kilograms was being cut up. Without any big expectation, I inquired with the stand's owner about the Pla Beuk. To my great surprise he walked to a freezer and brought back a big Pla Beuk head with the explanation:

"It is difficult to get hold of a Pla Beuk these days. You're lucky to come at the right time. This Pla Beuk caught in the Mekong only weighs 45 kilograms and was rather small. A regular size one could be more than 300 kilograms."

In the closing days of the year 2000, at the Nong Khai market, I was fortunate enough to have a look at the carcass of one of the last Pla Beuks living in the deep crevasses of the Mekong.

When in Nong Khai one must pay a visit to the Buddhist temple named Phrathat Klang Nam that has fallen into ruins since 1847. Submerged in the middle of the river, it is continuously sinking due to the pressure of the current and becomes visible only during the Dry Season. One hundred forty years ago, on his journey from Bangkok to Laos via the Isan plateau, Mouhot wrote in 1860 while sailing up the Mekong: "The Buddhist temple was swept from the bank of the river by the current. Nowadays, only half of it remains above the water looking like a sunken boat."

A mere 5 kilometers east of Nong Khai, a totally different landscape unfolded before my eyes: Wat Khaek. This group of colossal monuments built just recently in the 1970's, offers another facet of the varied cultures along the Mekong. The statue of the Sacred Seven Headed Naga Serpent which protected the Buddha during a violent storm as narrated in an old story stared down at me from at least 30 meters high. For me, Naga also reminds me of the rain forests that store the water of the Rainy Season and release it during the Dry one to regulate the flow of the Mekong. That way there would be fish for the fishermen and water for the farmers to work their rice fields during the two annual harvests.

UDON THANI REVISITED

Udon Thani lies 50 kilometers to the south of Nong Khai. An often mentioned American strategic airbase during the Vietnam War, it was swarming with young Thai girls from the countryside who came to work at the bars, massage parlors, hotels with air conditioned rooms primarily built to cater to the American GIs stationed there. The electricity supplied from the Nam Ngum Dam located on the Laotian side of the Mekong had played a major role in the extraordinary development of Udon.

After 1975, although hostilities have ended, hundreds of American soldiers married to Thai women refused to repatriate and chose to stay in Udon. A quarter of a century later, no traces could be found of those military families. They had dispersed to the four corners of the world: some went back to the U.S., others accompanied their spouses and grown children to different locations to work and live. The "Fast Food T&J" serving hamburgers and French fries" was the only store owned by an American veteran left standing. It was doing brisk business.

Today, unlike Bangkok, Udon is acclaimed as a beautiful city untouched by pollution. The Americans have departed but they left behind a very visible Americanized lifestyle noticeable in stores like Pizza Hut, Kentucky Fried Chicken and Mac Donald...dotting the shopping malls.

Thanks to the Mittaphap Bridge, Udon is chosen as an ideal destination for people from Vientiane to visit and shop during the weekends. The goods here are attractive and inexpensive. Besides, they also please the fashion taste of the Laotian girls of the X generation. My friend, a French trained Laotian doctor remarked:

"It will take a mere two or three weeks for the latest fashion styles shown in Paris, New York or Hong Kong to show up in the department stores of Udon."

Pointing to a huge sign on the sidewalk that proclaimed: "We Care. Ask Udon International Hospital", the Laotian doctor added:

"Patients from the Mahousot Hospital in Vientiane who need

emergency care are brought to The Udon International Hospital for treatment so that they don't have to be sent to Bangkok."

On the other side of the Mekong is Thailand, Laos' dynamic neighbor with whom it also shares the same language. Through the process of economic and cultural osmosis, silently but surely Laos is gradually being transformed into a mini Thailand.

THE PREHISTORIC VILLAGE OF BAN CHIANG

Ban Chiang sits at the top of a triangle with Nong Khai and Udon Thani forming the two ends of its base on the Korat plateau. Located 56 kilometers to the east of Udon Thani on route 22, it takes barely an hour to drive from one city to the other. To visit the excavation site of Ban Chiang is to travel back in time to the Bronze age because at this location was buried probably the oldest civilization of the Mekong. Ban Chiang is considered the most important archeological find in Southeast Asia after World War II. In 1992, UNESCO designated it a World Heritage Site.

Everything happened like in a fairy tale. In 1966, an archeology student from America was walking in the fields of Ban Chiang village when he tripped against the roots of a kapok tree and fell. Unwittingly, he landed face down on an archeological treasure as he found himself surrounded by a multitude of porcelain fragments sticking out from the ground. He picked a number of them to send to Bangkok before returning to the University of Pennsylvania to carry out additional researches.

Those porcelain, glazed terra cotta fragments and human bones were no strangers to the villagers of Ban Chiang as they often struck at them while digging or shoveling in the fields. When rumors about the newly found "prehistoric village" reached their ears, the villagers rushed to the site. They unearth those ancient objects and sold them to foreign collectors without any idea about the high prices they could command. Years later, a number of those artifacts were found to be illegally in the possession of several museums in California. As this fact comes to the attention of the public, it is expected that some of them will be eventually returned to Thailand.

It took four more years before the Thai and American archeologists began systematic excavations of the site. In two short years, they dug up eighteen tons of objects like bronze instruments, porcelain vases or pots, and even woven cloths and human remains in ancient tombs. Preliminary studies using the thermoluminescence technique indicated that these objects dated back to at least 3600 BC - which is 600 older than the oldest bronze objects from the Middle East. This discovery refutes the argument that the technology of bronze making originated in the Land of Two Rivers (Tigris and Euphrates) in the year 3000 BC. It concurrently disproves the theory purporting that bronze objects were imported into the southern regions from China because the oldest bronze objects found in that country were dated to around 2000 BC only. In another word, we can safely conclude that the technology for bronze making migrated from Southeast Asia into China instead of the other way around.

Traditionally, it was erroneously assumed that the civilization of Southeast Asia lagged far behind that of China. Curiously, no due importance has yet been given to those very artistically made bronze jewelry which spoke of a harmonious society possessing an advanced civilization not at all primitive compared to the Chinese one. The same holds true for agriculture. From C14 carbon radioactive dating in the study of rice husks found in Ban Chiang's porcelain vases, scientists were able to determine that agriculture took root in Southeast Asia at an earlier time than in China

Using the Ban Chiang human skeletal remains currently kept at the Department of Anthropology of the University of Hawaii, anthropologists were able to reconstruct a prototype of this prehistoric man. He was endowed with a wide forehead, prominent cheekbones, and long feet. Our man was healthy, living an average life span of 30 years. His death was usually attributed to illnesses like malaria rather than violent causes. He probably came from the Hoabinhnian stock (Vietnam) during the stone age and inhabited the region of Southeast Asia in the period between 12000 to 5000 BC. Joyce White suggested that the prehistoric villages of Ban Chiang succeeded in establishing a stable agriculture-based social system since 7500 BC while the earliest signs of rice cultivation upstream of the Yangtze River in China was dated at about 6500 to 5800 BC. Her finding was further supported by Peter Bellwood who argued that if you add the weather factor to the equation, then "the first cradle of rice cultivation" must be the tropical region of SEA Monsoon.

Suddenly as if things fell into a black hole, one is at a loss to explain why in the second century, for unexplainable reasons Ban Chiang was abandoned by its inhabitants and turned into a desolate place. For the moment, let's turn the page on the prehistoric origin of the Southeast Asian region that conventional textbooks dealing with the origins of world civilizations seemed to have practically ignored as they had done with the Plain of Jars, another civilization of the Mekong.

Upon my return to the U.S., my attention was caught by the news on the front page of the Người Việt Daily. It was about an explosion on the Mittaphap Bridge, the very place where only a few days ago I had stood to look down at the Mekong's current, in the hope of seeing a Pla Beuk.

BANGKOK (Kyodo News) - A bomb explosion on the Mittaphap

Bridge at the border between Laos and Thailand injured 11 tourists coming from Thailand. Immediately afterward the traffic on the bridge was interrupted. The explosion took place at 4:05 in the afternoon Wednesday, 01/25/2001. Evidence found at the scene indicated that the bomb was detonated from a control point at the foot of the bridge on the Laotian side.

Vientiane - Luang Prabang - Nong Khai
12/2000

Lao PDR White House - Year 2000

Mittaphap Friendship Bridge - Vientiane, Nong Khai

Arc de Triomphe Pantouxai - Vientiane

Cultural Pavillon - Made in China

*The golden stupa of That Luong - A symbol of Laos'
historic past*

Old Royal Palace - Luang Prabang

Ban Phanom famous for their woven fabrics

Henry Mouhot Tomb hidden under a dense foliage

Nam Ngum - first hydroelectric dam thirty years later

Year 2000 - Year for Tourism in Laos: Going from Green Tourism (Ecotour) to Black Tourism (Opium and Sex Tour)

The Buddha Cave of Pak Ou

A view of the Mekong from Pak Ou Cave

THE RISE OF THE PHOENIX WALKING THROUGH THE KILLING FIELDS

"The sufferings of the people are the sufferings of the monarchs"
Jayavarman VII

A "COME BACK TO SORRENTO" – ANGKOR KHMER

After 30 years, a return visit to Cambodia still proves to be quite a unique experience in itself. I first went to this country in 1970. At that time the Vietnam War had crossed its national boundaries and its tentacles reached into this land. In other words it had become a "guerre sans frontières". Rockets and mortars rained down on the city of Krek that had the misfortune of being located near the Vietnamese border. In the aftermath, the Lon Nol government instigated several years of terror known as the "decapitation" campaign against the Vietnamese. It was to be replaced by the atrocities of "ethnic cleansing" under Pol Pot's rule.

Lon Nol was a soldier and politician. In 1970, as Prince Sihanouk was traveling on a diplomatic mission in Europe, General Lon Nol staged a coup d'état and proclaimed himself president of the new Khmer Republic. Frustrated with Prince

Sihanouk's pseudo neutral policies, the United States threw its support behind Lon Nol's right wing government.

Prince Sihanouk was popular then. By overthrowing him and abolishing the monarchy, Lon Nol lost the support of the mass. As an ally of Washington, he was supposed to maintain friendly relations with Saigon. On the contrary, the general brutally mistreated the Vietnamese living in Cambodia. Thousands of Vietnamese including women and children were barbarously murdered. Their throats were cut and bodies thrown into the Mekong. All the while, with strong backing from China, his opponents, the Khmer Rouge, continued to expand their control in the countryside. By 1975, his government's authority was reduced to the limits of the capital city. Finally, before the fall of Phnom Penh on April 1, 1975, Lon Nol fled the country to go into exile, first in Hawaii then in California. He passed away in November of 1985. Lon Nol found his nemesis in the leader of the Khmer Rouge named Pol Pot (1925-1998), alias Brother Number One. Pol Pot's regime gained infamous notoriety for its grim determination to start an utopic society in the "Year Zero". To that end, Pol Pot directed the Khmer Rouge to enforce a version of agrarian collectivization calling for the compulsory relocation of city dwellers to the countryside to work in collective farms. Such a harsh policy of hard labor inevitably led to starvation, lack of medical care and mass executions resulting in the death of approximately 2 million persons. The invasion by Vietnam in 1979 put an end to all that. Pol Pot had to flee to the jungles in northwest Cambodia where he was stripped of all power by his Khmer Rouge comrades. He breathed his last at the age of 73 while living under house arrest.

In 2001, I returned to this country with the memories of the nightmarish years of the Killing Fields still fresh in my mind. Peace was a new comer and the country still littered with unexploded mines and explosives – the unfortunate inheritance from a drawn out bloody civil war. Happily, like a phoenix, Cambodia rose from its ashes to take flight toward brighter skies.

In the travelers' eyes, Cambodia had reclaimed her place on the tourism map of Southeast Asia thanks to the magnificent temples of Angkor, a tourist attraction that is unrivaled in Asia.

A promising prospect could come knocking at the door in 2002 with the proposed introduction of the ACV (Air Cushion Vehicle) tour lasting 14 days from the 3rd to the 17th of November each year. The craft is supposed to run the round between two terminal points: the port of Cần Thơ in the Mekong Delta and Simao in the province of Yunnan. Sailing upstream the Mekong, the tourists would start the trip at Cần Thơ to head for Phnom Penh then continue on to Siem Rap and the Tonle Sap Lake in Cambodia. Leaving that country behind, they would enter Laos to visit the Khone waterfall before moving on to Pakse, Vientiane then Luang Prabang. Their next stops would be in Thailand, Myanmar, and the Golden Triangle at the Chinese border. Afterward they would proceed to Jinghong and reach their final destination in Simao, China. The trip would not cover all the seven countries that border the Mekong because a section of the river that runs through the mountain gorges from Tibet to Yunnan is not navigable. Nevertheless, this 2,900 kilometer Ecotour through six countries still promises to be extremely appealing. Tourists could expect to catch the last glimpses of the Pla Beuks and the Irrawady Dolphins that inhabit the Mekong before they become extinct. But we are discussing here a thing that still belongs in the planning stage for the year 2002. (At the time of this writing, it was reported that this tour had been successfully offered to the tourists for the first time).

We were then in the first December of the 21st century. I did not come to this part of the Mekong for sightseeing but rather to conduct a fieldtrip. This section of the current was once dyed red with blood and choked with headless bodies of Vietnamese, the victims of the "decapitation" campaign. For ages the Khmers and Vietnamese regard each other with animosity stemming from a past history of rancorous interactions.

Cao Xuân Huy, the author of "Tháng Ba Gẫy Súng / Broken Guns in March", asked me: "Don't you fear decapitation? As a group, Laotians are without doubt more gentle than the Khmers." With those words, Huy wanted to compare my recent trip to Laos that went on smoothly to my upcoming journey to Cambodia. Huy had an interesting background. Born in North Vietnam in 1947, he joined the elite South Vietnamese Marines. After the fall of South Vietnam, he was imprisoned by the Communists and became one of the boat people who fled the country in 1982 to resettle in the United States a year later.

Another friend, Hoàng Khởi Phong, also jumped in with a similarly unfavorable comment: "Your book is written. Why do you have to go to Cambodia? You still have time to change your mind". Though his remark was not in itself an outright dissuasion, it could not be taken as being an encouragement either. In addition to being a poet and writer, Phong also worked as a journalist. Four years older than Huy, he served as a former officer in the Armed Forces of the Republic of Vietnam. In early 1975, he sought refuge in America where he became the editor of Văn Học Magazine from 1989 to 1991. His works include: "Ngày N+ / D Day", a memoir; and the novel "Người Trăm Năm Cũ / Men of One Hundred Yesteryears."

Dohamide, my Chăm friend from the time we were colleagues at the Bách Khoa / Encyclopedia magazine prior to 1975, was even more emphatic. He ventured that I should drop the idea altogether because we were so close to post 9/11. He turned more vehement when I told him of my intention to visit the Chăm Islam community of almost 500,000 living in the midst of eleven million Khmer Buddhists. Dohamide or Đỗ Hải Minh, his Vietnamese name, was born in 1934 in the city of Châu Đốc, Mekong Delta. A graduate of the National Institute of Administration in South Vietnam, he also earned an M.A. in Political Science from Kansas University. He was a contributor to Bách Khoa in Saigon and the magazine Thế Kỷ 21 / Twenty-First Century in California. In his later years in America, he founded the Vietnamese Islam Association as well as authored two research books: "A Condensed History of the Chăm People" and "Bangsa Champa: In Search of a Remote Root".

My American colleagues at the hospital where I work – several of them former Green Berets and veterans of the war in Cambodia - also expressed their astonishment about my choice of "vacation spot".

My eagerness to go on with the trip was somewhat dampened by an unexpected development when I learned that my travel companion, Nguyễn Kỳ Hùng, had to drop out at the last minute. An end of year project at Gateway, the electronic company where Hùng worked as a planning engineer, required his presence at the office. He is an accomplished young photographer / reporter who came along with me during our trip to the Mekong Delta two years back.

I fully realized that a reporter, even when not working in the battlefields, still has other fronts to face. The RWB (Reporters Without Borders / Reporters Sans Frontières) recorded that in 2001 there were thirty-one newsmen who lost their life in the line of duty. This figure was equal to the one reported for the previous year and did not include those held in captivity.

Being aware of the danger does not mean in any form or

shape refusing to accept one's responsibilities. Therefore, although one is naturally expected to face the uncertainties of one's profession whenever they arise, at a certain point down the road, one has to ask oneself whether one's death would serve a meaningful purpose or not. Consciously or not, each of us is facing that question in our daily life because death remains the final destination of our personal journey on this earth.

For me, coming to the Mekong is like responding to a siren's call: To go back, to come to the Tonle Sap Lake and other parts of the Mekong. Future generations may not be fortunate enough to behold the rich yet extremely fragile ecology of a river that may be called "The River of the Past" in a not too distant future.

RECENT NEWS BEFORE DEPARTING
President Bush removed Cambodia from the list of the world's major nations trafficking in drugs. Nevertheless the watch list of the DEA / Drug Enforcement Agency still contains 23 countries - Among them: China, Laos, Myanmar, Thailand, and Vietnam.

The mission of the DEA is to enforce the controlled substances laws or regulations of the United States and prosecute violators before the American courts. This Agency also recommends and supports non-enforcement programs aimed at reducing the availability of banned controlled substances on the domestic and international markets.

At the time of my visit, Cambodia was actively implementing a rather costly Demobilization Plan to return 30,000 servicepersons including officers and generals to civilian life by the end of 2002. The World Bank provided the lion's share of the fund earmarked for that Plan in the hope of reducing the quantity of weapons and ammunition that proliferated in Cambodia and secure the foundation for a lasting peace. A secondary objective of the planners was to improve "human rights" conditions while at the same time save US$ 10 million a year to be used for social and economic development projects. However, corruption still proved to be the most intractable impediment to the effective use of the US$ 42 million budgeted for that Plan.

Recently, prime minister Hun Sen signed a law calling for the closure of Karaoke parlors in order to eradicate social evils like: violent crimes, widespread prostitution, and a growing HIV epidemic in the countryside brought about by infected Karaoke waitresses as they returned to their villages. In the post 9/11 era, Cambodia's tourism industry was already experiencing a 20% drop in the number of visitors mainly from Europe and North America. The new law represented another serious "hurdle" to the tourism sector since the Asian vacationers who were expected to make up for the slack unfortunately enjoyed frequenting those banned Karaoke nightclubs.

The visit of Mr. Trần Đức Lương, President of Vietnam, coincided with huge fires that burned down a large number of thatch huts belonging mostly to the Vietnamese residents in two neighborhoods of Phnom Penh. Those two areas were part of a relocation plan that was previously adopted by the city government. At that time, diplomatic relations between the two countries were taking a turn for the worse due to a border dispute, a perennial curse that pervades their long history.

The people and government of Cambodia always maintain that the Mekong Delta and its millions of Khmer Vietnamese, also known as Khmer Krom, belonged to them. They lost that land to the Vietnamese during the latter's Southward March that began in the 17th and lasted until the early 19th century. In the initial phase, Vietnam laid claims to all the territories of the Kingdom of Champa, which for all practical purposes totally disappeared from the map of the world. In the ensuing years, the Vietnamese came face to face with another neighbor: the

Khmer. As a result, the Mekong Delta changed from Khmer to Vietnamese hands. The Southward March came to an abrupt stop with the French conquest of Vietnam, Cambodia and Laos and the establishment of French Indochina. Without the arrival of the French, the Cambodians had every reason to believe that their homeland would eventually be swallowed up by both the Thai and Vietnamese.

THE ROAD TO SIEM REAP
During the Thai-French war of 1941, the Japanese forced the French to cede a part of Cambodia's territory to the Thai. However, in the aftermath of Japan's defeat in 1945, the Thai had to return it to the French. This was probably the reason why the name Siem Reap meaning the "defeat of Siam" was coined for a small city located in the countryside to the northwest of the Tonle Sap Lake. Its verdant landscape was dotted with coconut, areca and tamarind trees...just like in the Mekong Delta. The disposition of the surrounding hills gave the area a strategic importance that prompted successive Khmer kings to build there the temples of Angkor to serve as their capital from the 9th to the 13th century. During the last civil war, the opposing parties often confronted each other and settled their accounts at this location.

In the "post-Khmer Rouge" era, the sleepy city of Siem Reap began to stir and became the staging area for tourists who wished to visit the wonder of Angkor. The introduction of a direct flight between Bangkok and Siem Reap spared them a stop over at Phnom Penh. No wonder why the flights to Phnom Penh were emptying up while those to Siem Reap were getting fully booked causing its airport to become overcrowded. Construction works were under way to expand that facility.

Golf courses and hotels, including the five-star Sofitel, were rushed into construction. Malaysian entrepreneurs planned to set up a grand scale "sound and light" show at the Angkor Wat site. However, due to the most recent economic crisis in Asia, they had to shelve the project.

The post 9/11 years also witnessed a change in the make up of the tourists in Cambodia. The country saw a sharp decrease in the number of visitors from North America and Europe. On the other hand, the gap was filled by a growing number of tourists from Asian countries like Japan, Taiwan, South Korea, China...

Visas on arrival – The airport police at Siem Reap was professional and organized to perform their tasks in a chain-work fashion. Robust Khmer men with curly hair and sun burnt skin looked neat in their well-pressed uniforms. In spite of my American passport, I was kept waiting there for a long while by the section head, a captain with a pair of bright but cold eyes. When he finally handed the passport back to me he thanked me using the short Vietnamese words *"Cám ơn"* in a tone pregnant with insinuation. By his attitude I was to understand that in the land of Angkor Wat my identity is that of a Vietnamese national regardless of the type of passport I bear. I came to the Khmer and Chăm peoples carrying on my shoulders the burden of almost three hundred years of past animosities. Could the debt we owe these peoples ever be repaid?

MALRAUX AND ANGKOR

To see all the Angkor monuments that were built along a circumference of 35 kilometers, would require at least three days to a week. Unfortunately, I had only one day in my itinerary to spend with this splendid but defunct civilization along the Mekong.

I followed the same road André Malraux called the Royal Way to reach the temples of Angkor. Since the time I first read his book, "La Voie Royale", I immediately took a liking to this man of adventure and action. For a long time I only knew him as an accomplished writer and politician. However, just recently by pure coincidence the American writer Walter Langlois through his book "André Malraux: The Indochina Adventure" (New York 1966) introduced me to a different Malraux.

More than 78 years ago (1923), this down-to-earth Malraux landed for the first time in Saigon at the young age of 23. Prior to that, he had gone to Hanoi to meet the members of the École Francaise d'Extrême Orient and learned that the temples of Angkor were classified as protected monuments. Nevertheless, once in Saigon, he undertook a journey up the Mekong to Phnom Penh in the company of his wife, Clara, and friend, Louis Chevasson. From there the trio sailed upstream the Tonle Sap River to arrive at Siem Rap via the Tonle Sap Lake then transferred to a land route to reach Angkor.

With premeditation, he carefully planned his moves by renting ox driven carts and hiring Khmer hands. At Angkor, they went to the Banteay Srei temple area where Malraux provided his workers with stone saws to cut out a steal depicting a beautiful apsaras along with a number of smaller statues. They packed their bounty in crates mislabeled as "chemical containers" before transporting them by carts to the Tonle Sap Lake for shipment to Phnom Penh with Saigon as the final destination.

If everything had gone smoothly, those art works would have fetched a fortune from New York collectors to the great satisfaction of the young Malraux who could in no way be described as well off at the time. Unbeknownst to Malraux, since the start, his group was put under surveillance every step of the way. The moment they set foot in Phnom Penh they were caught red handed with all the incriminating evidence. Except for Clara who was set free on account of her sex, her two male companions had to face trial. Malraux received a three-year jail sentence while Chevasson was given a shorter time of 18 months. Claiming that the Banteay Temples were not on the protected list the two appealed and were transferred to Saigon for a new trial. His reputation in the literary circles at the time brought his colleagues in Paris to his defense and the case took on cultural and political implications. The Saigon Court still found the pair guilty but reduced the lower court's verdict for Malraux to a suspended sentence of one year. Soon afterward Malraux returned to Paris.

The "rich irony" of all this (to borrow the terms used by Milton Osborne) is that the very person who was found guilty of committing "cultural vandalism" in French Indochina during colonial times later became the Minister of Culture in the government of General De Gaulle for quite a long time.

Nguyễn Hiến Lê (1912-1985) was born in Hanoi, then moved to the South of Vietnam in 1935. A self taught man, this scholar turned out to be a prolific writer with more than one hundred published books in his name. He was one of the main contributors to Bách Khoa / Encyclopedia magazine in Saigon prior to 1975. In 1943, at the age of 31, while on a mission for the Bureau of Public Works to Siem Reap, he had the opportunity to pay a visit to Angkor Wat and wrote an interesting short travel book about this place.

More than a half-century later, I also came to the massive stone blocks of Angkor. Though inanimate by nature, somehow they were arranged in such an artistic way that they formed a harmonious architectural whole, whose beauty was enhanced by myriads of intricate carvings. In its totality, this is an imposing achievement by master architects and an army of gifted carvers with very keen eyes for the human anatomy. Countless quantities of ink and paper have been spent in the praise of Michelangelo of the Renaissance in the West. When standing in front of the temples at Angkor, one could only watch in silent admiration for those anonymous great artists and could not help wonder where they came from and where their souls have gone to now. Their works predated Michelangelo five long centuries.

Sunrise at Angkor is something beautiful to marvel at - a quiet symphony lauding the communion between nature and human achievements. Five stupas stood out against a grayish sky that was blushing red as the sun rose over the horizon. Rows of sugar palm trees, the traditional symbol of Cambodia, cast their profiles on the reflecting surface of the lake as if to bear witness to the millenniums that had gone by. The lingering dewdrops from the previous night sparkled on the leaves and petals of the floating water lilies. Going up the steps leading to the temple and palace compound amidst towering and imposing stone statues, I walked by thousands of carvings. They reminded me that, like a history book, those stone tablets were the record keepers of actual life scenes in the past. Awed by the entire setting, I had the impression that time had come to a standstill. Then, overtaken by a moment of deep recollection, I pondered the ephemeral nature of dynasties and human existence. Raising my eyes to admire the compassionate look and enigmatic but serene smile of the Buddha statues I could not resist the temptation of comparing it to the much talked about smile of the Mona Lisa. For me, her smile could only rate a distant second to what I was looking at then.

As I was admiring dawn breaking out over the landscape, the ironic thought that I had before my eyes the vestiges of a civilization at its sunset came to my mind. No – actually of two civilizations: Angkor-Khmer and Champa. Meeting today's Khmers, for some unexplained reason, I entertained the same thought as Mouhot, the explorer who "rediscovered" the temples of Angkor more than a century ago. Like him I thought it would be difficult to believe that today's Khmer could actually be the descendants of or in any way related to the builders of the wonder of Angkor. In 2000, just one year ago, I came looking for Mouhot's tomb located in a deserted stretch of a tributary of the Mekong called Nam Khan River in Upper Laos and sat by its side.

I was overwhelmed by a strange and haunting feeling at the sight of several Catholic nuns sitting on a high stone platform of an ancient library that had fallen in ruins. They faced the rays of the rising sun singing a cheerful religious hymn as the wind carried their carefree, ethereal voice to far away places.

FROM THE VIETNAMESE FLOATING VILLAGE

From Siem Reap we boarded a motorboat heading south toward Chong Kneas, also known as the Vietnamese Floating Village northwest of the Tonle Sap Lake. On arrival we were greeted by a group of people who prefer to live in the rich and varied eco-environment of a river.

Like a magnet, the abundant resources of the Tonle Sap Lake attracted different peoples from all over the place to come and establish floating villages in the flood plains or on the lake. Their lifestyle seemed to have remained untouched by time for hundreds of years. They were fishermen whose principal source of income was derived from their catch. Besides fishing they also engaged in running fish farms; raising crocodiles, snakes, and ducks; wood cutting; hunting birds and games; even harvesting water plants.

I came to this floating village in search of the beauty of a natural ecology of a wild marshland. These floating villages migrate with the changes in the seasons and water levels. Sunrises and sunsets count among the most beautiful sceneries the Tonle Sap Lake has to offer.

TO THE BIRD SANCTUARY IN THE BIOSPHERE OF PREK

TOAL

The motorboat was cruising at full speed for almost two hours on the Tonle Sap Lake. A strong wind, high waves, and dark clouds gave me the impression I was sailing on the high sea. The water of the lake incessantly splashed on board. I did not mind getting soaked but had to struggle really hard to keep my Canon camera which was not waterproof from getting wet. Just a while back its lens got splashed when I was trying to take a picture of a rare bird that perched on a cluster of blooming purple water hyacinths. Probably the bird was tired and landed on the hyacinths for a short rest in the midst of that boundless body of water.

The boat crossed the width of the Tonle Sap Lake then veered south to berth at a floating village belonging to the Khmers named Prek Toal in the province of Battambang,. The office of the Environmental Research Station for the Tonle Sap Biosphere Reserve was located there.

The Prek Toal ecology with its Bird Sanctuary is one of the three biosphere zones of the Tonle Sap Lake. It is the gathering point for a great number of rare birds. I could see in the distance flocks of waterfowl of all sizes and kinds hovering over the lake.

It's an amazing phenomenon to watch the area of the lake change with the seasons. During the Dry Season the lake dries up and measures only 2,500 km². Come the Rainy Season, starting in June or July, the water level of the Mekong rises forcing the Tonle Sap River to reverse its course and flow into the Tonle Sap Lake causing the water level to swell from 8 to 10 meters and overflow its banks. Consequently, the lake's area expands to almost five times its size or to 12,000 km². The Mekong and Tonle Sap Lake were once the cradle of the Angkor civilization.

The royal decree of November, 1993 classified the Tonle Sap Lake as a Multiple Use Protected Area. In spite of the relentless efforts of prince Sihanouk it was not until October of 1997 that UNESCO recognized it as a Biosphere Reserve.

To better manage this Biosphere Reserve, the Tonle Sap Lake was divided into three categories: core, buffer and transition zones. The long-term objective is to protect the core and eventually turn it into a national park.

The three zones with a high degree of conservation efforts are:
- Prek Toal area: 31,282 ha
- Boeng Chhmar or Moat Kla area: 32,969 ha
- Stung Sen area: 6,586 ha

This trio forms an extremely varied ecology endowed with streams, lakes, marshlands, and swamp vegetation. In addition, they also represent an aquatic system unique to the Tonle Sap Lake giving sanctuary to a limitless number of fish, waterfowls, reptiles, amphibians, mammals, water vegetations, and microorganisms.

During the high water season, almost 2/3 the area of the marshlands in the Tonle Sap Lake is populated by an agglomeration of plants which consists of over 190 species. The flooded forest plays a vital role in the nurture and procreation of living organisms. It provides an environment for mutual symbiosis in the form of a giant food chain.

The Tonle Sap Lake is home for some 200 species of fish alone. Of those 70 are deemed of nutritional value and great commercial potentials. Consequently, the catch from Tonle Sap Lake accounts for more than 60% of the fresh water fish harvest in Cambodia.

However, there was a growing concern that the quantity of fish caught is declining and that big fish are growing scarcer. As for birds, these waterfowls find an ideal sanctuary in the lake on account of its abundant food source and the varied ecology of its marshlands and flooded forest. Preliminary studies show that there exist in the lake hundreds of bird species including twelve which are classified as rare in the world.

The lake's ecological system also provides a friendly habitat for reptiles and mammals: 23 species of snakes; 13 turtles; crocodile, monkey, leopard, and otter.

To date not much is known about the multifaceted and changing nature of the Tonle Sap Lake. To fill this gap of knowledge, we propose that a project be conducted immediately to study, record and monitor the birds, fish, vegetation, water plants, and the changes in the water quality of the lake. In summary: an in depth and systematic study of the entire ecology of the place. Considering the present day excessive rate of exploitation of its natural resources some species may become extinct before we even realize it. A case in point could be found at the Khone waterfall in southern Laos.

We were in the middle of December, the water level dropped to the one meter mark on the trunk of a 10 meter tall tree. Dried lumps of trash hanging on tall branches indicated that at the peak of the high water season three months ago the water level must be 3 meters higher. Except for the low bushes that appeared to be floating on top of the waterline, we could not make out a single clear path in between the tree clusters ahead of us. Probably a sampan would be more suitable to navigate in that flooded forest. Considering its rather large size, the boat we rented must be meant for sailing in the Tonle Sap Lake.

I was the only Vietnamese riding on the boat with three Khmer companions in the immensity of the flooded forest. Every now and then the engine choked because the propeller got enmeshed in small bushes. Right away, the steersman or his aide jumped into the water and struggled with noisy splashing sounds to free the propeller. They looked angry and argued loudly with each other. Their face betrayed the fierceness they felt inside. All the while the austere looking guide with a dark sunburn who went onboard at the Reserve Station was sitting motionless at the bow of the boat. At times he shook his head to show that his patience was wearing thin.

Under the scorching sunlight the birds were flying nonchalantly in the dense flooded forest. At that moment I was at a loss and did not know whether I should press ahead or turn back. I truly could not tell which choice would be the wiser. My imagination was wild enough to let me think that should anything happen to me in that remote, no man's land like place I would be utterly helpless. I also realized that human nature is like that of a fierce dormant beast and all visible signs of fear could wake it up. So I just played it calm to the point of manifesting a "let go" attitude. In the end the motorboat did dock safely at the Bird Sanctuary Center.

A very young Meas Rithy was expecting me because he had been forewarned of my arrival by a telephone call from the Reserve Office. He could not imagine that it could take that long for a motorboat to complete the trip. Meas held a Bachelor Degree in Forestry from the Royal University of Phnom Penh. Upon graduation, he was assigned to the position of station chief at the Prek Toal – Tonle Sap Biosphere Reserve. Thanks to frequent contacts with UNESCO officials, Meas spoke fluent English. His experience working with foreign delegations and tourists allowed Meas to give me a complete yet concise briefing that helped me arrive at a better understanding of the Bird Sanctuary and the Reserve. I had done my homework prior to departure so what I heard allowed me to systemize the information I already had. Most importantly, Meas arranged for me to go with a guide on an on-the-site observation tour.

To put me to the test, Meas took me to a flimsy thatch box

hanging down from a tall tree branch he called a watch station with a rope ladder providing the only access to it. With my years in the military and three years in the concentration camps this could hardly represent a formidable challenge for me. With agility I climbed up first. The place barely had enough room to accommodate a hammock and the floor was made of wooden planks tied together with ropes. This was probably the highest spot with a panoramic view of the Bird Sanctuary. From there, using a pair of binoculars I could make out each cluster of trees or flocks of birds of all sizes perching on the branches in the distance. Meas gave me a lecture on each species of birds and added that the Dry Season (January to March) would be the best time to visit the Bird Sanctuary. This time coincides with that of the Bird sanctuary at Tam Nông in the Đồng Tháp Mười Province of the Mekong Delta in Vietnam. During this time, the flooded forest was transformed into mud fields spotted with water puddles and shallow lakes teeming with fish and shrimps. This was also the appointed time for birds and beasts to converge to the place in flocks and hordes. That ecological scene must have surpassed by far the horror movie "The Birds" of the film director Alfred Hitchcock. It sure is an ecological wonder!

To make it here on time I missed both my breakfast and lunch. Out of compassion the steersman shared with me half a box of white rice and a slice of Chinese sausage soaked in fat. Each mouthful of rice tasted sweet and delicious on an empty stomach.

Next, Meas and I boarded a small sampan propelled by the "arm-power" of a rower to get closer to each tree cluster and flock of birds. The small craft glided effortlessly on the water in the midst of the wild and untouched beauty of the flooded forest. We stopped in stages for me to observe each species of birds including some classified as rare and included in the endangered list like the Spot-billed Pelican, Oriental Darter, Lesser Adjutant, Greater Adjutant, Black Necked Stork, Painted Stork, Milky Stork, Glossy Ibis, Grey-headed Fish Eagle...

I was told very early that morning a group of French ornithologists had gone by small boats to the more distant spots to photograph and film the White-winged Ducks known to be an extremely rare species.

On the return trip I learned more about Meas' background. He earned a meager US$ 15 Dollars a month that prevented him from severing his financial umbilical cord with his parents. Nevertheless he felt passionately devoted to his work to save the flooded forest and its birds and beasts. He did not have the slightest inkling about the series of dams in the gigantic Yunnan Cascades or the fact that should the water level in the Tonle Sap Lake drop by one meter the immediate result would be the disappearance of 2,000 km^2 of flooded forest and the entire Prek Toal Reserve as well.

Meas's world does not reach beyond the Bird Sanctuary. His modest desire was to meet the right people he called "connections" that would help him go and study abroad – especially in the United States. Before we left Prek Toal to return to Siem Reap, I bid my farewell to Meas without neglecting to leave a token contribution of US$ 20 toward the preservation works of the Reserve.

JAYAVARMAN VII SIEM REAP

I used my remaining time in Siem Reap to visit the children hospital Jayavarman VII that was inaugurated by Prince Sihanouk and prime minister Hun Sen during a ribbon cutting ceremony in 1999. This is the third hospital of its kind in Phnom Penh. The director of not one but all three is the legendary Dr. Beat Richner. A Swiss national, he worked as a pediatrician at a children hospital in Phnom Penh from 1974 to 1975, the year the Khmer Rouge marched into the capital.

In 1991 prince Sihanouk asked Dr. Richner to restore that children hospital to its former state. The following year, the Kantha Bopha I hospital went back into operation. Then in 1996 another hospital named Kantha Bopha II was inaugurated in Phnom Penh. Three years later came the turn of a third hospital this time in Siem Reap-Angkor: the Jayavarman VII hospital. That name was chosen because it conveys a deep historical connotation.

Jayavarman is the last hero king of the Khmer-Angkor dynasty in the 12th century. He was the ruler who expanded the kingdom's borders to its largest reaches. Besides being a builder of fabulous temple areas like the renowned Bayon, he also funded useful projects like the construction of roads, clinics and hospitals.

Medical treatment at the Jayavarman VII are up to standards and totally free to the poor children of Cambodia. The hospital also houses teaching facilities for medical students and interns. To run the three hospitals requires an annual budget of US$ 9 million coming mainly from private donors in Switzerland. Doctor Richner observes a rigid work schedule: three days in Phnom Penh and the last three days of the week in Siem Reap. Besides being a pediatrician he also plays the cello and excels in performing Bach's works. In spite of his busy work load Dr. Richner still finds time to do a Bach performance every Saturday night at the hospital. He personally executes Beatocello in Concert to raise fund for the hospital even though attendance at the event is free. The audience consists mostly of foreign tourists who are on sightseeing tours at the temples of Angkor.

In this small town, not very far from Angkor Wat and Angkor Thom, in the warm climate of the continental Asia Monsoon I immersed myself in the melody of J.S. Bach's music that found a new life in the vibrations of Dr. Richner's cello. At that moment I no longer believed there existed an irreconcilable divide between East and West as proclaimed by Rudyard Kipling in one of his famous sayings. On the contrary, I felt in my heart a sudden merging of the Mekong and Danube into a single harmonious current. That physician artist had introduced Bach's music, full of rhythm and intellect, into the temples of Asia. The musical notes from his program, "Bach at the Pagoda", resounded to distant corners reaching the Killing Fields to soothe, console, and comfort the restless souls that still haunt the place.

Leaving the spacious and well kept hospital at Siem Reap behind, I could not erase from my memory the image of Khmer mothers stepping confidently through its doors with their babies in their arms while the Buddha like bust of Jayavarman VII tinted crimson by the emerging sunrays looked down from the red roofs. Below it, a plaque bearing a meaningful message in French, probably chosen by Dr. Richner himself, reads: "*Les souffrances des peuples sont les souffrances des rois* / The sufferings of the people are the sufferings of the monarchs" Jayavarma VII. Could his Majesty Sihanouk the symbol of a declining epoch and his Majesty Hun Sen the symbol of an emerging era feel any of the pains of the Khmer survivors who are coming out of the Killing Fields?

Richner evokes the memory of Albert Schweitzer (1875-1965), the 1952 Nobel Peace Prize laureate, who came more than a century earlier to the Lambaréné hospital in Gabon to tend to those afflicted with leprosy in Africa. Interestingly enough, Schweitzer was also a gifted organist well versed in the music of Johann Sebastian Bach.

For the rest of the day I visited a crocodile farm located 2 kilometers from the center of town. I could not see anything extraordinary or unusual about a crocodile farm. But according to a story, the "unbelievable but true" did happen under Pol Pot's rule. I was told that soldiers of the Khmer Rouge had thrown people alive into the pit to be devoured by those reptiles. Nowadays, they are raised for export to Thailand where their leather fetches US$ 2,000 each. Gone is the sight of crocodiles feasting on human flesh, still, watching their weekly feeding on Fridays is enough to turn one's stomach.

PHNOM PENH – THE FOREIGN CORRESPONDENTS' CLUB

During the war years, foreign correspondents were quite familiar with the FCCC (Foreign Correspondents' Club of Cambodia) located on Preah Sosovath Boulevard. It consisted of a complex of buildings constructed during French rule with rooms and balconies overlooking the Tonle Sap River. For foreign correspondents, this was the place to meet and socialize.

Three days prior to my arrival, I telephoned the Club from Siem Reap to reconfirm that a room was reserved for me and a car would pick me up at the airport. None of those things materialized on my arrival. The only option for me then was to take a taxi from the airport to the Club to discover that I could not book a room there either.

I did not let my imagination run wild when I forewarned myself that Phnom Penh was not a very safe place for foreign visitors. Taking a ride on a Honda motorcycle-for-hire or stepping into an unlicensed taxi without a commercial sign meant that you were embarking on a trip with unknown destinations. The reason? Armed robberies were commonplace here. Advisories were out that under no circumstances should tourists put up a fight. They should hold their hands up and surrender anything the robbers asked for be it money or valuable jewelry and all. Most of the time, the robbers would throw back the credit cards and passports to their poor victims before fleeing the scene. Rumors were ripe that a number of rogue Cambodian policemen worked in cahoots with those criminals.

A rapacious group of Honda motorcycle and unlicensed taxi drivers was waiting at the gate of the Club. Like a flock of vultures they fought for customers with a total disregard for manners. One would grab the camera, another would pull at the luggage while at the same time noisily asking questions as if to size up their preys: "You are Chinese?" " You are Thai?" "You are Japanese?" No matter what interpretation you might draw of the situation, it is quite unwise to let them know that you are Vietnamese. Seeing a Café Internet next door to the FCCC, I told them I had already booked a room at the hotel and only needed to use the Internet. My intention was to get rid of them so that I could find a telephone and contact the taxi driver who picked me up at the Pochentong International Airport. In my view, it would be a safe bet to use a licensed taxicab driver who can speak some English. Besides, he also had a cellular phone for me to call whenever I needed his services.

Sok Thon, the taxi driver, immediately recognized my voice over the telephone line and with a brief reply: "No Problem" offered to come pick me up right away instead of driving to the airport to look for customers. I breathed a sigh of relief and went back to my cup of cappuccino in the air-conditioned room of the Café while trying to block from my mind the hustle bustle and sweltering heat of the street. I also took this opportunity to go on the Internet and send an email to my friend Khánh Trường to congratulate him on the 12th anniversary of his Hợp Lưu magazine as well as the painting exhibition showing more than 100 of his works.

Khánh Trường, pen name of Nguyễn Khánh Trường (1948 Quảng Nam), is an artist, painter, and writer. He joined the

Airborne Division of the Armed Forces of the Republic of Vietnam in 1968. Wounded in 1970 he was then discharged. In 1987 he escaped Vietnam by boat. One year later the publication of his poetry debut 'Đoàn Thi Khánh Trường' promulgated him into the Vietnamese literary circles. He founded Hợp Lưu / The Confluence magazine, and became well known as an editor who supported the confluence of two Vietnamese literary streams: in and outside of Vietnam. His published works include: Đoản Thi / Short Poems of Khánh Trường, Chung Cuộc / The End (a collection of short stories)...A writer friend, Mai Thảo, gave Khánh Trường the nick name of *"The Sidewalk Artist of New York"*.

For his part, Mai Thảo - the pen name of Nguyễn Đăng Quý (1927-1998) is a celebrated writer, poet, and publisher in his own right. Born in Nam Định, North Vietnam, he sought refuge in the South when the country was partitioned in two in 1954. There he founded the avant-garde, influential literary movement named Sáng Tạo / Creative Group. After the Communist take over of the South in 1975 he went underground and fled by boat to Malaysia in 1978. He resettled in the U.S. and passed away in California in 1998. A short list of his works includes: Đêm Gĩa Từ Hà Nội / Hanoi Farewell Night (a collection of short stories, which shows him at his best), Tháng Giêng Cỏ Non / Green Grass of January, Bản Chúc Thư Trên Ngọn Đỉnh Trời / The Testament on the Highest Peak, his favorite story; and his last but not least publication: Poems of Mai Thảo.

THE TAXI DRIVER NAMED "NO PROBLEM"

Half an hour later Sok Thon showed up at the Café Internet and helped me carry my luggage to his cab, a 1988 air conditioned Camry. Its second paint was still shiny. I suggested to him that I would like to look for a hotel comparable to the FCCC with a view of the river. Again, "No problem" came back to me - his usual, self-confident way of answering.

He took me to the Sunshine Hotel located on the same street that ran along the river and next to the Indochine Hotel. The owner of the place was Chinese. The window in my fourth floor room overlooked the Tonle Sap River that flowed south to the Quatre Bras in front of the Royal Palace.

Quatre Bras / Four Arms in French or Chatomuk / Four Faces in Khmer, is a confluence of four rivers: the Upper Mekong and the Tonle Sap Rivers join together at this place then split into The Lower Mekong and the Bassac. The last two flow side by side through southern Vietnam and are renamed Sông Tiền and Sông Hậu by the local inhabitants. They then form a network of nine tributaries or commonly called the Nine Dragons (Cửu Long in Vietnamese).

Quatres Bras is the site of the most spectacular festival in the Cambodian year: Bon Om Tuk or the annual Water and Moon Festival (a Cambodian version of the Mardi Gras). It is the traditional way the people celebrate and pay homage to the Tonle Sap River as its current successfully defies the law of gravity and flows uphill into the Great Lake during the Rainy Season.

The incompetence of the FCCC staff proved to be a blessing in disguise for me since it allowed me to find the companion of travel I needed. Sok Thon, a full fledged Khmer, had worked as a taxi driver for ten years. He spoke English with a complete disregard for grammar but possessed a vocabulary large enough for the two of us to communicate with each other. Besides, he loved to speak foreign languages including a sprinkling of French words.

It was not until later that I learned Sok Thon had served in the military for eight years as an officer – probably in a junior rank. He had lived in Vietnam for two years so could speak some

Vietnamese. On that point I made up my mind never to avail myself of his skill with the Vietnamese language.

The last afternoon before my departure, as we were leaving the "Tuol Sleng" Museum of Genocidal Crime, Sok Thom confided in me that his hometown is Kompong Chhnang. He added that his father was killed in 1974 by the Khmer Rouge because he was a village chief. His brother also met the same fate for being a teacher. Sok Thom only escaped death by pretending to be a peasant. An interesting detail here: two members of his family were able to make it to Thailand and later immigrated to the United States where the older sister found a home in Long Beach while the younger brother settled in Fresno. Both had returned to Cambodia for family visits.

Sok Thom and his wife had three children. His oldest son - 17 years old of the post-Khmer Rouge generation, was studying for his university entrance test. Sok Thon encouraged him to learn English and bought him a computer to help him in his studies. "No Problem" was optimistic about the future of his children and that thought was the joy of his life.

The check-in at the hotel done, I entered the elevator and came face to face with a Western backpacker in the company of a local young girl. He greeted me first and said he knew I came from Long Beach. My astonishment was total at this unexpected turn of event. It was true that I was living then in Long Beach. However, I did not believe I had ever met or known that young man before. Puzzled, I asked how he could tell I came from that city? He replied that I left Phnom Penh 26 years ago and went back for a visit. Suddenly it dawned on me that I was dealing with a Western backpacker cum fast talker who tried to be smart. He knew that the largest community of Cambodian expatriates lived in Long Beach and assumed I must be one of them. He then proposed for us to meet that night at the Bar Indochine next door but I was too busy to afford the luxury of killing time with him at such a place.

After dumping my luggage in the room I rushed downstairs to meet the driver who was waiting for me. I spent the entire afternoon of my first day in Phnom Penh at the bookstore named Monuments Books on Norodom boulevard to buy an updated map of the land of Angkor along with a detailed one of Phnom Penh and other newspapers like the Phnom Penh Post, the Cambodia Daily in English and the afternoon edition of the Cambodge Soir in French.

When reading the Phnom Penh Post, it would be hard for the reader's attention not to be drawn to the "Police Blotter" section that was full of news of violent deaths by stabbing and, especially, firearms:

November 11: Kong Chak, 27, a motorcycle-for-hire driver, was found dead in the forest in Prey Sleuk village, Chhbar Morn district, Kompong Speu. Police said that Chak had been killed several days earlier, and the suspected motive was robbery as his motorbike had been stolen. [sic]

November 12: Khan Chlem, 30, a paratrooper, and Kong Mun, 31, a military policeman, were arrested on suspicion they shot to death William Tay, 48, the owner of Phnom Penh's Holiday Club, the previous week. The police alleged that a Taiwanese national named Lee Han Shin promised the men US$ 10,000 to kill Tay. [sic]

November 13: Ouk Kimdoeun, 52, was knifed to death at 7:10 pm after stepping out of his tourist car in Sei Ma village, Takeo Province. Police alleged Kimdoeun, who had emigrated to France, was visiting his sister-in-law when he was chopped eight times and had his throat cut by his nephew, Srey Lalin, 22...[sic]

The above list was followed by other horrific crimes including throat slitting, rapes... They occupied an entire page of the newspaper. Phnom Penh, the capital of Cambodia, seemed to project an image of the Wild West in Southeast Asia.

As soon as I finished getting my bearings on the map, I took the initiative to ask Sok Thon to take me to the notable locations in Phnom Penh about which I probably have done more research than him: the Chruoy Changvar Bridge, the Cambodia-Vietnam Victory Monument built in the late 1970s to commemorate the Vietnamese invasion of Cambodia resulting in the demise of the Khmer Rouge, the Monivong Bridge, the Chăm and Vietnamese enclaves along the Bassac riverbanks and also the sites of the two recent fires…Enough for me to use up two rolls of film on the first leg of my journey. The information Sok Thon gave me concerning the history of those places did not add much to my existing knowledge about them.

THE CHRUOY CHANGVAR BRIDGE AND THE KILLING FIELDS

This bridge is also known by another name: The Japanese Friendship Bridge. Chruoy Changvar was formerly a peninsula which lied in between the Mekong and Tonle Sap River near Phnom Penh. It is the area where the Chăm Islam community chose to make their home and it also bore witness to the slaughter and miseries they suffered at the hands of Pol Pot's henchmen. North east of Phnom Penh, this 700 meters long historic bridge connects the two banks of the Tonle Sap River. The distance from this bridge measured in kilometers to Kompong Cham is 144, Kompong Thom 165 and Siem Reap 311. From the bridge I could see two or three domes of the Muslim mosques.

This famous bridge was destroyed by mines during fierce combats in 1975. Nowadays it stands as a symbol of the devastations that were wrought on Cambodia. This country also served as the background for the movie "The Killing Fields" depicting the scene the Khmer Rouge entered Phnom Penh on April 17,1975. It was at this place that Sydney Schanberg of the New York Times, the British journalist John Swain of the Sunday Times and three others were captured by the Khmer Rouge. They would have been shot on the spot were it not for the courage and quick-wittedness of Dith Pran, Schanberg's interpreter. This story full of suspense was later narrated in details by John Swain in his book "River of Time" first published in the United States in 1997. It took until 1997 for the bridge to be rebuilt by the Japanese at a total cost of US$ 23.2 million in non-refundable funds.

THE MONIVONG BRIDGE AND TWO SUSPICIOUS FIRES

Also called the Vietnamese Bridge, it spans the Bassac River (named Hậu River after it crosses into Vietnam) and is located northeast of Phnom Penh. From this bridge we can take National Route 1 to Svay Rieng or to Saigon which are 110 and 220 kilometers away respectively. This is the second historic bridge which saw incessant shelling and vicious battles before the capital Phnom Penh fell into Khmer Rouge hands. Not far from the foot of the bridge you could see slums spreading out along the riverbanks. Most of their inhabitants were Vietnamese. Recently, the local newspapers had reported that this area was ravaged by two big fires.

Tens of thousands of the most destitute residents in Phnom Penh – the majority of them Vietnamese – saw their properties go up in smoke in two successive fires on the 26th and 27th of November, 2001. The first fire which destroyed more than 2,200 houses started in the vicinity of the Bassac Theater also known as the Building area. The following night, a second fire which took place in the Chhbar Ampoe neighborhood at the other side of the Monivong Bridge's riverbank burned more than 1,000 homes to ashes and caused the death of one person. The headline in large type on the front page of the Phnom Penh Post ran: "Suspicious Fires Raze Slums".

The above event occurred at the same time President Trần Đức Lương of Vietnam arrived on a state visit. According to the AFP dispatch of December 6th, Western diplomats viewed the two fires as an "unequivocal message sent to Hanoi". A number of the victims of the fire on Chhbar Ampoe were convinced that it was started deliberately. On the other hand the Vice Chief of Police of Phnom Penh asserted that both fires were accidental and the second one resulted from a gas tank explosion.

An eye witness who wished to remain anonymous told a Phnom Penh Post reporter: "In the dark of the night I saw with my own eyes a burning torch being thrown from a speeding motorboat toward the bank. It hit the hut that belongs to Mr. Thanh and set it on fire.". Thanh was the person who burned to death. "The explanation that a gas tank exploded at Mr. Thanh's place could not stand on its feet because he is very poor and sick. He does not have enough food to eat and has to rely on the neighbors' largesse to live. How could he own a gas tank?". Another victim added: "We only use coal or firewood. Nobody here can afford to buy gas tanks. Moreover, when the firemen arrived at the scene they demanded bribes from the victims before turning on the water hoses to put down the fire."

On my visit to the sites of the two fires I could still detect the smell of burning. Debris and broken bricks or mortars were scattered all over the place along with smoldering beams, a few corrugated tiles blackened by the fire and bent by the heat. The once green coconut trees now stood with their scorched trunks barren of leaves. The victims and their families were herded into trucks to be transported to the city outskirts. Amidst such desolation and despair the only living creatures were a couple of wild dogs roaming around to scavenge for food. But what food was there to be found in the ashes and burning coals of the place? Who could imagine that those two small areas could at one time provide shelters around the clock to almost 20,000 souls for God knows how many years.

"Accidental or intentional" all this is now fait accompli. The task of coming to the aids of the victims however was assumed by international organizations: Urban Poverty Reduction Group, Department of International Development, and the UNDP / United Nations Development Plan.

Mark Mallalieu, the president of the Department of International Development South-East Asia, stated that his organization will be guided by the desire to help the poor in its reviews of the data it collected "...Naturally we want to know what did actually happen and the underlying motives behind these incidents so that we could take appropriate actions."

Based on initial estimates, 16,500 individuals were rendered homeless by the two fires. The government immediately moved all the victims of the first fire and half of the second one out of the capital city. This decision drew quick criticism from non-governmental organizations (NGOs) as they believed that the government acted too hastily when it relocated these people to an environment devoid of any facilities that were indispensable for day to day living.

A great number of people adamantly maintained that both fires were the work of arsonists not withstanding a denial from Phnom Penh's mayor, Mr. Chea Sophara. He went so far as threatening to prosecute those who were caught spreading such rumor. I beg the reader to forgive my audacity to pen a Confucius-style saying of my own: "He who starts a fire then confesses his crime, doesn't exist in life".

For a long time the government made it plain it wanted to get rid of the chaotic and unsanitary residential neighborhoods of the capital city it deemed an impediment to the development of the tourism industry. The fire areas in question were part of the slums running along the Bassac River all the way to the south of the Monivong Bridge. The dwellers of those thatch huts were mostly poor Vietnamese who were traditionally looked down upon as illegal squatters.

Moreover, according to the same Phnom Penh Post reporter, in the immediate aftermath of the fire, the Phnom Penh administrators barred international non-governmental organizations from getting access to the sites to aid the victims. They were only permitted to do their work at the relocation centers outside the city limits. In spite of the relentless intercessions from foreign embassies and the endless telephone calls back and forth by the non-governmental organizations (NGOs) the end result still remained to be desired: during the night of the 3rd of December more than 500 families that stayed on at the two sites were put in a convoy and evacuated to different relocation camps outside of the capital. Owners of the houses spared by the flames received orders to tear them down and vacate the place within two weeks time.

The families of the victims were taken to two sites on the city's outskirt: Anlong Kngah (154 ha) and the somewhat smaller Anlong Gong. Both were located in the flood plains and devoid of roads or access ways. Foreign aid experts unanimously agreed that the locations were utterly unsuitable for relocation purposes and required at least 6 months of repair or maintenance works before those people could move in. They pointed to the fact that those two places were wastelands lacking all means of communication, marketplaces, schools, medical stations and job opportunities for the victims.

Peter Swan, technical advisor for the Phnom Penh Urban Poverty Reduction Group, observed that when the victims could not find employment at their place of relocation, sooner or later they will find ways to move on. He cited the experience with the May 2001 fire which devastated the village of Basaac forcing 500 families to lose their homes. They were resettled in Chungruk, an area not amenable for normal living: far from the cities, no facilities, no employments...End result? More than half of them decided to move on to brighter horizons.

The forced relocation of this group of poor people to wasteland areas outside of Phnom Penh ran the risk of creating slums that eventually would form a belt encircling the capital city. A more viable alternative would be to provide temporary shelters for the victims at the site of the fire enabling them to keep their jobs and their children to continue with their schooling.

The authorities in Phnom Penh had created a new vicious circle that helped perpetuate poverty and they were forcing it on this destitute group of about 20,000 predominantly Vietnamese victims of the recent fires.

Throughout the ups and downs of Cambodia's history, the Vietnamese expatriates have been relegated to the status of "second class" citizens in the land of Angkor. Regrettably, they could not detect the faintest signs of welcome or succor from Vietnam, their far away homeland.

THE VIETNAMESE CAMBODIA VICTORY MONUMENT
In 1979 more than 100,000 Vietnamese troops invaded Cambodia to defeat the Khmer Rouge and occupy that country.

In 1989, after more than 10 years of occupation, international pressure and considerable losses compelled the Vietnamese to withdraw. They left behind a so-called friendly government headed by Hun Sen. Meanwhile in their hideout at Pailin in the southwest of the country, the Khmer Rouge started on a path of decline and disintegration: Ieng Sary, the number two man, surrendered to government troops; Son Sen was executed on Pol Pot's orders then Pol Pot himself was put under house arrest and subsequently died of illness.

Following an election supervised by the United Nations, Hun Sen emerged as the strongman who confidently and gradually distanced himself from Hanoi's influence.

Ten years later, from a deployment of 100,000 troops, the Vietnamese presence in Phnom Penh was reduced to its Embassy compound and the Vietnamese Cambodia Victory Monument on Norodom Sihanouk square. How long the monument will continue to stand there remains an open question.

The date of 'January 7th 1979' was chosen to commemorate the defeat of the Khmer Rouge rule by the Vietnamese. At first it was celebrated as the Independence Day of Cambodia. However, starting in 1993 the Phnom Penh government renamed it the Victory Day Over the Genocidal Regime. The Minister of Information of the Hun Sen administration severely admonished the owner of the luxury hotel Cambodianna, a joint venture with Singapore, for distorting the history of Cambodia when he allowed the phrase "The seventh of January is the day the Vietnamese liberated Cambodia" to be printed on the 2002 calendar of the hotel.

In all fairness, even the most ardent anti-Vietnamese Khmers must admit that no one could tell what could have happened to their people after those ten years if the Vietnamese had not "invaded Cambodia" and overthrown the Khmer Rouge. This "love hate" relationship with the Vietnamese is also the ambivalence the Khmer survivors had to bear when they walked out of the Killing Fields.

At the present time, as it is the case with Laos, the Phnom Penh government is not only distancing itself from but also adopting a defiant stance toward Hanoi thus finding itself increasingly falling into China's orbit.

LATEST NEWS: 02 AUGUST 2007
Occasionally, the Vietnamese Cambodia Victory Monument became a political issue.

On August 30, 1998, several Khmers climbed the monument with hammers, poured gasoline on it and set it on fire. The damage was later repaired by the authorities.

Again, on July 29, 2007, unknown party(ies) planted several kilograms of TNT in an attempt to topple this massive Vietnamese Cambodia Victory Monument. Some Khmers hate this monument and called it useless, others "believe the Yuon (a derogatory name for Vietnamese) themselves planted the TNT and then blamed it on the Khmer Krom people - it is old tactics the Vietnamese use to look for a pretext to destroy our Khmer Krom brothers." [sic]

THE VIETNAMESE ON THE LAND OF NO "MILK AND HONEY"

The Vietnamese have lived in Cambodia for many generations along the banks of the Mekong, Tonle Sap River and the Great Lake. Unlike the Chinese, they find it difficult to assimilate into the main stream because they are looked at with suspicion if not hatred. The Khmer people contemptuously call them "the Yuon" which means "those from the north". The Thai do not particularly like the Vietnamese but show no such open hostility and animosity toward them. "Decapitation" is the term used to refer to the campaigns the Khmers engaged in to massacre or behead the Vietnamese not only in Cambodia but also in the Mekong Delta in Vietnam during the *"Mùa Thổ Dậy /* the Uprising Season of the Khmer Krom". Those were terrifying and bloody times that anybody who had the misfortune to live through would not soon forget.

At the peak of the Vietnam War, though Cambodia and Vietnam were presumed allies, the pro-American government of Lon Nol engaged in an atrocious nationwide drive to capture and decapitate the Vietnamese. When the Khmer Rouge took over the reins of power they replaced it with what was known as "ethnic cleansing". Once more the Vietnamese had to live through the same nightmare albeit with a different name. There are no statistics that give an accurate figure of the Vietnamese who survived and still lived in Cambodia. The number ranging from 200,000 to one million of them in a population of 11 million is at best an estimate.

"Against the Vietnamese" rightly or wrongly always proves to be a popular and vote getting campaign slogan in Cambodia. It is rare to meet a local person who has something good to say about the Vietnamese. A member of the Human Rights Organization once told a reporter of the Far Eastern Economic Review (1994): "Given a choice, the majority of people in this country would expel every single Vietnamese." [sic]

In cases of murders or violent brawls even when all the parties involved are Khmers this animosity against the Vietnamese again shows its ugly face with the guilty perpetrators being depicted as those with *"Khmer bodies and Viet souls."*

The anti-Vietnamese bias of the Khmers predated the arrival of the French in Indochina. It took root at the time Cambodia was mercilessly torn apart by her two larger neighbors: Thailand and Vietnam. Under the expansionist policy of emperor Minh Mạng, Vietnam established a protectorate rule over the land of Angkor. This policy was not only harsh but also presumptuous and high handed as exemplified by these words uttered by the Vietnamese emperor: "Those primitive Cambodians are now children of the realm. We must teach and help them understand as well as appreciate our customs". The mandarins of the Nguyễn court from Trương Minh Giảng to "proconsul" Thoại Ngọc Hầu administered the land with an iron fist enforcing a policy at best described as draconian. The wrongs those mandarins inflicted on the Khmer people had accumulated over time and led to a "historic hatred" which is further intensified by a constant fear that the Vietnamese will continue to expand at their expense.

The policy of "divide and rule" during the French colonial rule only helped deepen the existing hatred. It is worth mentioning that the Mekong Delta which was integrated into Vietnam during the Vietnamese Southward March is still claimed by the Khmer as part of their territory. In the eyes of the Khmer and Chăm people, the Vietnamese Southward March in essence is nothing more than an expansionist invasion or land grab on the part of the Vietnamese.

In general, life for the Vietnamese in Cambodia is neither easy nor prosperous. Most earn their living as fishermen, small business owners, and hired hands. If they live in Vietnam their life could not be harder. More than 70% of the prostitutes (including the under-age) practicing the oldest trade of the world in Cambodia are Vietnamese. Recently not a few under-age girls are bought in the Mekong Delta and taken across the border to Cambodia, a fact that surprises and saddens those who proudly call themselves the offspring of the pioneers of the Vietnamese Southward March.

FROM THE UNIVERSITY OF PHNOM PENH TO THE UNIVERSITY OF HANOI

Despite the tribulations and sorrows that pervaded this entire land, the palm trees still bloom and give juicy fruits and sweet honey. Like those palm trees, the post-Khmer Rouge youth though born in the ashes of war and a far from perfect society have taken roots, blossomed and grown tall under the blue sky. Within the premises of their campuses, they have courageously voiced their concerns and discontent about the inequities and corruption they saw around them. The issues they raised closely affected their future. At the same time it demonstrated their willingness to go beyond their selfish interests and fight for the greater good of their country. Numerous were the demonstrations demanding democracy and the return of their land from Vietnam.

What a stark and sad contrast when one turns one's attention to the young generations in Vietnam. Twenty seven long years have gone by since the unification of Vietnam in 1975. Yet one could only hear the dead silence of a deep slumber pervading the campuses of the state universities from Hanoi to Huế, Saigon and Cần Thơ. It's enough to make one shudder in disbelief and despair.

ROUTE NUMBER 5 – THE INDUSTRIAL ZONE OF TONLE SAP

For centuries rice and fish form the backbone of Cambodia's economy. After the restoration of peace, the dream of industrialization became the trumpet call to all Cambodians. Industrial zones were set up along the banks of the Tonle Sap River and they never ceased to expand: chemical plants, alcohol distilleries, saw mills, cotton factories, clothes manufacturers... Sok Thon explained that the plants were built along the river because they needed a constant supply of water. But it is left for me to further understand that like in the case of the export zones located along the banks of the Lancang Jiang in Yunnan, the Tonle Sap River, albeit at a smaller scale, will inexorably be turned into a sewage pipe for industrial waste to be discharged either into the Great Lake during the Rainy Season or the Mekong Delta via the Sông Tiền and Sông Hậu Rivers during the Dry one.

Fish can still swim downstream from the Great Lake to the Mekong Delta as long as the pollution level of the Tonle Sap River stays below the "lethal threshold". However they will arrive in smaller number and no longer be "clean fish" for tainted they have become from pollution! A perfect example of another "unlearned lesson" of history: development of industrial zones along the riverbank, dumping of harmful waste, and destruction of the ecology.

To this day people still cannot forget the most calamitous ecological disaster which befell Thailand in March of 1992 when 9,000 tons of decaying molasses from the Khon Kaen plant were dumped into the Nam Pong River which flows into the two tributaries of the Mekong: Chi and Mun. This catastrophic incident caused the complete disappearance of the fish in those tributaries. The effects of all this on the Mekong Delta still remained to be seen.

At the close of 1998, a second disaster - this time "made in Taiwan" - struck Sihanookville. Cambodian customs officers on the take turned a blind eye and allowed a Taiwanese industrial firm to release tanks of industrial waste with extremely toxic mercury contents into the area close to Sihanoukville resulting in the death of a number of workers at the local harbor. Though the guilty party, Formosa Plastics, subsequently accepted responsibilities and removed the harmful materials, the ensuing bad publicity caused the tourism industry in Sihanookville to register a drop in its business.

Numerous similar "scandals" - the dumping of toxic substances into the sea, rivers and even on land - still go unreported. Unfortunately the Mekong Delta invariably serves as the final depository for all this waste.

The latest news on the Nation – Thailand December 14, 2001: The local authorities advised people to abstain from eating the contaminated fish in the Lop Buri, an affluent of the Chao Phraya which is the second largest river in Thailand after the Mekong. The chemicals in the water used to extinguish a market fire ran into the Lop Buri River and killed many species of fish. These toxic materials will eventually dilute when they flow into the currents of the main rivers. However, government officials feared that greedy local merchants would still offer the contaminated fish for sale to the public. Preliminary tests of water samples showed that their oxygen content was reduced by half.

A day will come when the oxygen content of the Tonle Sap current will dip below 50% before it reaches the Quatre Bras. Then, not a single fish from the Tonle Sap Lake will be able to survive this "fatal ecological threshold" to arrive at the Mekong Delta.

Chiều chiều quạ nói với diều
Cù lao Ông Chưởng có nhiều cá tôm

In the afternoon the raven reminds the migrating kite
On the island of Mr. Chưởng fish and shrimps thrive
(Vietnamese proverb)

There will be a time when nowhere can an abundance of shrimps and fish be found. The Mekong Delta will cease to be a hospitable place for the birds to visit.

THE WAY TO KOMPONG CHHNANG - TO THE TONLE SAP LAKE

In April of 1975 on Route Number 5, people were ordered in drove to leave Phnom Penh empty handed and march to the Killing Fields. This was one of the main national routes that ran south along the Tonle Sap River to the city of Kompong

Chhnang, up to the Tonle Sap Lake then to Chhnok Tru, the floating fisherman village where a large number of Vietnamese lived.

We left the capital city in the morning before the early rush hour. Approaching from the opposite direction were motorcycle-trailers, a type of motorcycle pulling four-wheeled trailers resembling long wooden boxes that can carry 25 to 30 passengers. The local people preferred this means of transportation because it was inexpensive. Tightly packed on those boxes were very young female workers at the clothing factories in the export and industrial zones on the Tonle Sap riverbanks. Sharing the ride with them were boys and girls on their way to school.

The road was narrow, full of potholes and sorely needed repairs. However, it did not prevent cars small and large from going really fast. Our driver, Sok Thon, revealed to me that accidents and car rollovers often happened on this road. Last year almost a whole load of 20 passengers in a motorcycle-trailer lost their lives in one single accident.

Probably we should pause here to consider the case of the tens of thousands of female workers in the garment industry. They flocked from the countryside to look for employment in the cities where dangerous temptations abounded. A good number of them quit their low paying jobs to work as bar girls or prostitutes. Once they did that, they reached a point of no return and had to stay the course until they became too sick to work. Back to their villages, they became ticking bombs and began to spread the HIV virus around. After Thailand, other countries like Cambodia, Laos and Vietnam came to the realization that HIV epidemics were too high a price to pay for the development of their tourism industry.

Convoys after convoys of eighteen-wheelers loaded with gigantic logs from the rainforests of Kompong Thom crossed the ferry to roll on Route Number 5 toward the sawmill grounds, a joint venture between Japan and Cambodia. This country's suicidal deforestation - legal or not - proceeded at a dizzying pace with no sign of abating. The Japanese were not alone in this game. Fabulously rich log developers from Thailand, Malaysia, and Indonesia joined in the fray. They worked in cahoots with corrupt generals and local government officials in Cambodia to cut down its precious rainforests at a fast pace in complete disregard for the existing laws which specifically banned such practices.

In the 1960's, 75% of Cambodia's area was covered by rainforest. Going into the 1990's this figure took a nosedive to 50%. Incredibly, if anything the rate of illegal deforestation during the coming years would pick up speed. This state of affairs led environmentalists like William Shawcross to lament: "Illegal deforestation probably represents the most devastating aspect of corruption in the government". With the forests gone, rainwater will erode the hills and mountains, carrying the soil down into the Tonle Sap Lake to render it shallower. Besides, we should not forget the mammoth dams in far away Yunnan which are lowering the water levels in the affected rivers. This dreadful combination of events could prevent the Tonle Sap River from reversing course and flow into the Tonle Sap Lake. This would result in an ecological disaster to both Cambodia and Vietnam. The Tonle Sap Lake is the largest fresh water lake in Southeast Asia. It may one day turn into a dead lake like the Aral Lake in Central Asia.

On that day the Camry and its passengers really took a beating from the extremely poor road condition of Route Number 5: loose rocks, potholes, and muddy broken road surfaces everywhere you go. The big holes on the road surface according to Sok Thon were old shell craters left intact from the fighting with the Khmer Rouge in recent past. In the beginning they were temporarily filled with earth. With the passing of heavy-duty trucks they grew bigger and deeper. The situation worsened as traffic increased with time. Route Number 5 was not unique in the category of bad roads. Statistics released by The Ministry of Public Works showed that before the war there were 35,000 kilometers of asphalted roads in Cambodia. Now only 350 kilometers of them were useable. The degradation of the road condition in this country was simply unimaginable. The French began to develop the road network during the 1930's but in the following decades it began to deteriorate due to flooding, wars, mines, and shelling.

The word "Chhnang" means pottery and glazed earthenware. Kompong Chhnang is the city located near the harbor on the Tonle Sap River where these objects were produced. True to its name; all kinds of jars, basins, pots and pans were displayed for sale along the roads. Further back from the road we could see houses on stilts being fenced in by rows of coconut trees, mango trees, longan trees, tamarind trees...and rice fields stretching to the far horizons with their ever present palm trees soaring into the vast blue sky. The trunks of those trees still bore in them shrapnel or bullets, relics of past hostilities. Some had their tops cut off leaving only trunks burned into a black gray color. It is a common scene to encounter men, women, and children walking with clutches on the roads leading to and from villages. The vast majority of them were victims of unexploded mines which lied scattered all over Cambodia.

It is worth noting here that the United States, the number one superpower in the world, armed with nuclear weapons and intercontinental ballistic missiles had refused to join the other signatories of the Ottawa Convention to observe the Ban on Anti-Personnel Landmines (APL). Also known as The Mine Ban, it outlaws the use of that type of weapons whose victims were mostly innocent civilians. Going one step further, the Bush administration quickly walked out of The Kyoto Protocol which represented a worldwide effort to curb the effects of global warming caused mainly by the industrialized countries. An increase of one degree Celsius in the temperature of the atmosphere is enough to melt the ice on the earth poles causing a rise in the sea level. The Mekong Delta, always lower than the sea level, is suffering from a dwindling supply of fresh water due to the construction of the mammoth dams of the Yunnan Cascades. Now, were the sea level in the East Sea to rise by 1 meter, the Paracels / Hoàng Sa and Spratlys / Trường Sa archipelagoes would disappear under the water and there would be no longer a bone of contention for the countries of the region to fight over territorial rights. It would also mean the disappearance of the "Civilization of Orchard / Văn Minh Miệt Vườn".

What we just surmised is not the work of an unbridled imagination but could actually take place in the real world as reported in this AP report of 3/24/10. The case in point was the tiny New Moore Island in the Bay of Bengal. For nearly 30 years, India and Bangladesh both claimed this island as their own. According to the scientists at the School of Oceanographic Studies at Jadavpur University in Calcutta, sea levels had been rising annually. As a result, this disputed island was completely submerged by rising sea levels leading the oceanographer named Sugata Hazra to observe: "What these two countries could not achieve from years of talking, has been resolved by global warming,"

Driving on this bad road, we were made fully aware of the heavy tolls cars had to pay traveling on it. On the way we passed several vehicles left stranded on the roadside because their tires blew up on sharp edged rocks. Our rickety Camry did not fare any better. A rear tire blew up as we crossed the city limits of

Kompong Chhnang. The cut was too large to be patched but it only took ten minutes for Sok Thon, our agile driver, to replace it with a spare tire.

Our journey barely started, yet we were reduced to driving on four worn out tires with no spare left. What would befall us on this country road covered with potholes and loose rocks if another tire blew up? I voiced my concern to our driver to be met with his customary reply: "No Problem".

There is certainly "No Problem" for Sok Thom because he is a Khmer. However, being a Vietnamese, I had no intention of finding myself forced to spend the night in a remote and isolated Khmer village.

As if nothing had happened, he drove on straight ahead on the road covered with rocks and red dirt. Sok Thon behaved like an officer in the operation room. He assiduously put himself to the task brushing aside all distractions so that he could achieve the operation plan I set for him. I was the one who had to hold him back. I reminded him that the Camry was not a Jeep. It was built for city driving and he should not drive it so recklessly. Nevertheless he always insisted that everything was OK. I realized that the money I paid him was not sufficient to compensate him for the days of "mistreatment" he put his "bread earning" car through.

From Chhnok Tru we drove 36 kilometers on a smaller stone road to reach Kompong Chhnang. It was a floating village located at the junction where the Tonle Sap Lake and Tonle Sap River meet. The inhabitants earned their living from fishing. This mixed community was made up of people from different ethnic origins with the Vietnamese representing the largest group followed by the Chăm then Khmer. They were easily distinguishable by their facial features and dresses. The Vietnamese women kept to their traditional short blouses, *"áo bà ba"*. They talked to each other in the Vietnamese southern dialect from one boat to another. Their loud voices resounded over the river and canals.

The skipper of the boat we hired that morning was a twelve year old Khmer lad. He masterfully guided the motorized boat to take Sok Thon and me through a maze of floating houses. I could not help but wonder what circumstances had forced those young boys to mature so early in life. More than half of the fiercest and most ruthless of the Khmer Rouge killers were between the age of 12 and 14. They were not much taller than their AK47 automatic rifles and yet their fingers were extremely fast on the triggers. At Tuol Sleng, the most ruthless torturers and jail keepers who were ready at a moment's notice to break the skulls of their victims with a swing of an ax also belonged to this age group. Not to forget the 13 year old mischievous group of peddlers in the Angkor area. Even the prostitutes who so expertly handled their customers could not be more than 15 years old. Those "virtuosos" could in no way be the products of the splendid Angkor-Khmer civilization of more than eight centuries ago.

Probably thanks to the abundant supply of fish in the Tonle Sap Lake, the Vietnamese at this place enjoyed a markedly higher standard of living than their compatriots who dwelled in the slums of Phnom Penh. Their spacious floating houses boasted bristling TV antennas on the roofs like in the Năm Căn region of the Mekong Delta. The front doors of several houses were adorned with pots of red pergolas or yellow chrysanthemum. Outside the house, the owners raised fish, fowls and dogs. Different religions were practiced here: the floating church of St. Anthony and the Quan Thế Âm pagoda were frequented by the Vietnamese. The place was teeming with businesses operated by them: barbershop, watch repair, variety store and gas stations... The local Vietnamese residents appeared to be self confident and proud of their identity even though they were no strangers to the calamities and losses that befell them under the Lon Nol and Pol Pot rules.

On our return trip, a truck broke its axle on the wooden bridge causing a huge traffic jam in both directions. How to handle the problem seemed to be the concern of everyone and the responsibility of no one. Breaking out of the line of waiting cars, Sok Thon found a detour on the dry rice fields for us to continue on our way.

Where in the world could they find such large quantities of logs? Back on Route Number 5 several lumber trucks transporting giant logs were heading in the direction of the industrial zone of Tonle Sap. On that same route, soldiers wearing the uniforms of the Cambodian Corps of Engineers were handling heavy equipment like rollers to compact the aggregate base in preparation for the laying of asphalt on a section of the route. With the cessation of hostilities and the ensuing demobilization plan, Hun Sen was using the Army for peacetime construction projects.

KOMPONG CHAM – THE JAPANESE BRIDGE

I have come to different bridges built across the Mekong: The Mittaphap Bridge linking Vientiane and Nong Khai (04/94), the Mỹ Thuận Bridge astride the Tiền River (05/2000), and the Laos-Nippon / Champassak Bridge (08/2000).

Before arriving in Phnom Penh I was aware that Japan was helping build the country's first bridge across the Mekong in the city of Kompong Cham. The bridge measured 1,4 kilometer in length and cost US$ 56 million in non-refundable fund. Thanks to it, the north and northeast regions of Cambodia will become more easily accessible. Besides it will serve as an important link in the super highway connecting Bangkok, Phnom Penh and Saigon.

The project started in 1998 and lasted more than three years.

The Mekong Hotel, the largest one in Kompong Cham, was reserved for the use of the Japanese experts working in the construction of the bridge. I was told that immediately in their wake came from nowhere large groups of Vietnamese girls to service them in Karaoke bars and massage parlors used as a front for prostitution. Prime minister Hun Sen attended the bridge's inauguration on December 4, 2001.

On this trip I had the opportunity to admire the splendid brand new Kompong Cham Japanese Bridge. I was not alone in my enthusiasm to have a look of the new bridge. Sok Thon, our driver, for one also shared that feeling.

We departed from Phnom Penh in the early morning. Route Number 7 from Skoon to Kompong Cham, probably the best asphalted road in Cambodia, was also built with the assistance of the Japanese. Kompong Cham ranked as the country's third largest port city after Phnom Penh and Battambang. Its abundant resources consisted of rubber, rice and fruits. The land here was rich and fertile. Along the road, vast rice fields covered with ripe golden rice stalks were ready for the harvest. Several groups of harvesters scattered around in the fields. Short and tall sugar palm trees stood against the blue sky adding a colorful touch peculiar to the Angkor countryside. Occasionally, I would see in the middle of the rice fields a lotus pond showing off its green leaves and red blossoms.

The stilt houses in the villages were built using an architecture that is suitable to the volume of water that fell down profusely during the Rainy Season. Every house had at least a big jar to contain rainwater.

Like in the Mekong Delta, even though water could be seen everywhere around their houses during the Rainy Season, people still show a need for these jars. This fact led engineer Nguyễn Hữu Chung of the Friends of the Cửu Long Group to describe it as the *'Civilization of Jars'* which is characteristic of the people living downstream the Mekong.

It was impossible for travelers not to notice the signs on the offices of political parties that sprang up almost in all parts of the country: on the streets of Siem Reap, Phnom Penh, along Route Number 5 leading to Kompong Chhnang, Route Number 7 to Kompong Cham. Everywhere you turned you could see them. They might be erected just for show nevertheless they were the welcome indications of a budding democracy. The most numerous signs belonged to the CCP (Cambodian People's Party), the government party of Prime Minister Hun Sen. The FUNCINPEC (Front Uni National pour un Cambodge Indépendant Neutre Pacifique et Coopératif), the opposition party led by Norodom Ranariddh, prince Sihanook's son, came in second place. Only very seldom would one encounter a sign of the KNP / Khmer National Party belonging to Sam Rainsy.

With a grin our driver, Sok Thon, remarked that there were not 3 but 32 political parties. I realized that, like in America, money and power are the two sine qua non ingredients to develop a political party's infrastructure. A number of Cambodians who became naturalized American citizens have returned with their money to try their luck in the local elections. They carried out campaigns "à la Américaine" but so far not one of them succeeded. On the other hand, quite a few of them with dual American and Cambodian citizenship were invited to hold important positions in the government on account of their scientific or technical know-how. This represents a bold move on the part of the Phnom Penh government in stark contrast to their Laotian or Vietnamese counterparts who still show signs of being over cautious and secretive.

There was no freedom of press in Cambodia considering the bloody liquidations, assassinations of newspersons or grenades thrown at the offices of opposition newspapers. Customarily, the party in power always wanted to keep the press and communication media under their thumb. Whether one loves or hates Hun Sen is not the issue. A former battalion commander of the Khmer Rouge, he was accused of being a stooge of Hanoi. Now as prime minister he clearly proved to be his own man and earned the grudging respect of Sihanook who had shown a dislike for him at first. In addition, the diplomatic corps also recognizes in him a de facto strongman who plays a crucial, stabilizing role in Cambodia.

Rising to the azure sky and hovering over the sugar palm trees were the roofs of the Khmer pagodas whose architecture is very different from those in Vietnam. In a land where Theravada Buddhism was recognized as the state religion, pagodas were ever present. From the king down to the common subjects, every man had to enter the monastery to have his head shaven and become a monk before he was deemed mature for normal life in society. Sihanook went through that process. In the 1930's even Pol Pot entered the Wat Botum Vaddei pagoda to lead a monk's existence for many months.

However by the time the Khmer Rouge came to power the situation changed drastically. In the wild expectation to achieve a primitive communist society where everybody had to work, the monks were looked down on as parasites and utterly useless as a group. "Buddhism is at the root of the decline of the Cambodian nation". The population was prohibited from rendering service to the monks and religious classes. Pol Pot was determined to institute a government imbued with nationalist extremism and sustain a population growing fast enough to allow him to retake the Mekong Delta which was formerly part of Cambodia and the border area to the west of Surin Buriram in Thailand whose inhabitants still speak Khmer. After 44 months of Khmer Rouge rule, from a high of 60,000 monks only 1,000 were left to return to their run down pagodas in January of 1979. Prior to that, those religious places had been turned into warehouses, prisons and even execution grounds.

After the long period of devastation and desolation that followed "Year Zero", Cambodia rose from her ashes to come out of the Killing Fields. For the surviving Khmers, to return to the merciful shadow of the Buddha is to find a closure to their nightmarish past, rediscover a source of comfort for this life and find hope for deliverance in the next ones.

We had no choice but to park the car far away from the head of the bridge. Under the steaming heat of the noontime sun, Sok Thon and I walked to the bridge. The traffic including motorcycles and bicycles was still light. Greed driven, the operators of commercial vehicles invariably overloaded their cars with passengers and freight. They sped by at terrifying speed at times crossing lanes or driving in the middle of the bridge with complete disregard for the safety of the passengers. We stood on the bridge to admire the majestic panorama of the Tonle Thom River, the Cambodian name for the Mekong. Before our eyes ferry boats crisscrossed up, down and across the current in all directions. On the side of Kompong Cham city, river boats were docked at the port waiting to take travelers to Phnom Penh or to northern cities like Kratié, Sambor…Nearby were small markets on the riverbank where sellers carried wicker baskets plying golden baguettes, a vestige the French left behind in all the three countries of Indochina. As we almost reached the other end of the bridge a scene made me stop dead on my track: rising from the green foliage was an ancient military outpost covered with moss. But new were the numerous bullet holes of all sizes that pock marked its walls. Some of them were made so deep by the spinning bullets that they revealed the dark red color inside the bricks making them look like bleeding wounds that had not healed. They were kept intact to serve as testimonies to the devastation of the war in contrast to the huge peacetime reconstruction efforts that were going on in the land.

We returned to the car to continue on with our journey across the bridge. Sok Thon was overcome with joy. It was the first time for him to drive on a new bridge spanning the Mekong in his country. The drive on the segment of Route Number 7 going north turned uncomfortable again due to numerous potholes, loose rocks and red dust. Choosing the land route to go to Kratié was a bad idea because it brought self-inflicted pains to the body and could be dangerous on account of frequent highway robberies. It would be many more years before the Japanese could help build a new segment of this route going north to Kratié then all the way to Stung Treng near the Southern Laos border. Until then, the river route also known as the "brown highway" would prove to be a more convenient and safe bet.

ON THE TONLE SAP RIVER - THE CHĂM ISLAM COMMUNITY

In the first half of the 18th century, the year 1720 marked the time the kingdom of Champa was erased from the map as a result of the Vietnamese Southern March. Those Chăm who were fortunate to escape the bloody massacre ordered by emperor Minh Mạng fled to Cambodia. The vast majority of them resettled in the cities of Kompong Cham and Kompong Chhnang while the rest chose to live in scattered areas along the Tonle Sap River or Tonle Sap Lake. They earned their living from fishing, rice cultivation, butchering cows, making medicine and a few by practicing witchcraft. In the beginning only a very small number of the Chăm practiced Islam. However, through contacts with merchants from Malaysia, Indonesia...they quickly converted to the new faith out of a desire to preserve their ethnic and cultural identity while living in a Khmer society that chose Buddhism as its official religion.

Since they do not share the same religion, spoken and written language, or history with their host country, the Chăm tend to band with the Vietnamese and form an opposing or countervailing force in regard to the Khmer.

Actually the origin of that odd union could be traced back to the Vĩnh Tế Canal. In the middle of the 18th century, the Vietnamese Southern March ran out of steam as it reached the city of Châu Đốc to the west of the Mekong Delta. This city sat on the border with Cambodia thus posing a high risk of confrontation involving the two neighboring countries. To deal with the new situation, the Nguyễn emperors, from Gia Long down to Minh Mạng, implemented the aggressive "đinh điền" strategy using peasant-soldiers to settle and defend the new territories. To achieve that goal the Vietnamese imperial court nominated "proconsul" Thoại Ngọc Hầu to build the Vĩnh Tế Canal linking Châu Đốc to Hà Tiên. He enlisted thousands of Khmer laborers to work day and night to do the job under the harsh supervision of the Chăm soldiers. This system of hard labor entailed immense sufferings and the loss of thousands of lives. It is no wonder that the Khmer people hate the "Yuon", a derogatory term they use to call the Vietnamese and their vicious allies the Chăm.

For the above reason the Chăm became the second ethnic group after the Vietnamese to be targeted by Pol Pot in his ethnic cleansing campaign. According to an estimate about half of the Chăm population were murdered by the Khmer Rouge along with the destruction of their mosques and schools. A number of survivors fled on the Mekong to Laos. In contrast, the Chăm Islam communities in the southern part of Thailand and Malaysia enjoyed a more tranquil and comfortable life. During the post-Khmer Rouge era, the Muslim mosques and schools in Cambodia were rebuilt with funds provided by Muslim countries like Malaysia, Saudi Arabia, Kuwait...

Social customs of the Chăm Islam were not as strict as those in the fundamentalist Muslim communities in the world. Women were not required to wear burqas, dresses that cover the entire body from head to toes with veils that hide the face except for the eyes, like in Afghanistan.

It is common to meet young Chăm girls of the X generation wearing short skirts showing their legs and T-shirts bearing parts of their breasts. Though strict religious rules forbade sexual relationship outside of marriage, a small number of Chăm men and women still fell victims to the HIV epidemic that was ravaging the cities or countryside of the entire land.

After the 9/11 attacks on New York and Washington D.C. to be followed by the American counterattack in Afghanistan, the Chăm Islam community in Cambodia understandably experienced difficulties in their dealings with the outside world. They soon discovered that foreign financial support for purely educational, social and religious developments were to be adversely affected. A case in point was a recent law promulgated by the Ministry of Cults and Religious Affairs of the Hun Sen government stipulating limitations on religious activities that clearly targeted the Chăm Islam communities.

Haji Yusuf, the respected leader of the Chăm Islam community in Phnom Penh, in an interview with a reporter of the Phnom Penh Post, voiced his disagreement with the massive bombings the Americans carried out in Afghanistan resulting in casualties among the civilian population. As he saw it, in the war on terror, a conciliatory approach would prove more effective than the hot war being pursued at the present time. He used this suggestive allegory *"While hot waters run shallow, cold waters run deep"* to advise the Americans to show patience and act with a clear mind instead of out of anger like now.

I came to visit the Chăm who inhabited along the banks of the Tonle Sap River. They lived in houses built on stilts, floating houses or even boats. They could not be poorer and it appeared as if the sole purpose of their existence was for procreation and their faith. I was able to take photographs of the Chăm Islam people prostrating in prayer on their boats on the Tonle Sap River during the fast of Ramadan.

From a moored boat, a Chăm woman was lowering a net a little larger than a plank bed that appeared really heavy each time she heaved it out of the water. Wriggling in the net were several silvery fish not larger than three fingers. Sometimes the net came out of the water empty. The way it looked, by the afternoon, she would be lucky if she could catch a pot full of fish to feed her family at dinnertime. Several fishermen took their boats to the middle of the current to throw their nets. Their catch was larger but no big fish were caught.

Our boat continued to sail along the banks of the Tonle Sap to reach the foot of the Chruoy Changvar Bridge. On the other side of the bridge was the river port used by passenger ships servicing Siem Reap or the northern cities of Kompong Cham, Kratié....

Our boat took a detour to go to Quatre Bras (Chatomuk), the place where four rivers congregate. At this site people celebrate the Bon Om Tuk water festival on the first day of November marking the end of the Rainy Season and the start of the Dry one. It is also the time when the Tonle Sap River reverses course to flow from the Tonle Sap Lake to Quatre Bras then to the Mekong Delta via the Tiền and Hậu Rivers.

Bon Om Tuk is the biggest annual water festival celebrated at Quatre Bras. The king and queen traditionally come to take part in the rituals of fireworks and the royal barge race marking the start of the fishing and sowing season.

Not far from the royal palace, a big casino ship christened Naga was berthed at the riverbank. This "Las Vegas" in Phnom Penh was financed by Malaysian entrepreneurs and reserved exclusively for foreigners. It was similar to the Ecocasino on the lake where the hydroelectric dam of Nam Ngum was built in Laos.

We went ashore to go back to the dyke road. I was deeply moved and felt for the skinny Chăm boy and girl I held in my arms. Those children were born under an unlucky star. They went barefoot and their bright and intelligent eyes only decried the fact that most of them did not have the chance to go to school. How could we ever pay our spiritual debt to the Chăm people?

THE SUGAR PALM TREES BY THE LOTUS POND

Before bidding farewell to Phnom Penh I spent my remaining time to visit the Olympic Stadium and the Tuol Sleng Museum of Genocidal Crime. The Stadium was located near two boulevards: Preak Sihanook and Monireth. In the 1970's the Lon Nol government used it as the gathering place for huge demonstrations to launch its nationwide campaign against the Vietnamese. Under the Khmer Rouge rule, it was turned into an execution ground for many of their victims. Among them were prince Sirik Matak and prime minister Long Boret who by their dignified refusal to leave with the Americans during the last hours of their government had shown that they were deserving leaders of the Khmer people. As for Lon Nol, he was quick to take to his heels and absconded to Hawaii with millions of US Dollars in tow. Now the stadium stood empty as it was being renovated and expanded to Olympic standards for the use of tourists.

In the eyes of the world the Tuol Sleng Museum was a reminder of the genocidal crime committed by the Khmer Rouge.

According to the Khmer dictionary this fateful name means "The Hill of Poisonous Medicine". The building was originally the site of a harmless school in the south of Phnom Penh. In May of 1976 it was converted into a prison named S-21 where those suspected of opposing Angkar, another name for the Khmer Rouge, were tortured. Two iron fences and rows of barbed wires electrified with high voltage currents surrounded S-21 to prevent the prisoners from escaping. Inside, classrooms were transformed into jail cells with their windows reinforced with iron bars and barbed wires woven into them. The rooms upstairs were used for common holding areas. Each classroom on the first floor was divided into smaller cells (measuring 0.8 meter by 2 meters) reserved for solitary confinement.

The warden of S-21, Kang Kek Ieu, also known as Comrade Deuch, formerly worked as a mathematics teacher in the 1950's. He saw life in the city of Kompong Thom and graduated from the French Lycée Sisowath. In 1965, his activities as a Communist agitator landed him in jail. Upon release he rejoined the resistance to carry on with his works.

The prison guards were boys and girls aged from 12 to 15. The Khmer Rouge enlisted those innocent and uneducated youngsters to train and brainwash them into the cruelest of fanatics. The victims at Tuol Sleng came from all social backgrounds. They arrived from every corner of the country and were of different nationalities: Vietnamese, Laotian, Thai, British, American, Canadian, Australian ... However most were Khmers of the educated class: intellectuals, doctors, engineers, lawyers, teachers... At a later date, Khmer Rouge accused of being traitors were also incarcerated there.

Instruments of torture were not lacking and living accommodations at S-21 pitiful. Besides being beaten females inmates were often raped. There were instances where an entire family was arrested then killed including newly born babies. The incredible thing was how diligent and thorough the guards at Tuol Sleng were in keeping the records of the jail: the victims were fingerprinted, photographed and required to write a detailed personal history from birth to the time of arrest before they were stripped naked and had all their personal belongings confiscated. Afterwards, with their feet in shackles, they were thrown into cells and left to sleep on the floor without any mosquitoes nets and blankets. From 1975 to 1978, at Tuol Sleng alone more than 10,000 people underwent torture and execution. That figure did not include children. Countless photographs were taken of victims with their arms tied behind their back. Their faces looked swollen from torture and their eyes showing indescribable fright. Other pictures depicted corpses lying in different positions in pools of blood. It seemed as if I could still smell the terrifying odor of blood, hear the screams echoing from some unknown corner in that cold and empty prison where time was transported back to a primitive and prehistoric past.

The jigsaw map of Cambodia during those four years of Khmer Rouge rule was constructed with Mounds of Skulls and Rivers of Blood.

Seeing that the Tuol Sleng Museum possessed an uncommon appeal to the tourists, in a stroke of imaginative creativity, Hun Sen wanted to capitalize on the idea. He was considering a project to convert Pol Pot's last hideout and the mass graves in the Southwest area of Pailin near the border with Thailand into a second tourism attraction. For Hun Sen the two million souls who perished under the genocidal rule of Pol Pot did not die in vain. Even in death they were contributing their share to the recovery of the country's economy, devastated by the years of hostilities.

Going through the gate of Tuol Sleng, I felt my heart and legs as heavy as lead. I told myself had I come to that place on my first day in Phnom Penh I probably would not have stayed a day longer in Cambodia. I wanted to forget Tuol Sleng, the gate to hell for tens of thousands of human beings; to leave behind me the Olympic Stadium; to wipe from my memory those frightful months and years when human bones piled up as high as mountains and blood flowed as deep as rivers; to erase from my mind the savagery of prehistoric time; the monstrous reign of evil; the betrayals and paradoxically not a few noble acts of sacrifice. But how could one ever ignore the most ignoble drama in human history of the "second half of the 20th Century" as one was about to step into the threshold of a new millennium.

On the plane taking off from the Pochentong International Airport I looked down at the city of Phnom Penh and the Mekong River at the Quatre Bras junction in front of the Royal Palace. The last image I wanted to retain in my mind of the land of Angkor was that of the rows of sugar palm trees growing by the ponds of fragrant white and pink lotuses. Their trunks may be pock marked by bullets yet they were still standing tall to reach toward the blue sky.

The sun will continue to rise and set on the Mekong, the magnificent beauty of the sky and earth will still be around despite all the upheaval and wars brought about by the dark side of the human heart. The trip only reinforces my fear that the Mekong is on the decline. Lest I forget I would like to say to my Khmer travel companion, Sok Thon: *"Thank you and let's meet again when I have the chance to return for a visit to the land of Angkor."*

Siem Reap –Prek Toal –Phnom Penh
Kompong Cham – Kompong Chhnang – Chhnok Tru
12/2001

Angkor Wat at sunrise

Siem Reap Air to Angkor with Visas on Arrival

Post-Khmer Rouge Angkor Dance revival

Apsara showing gun-shot-wound (GSW) by AK47 or M16

Chăm on Tonle Sap River near Phnom Penh

Ramadan in the ninth month of the Islamic calendar: Chăm Islam praying on Tonle Sap River

FCCC (Foreign Correspondents' Club of Cambodia) in Phnom Penh

Crossing the Tonle Sap Lake on the way to the Bird Sanctuary of Prek Toal

The Vietnamese in the land of no "milk and honey"

Olympic Stadium: the gathering place for mass demonstrations against the Vietnamese

Vietnamese-Cambodia Victory Monument in Norodom Sihanouk square

Tuol Sleng Museum: Mounds of skulls and River of bloods

Poor Chăm youngsters going barefoot

Kompong Cham-The Japanese Bridge across the Mekong

FROM THE MỸ THUẬN BRIDGE 2000 TO THE CẦN THƠ BRIDGE 2008

"From mountains to the sea, wetlands at work for us"
World Wetlands Day 02/20/2004

TO TAM NÔNG – THE BIRDLESS BIRD SANCTUARY

We left Saigon in the early morning to avoid its traffic jams and cacophony of noises. Heading southwest on National Route 1A, we drove through the provinces of Long An and Tiền Giang via the district of Cái Bè before switching to Provincial Road Number 30 to arrive at Đồng Tháp Mười. The bad condition of the road coupled with the fear of being gunned for speeding by the traffic police acted as a big inducement for our driver to slow down at certain sections of the way. It took us more than six hours to cover 200 kilometers. Bus drivers coming from the opposite direction constantly stuck their hands out of the window to greet us with a friendly wave. I soon learned that a downturn hand signified that the road ahead of us was clear of police giving the green light to our driver to accelerate and disregard the speed limit. Any traffic violation would result not only in a hefty fine but also a hole being punched on the driver license. Three holes meant an automatic suspension of the license...This measure proved to be quite a deterrent to the most daring drivers who liked to think of themselves as "top notch".

To visit Đồng Tháp Mười is to come to a vast area of depressed land. There is an interesting theory purporting that "probably in the old days the Cửu Long Giang, the Vietnamese name of the Mekong, used to run through this place and for some unknown natural reason it changed course to its present location. The huge natural depressions of Đồng Tháp Mười (Plain of Reeds) and Đồng Cà Mau (Plain of Cà Mau) are the two reservoirs where the Mekong stores its water during the high water season." (Trần Ngươn Phiêu – Đồng Tháp Mười 2006)

From the village of Cao Lãnh in the Đồng Tháp Mười Province, we drove up to the Thanh Bình District. From there we switched to Provincial Road Number 30 going northwest. At a three way intersection instead of heading toward Hồng Ngự we followed a sign and turned right to drive an additional 17 kilometers on a narrow and rather bumpy asphalted road before reaching our final destination: the Tam Nông Bird Sanctuary.

Along the road new and old houses were jostling for space – a sure sign that rapid population growth was posing a real threat to the Bird Sanctuary. Further back from the roadside, we noticed a tomb built not on ground level but on a dry cement platform raised higher than the surface of the road. The whole structure stood in a flooded rice field indicating that Tam Nông used to be a marshland area.

The Tam Nông Bird Sanctuary lies within a quadrangle of canals that dissects the Mekong Delta. Its "vital" statistics show it has a quasi-equatorial monsoon climate with an average temperature of 27 degrees centigrade and a variation of 3 to 5 degrees a year. Rainfall measures a rather low of 1,500mm/year and the Rainy Season extends from May to November. (Phùng Trung Ngân, Garrulas 6:3-5, 1989).

During the war, countless bloody battles were fought in Đồng Tháp Mười. The area proved to be extremely unresponsive to the South Vietnamese government's pacification efforts. The Americans did not fare any better. They had repeatedly attempted to destroy the Vietcong's safe haven to no avail by either draining the marshlands or using a combination of Agent Orange and napalm bombs in their defoliation efforts.

After the war, rapid population growth brought about severe scarcity of land. It then became indispensable for the people to embark on a continuous effort to drain the marshlands through a complex system of canals to come up with new arable land.

In 1985 soon after the Eastern Sarus Cranes were first spotted in the wetlands of Đồng Tháp Mười, world scientists convened an International Conference on Cranes in Kunming, the capital of Yunnan province. In attendance were representatives of various organizations like World Wildlife Fund (WWF), International Union for the Conservation of Nature (IUCN), International Crane Foundation (ICF)… They met to arrive at measures to conserve and turn the Bird Santuary of Tam Nông into a prototype "eco-tourism" site for Southeast Asia. Consequently the Tam Nông Bird Sanctuary was transformed into an important preserve for scientists to study the life and habits of migratory birds.

This sanctuary is located within a large depression on the left bank of the River Tiền and covers an area of 7,588 hectares. Depicted as a "scaled down model of the Đồng Tháp Mười landscape", it is the habitat for 130 kinds of plants, 120 species of fresh water fish, 40 kinds of amphibian reptiles, over 200 species of birds including 16 considered rare and precious. The Eastern Sarus Cranes or Grus antigone sharpie - also named Red-headed Cranes - were listed in the World's Red Book because they were threatened with extinction. Carvings of "dancing cranes" found on the bas-reliefs in the Bayon, the famed temple built in Angkor by Jayavarman VII in late twelfth century, testify to the fact that those birds form an integral part of the life of not only the now extinct and most glorious civilization of the Mekong but also of the area itself. Eight years ago (December 29, 1998), the Tam Nông Bird Sanctuary in the Đồng Tháp Mười region was officially designated the Tràm Chim National Park (TCNP).

The Bird Santuary consisted primarily of wetlands where Melaleuca woods coexist with wet grasslands. The Rainy Season lasts from August to November peaking in September. The water averages 2.50 meter in depth. Since the Bird Sanctuary is located in the lowlands it stays submerged even during the Dry Season.

From marker no. 17 on the road it was almost impossible to make out the office of the Tam Nông Bird Sanctuary. But that did not prevent us from finding it in the end. Our guide who had a very simple name Nguyễn Thị Được (meaning the OK or acceptable daughter of the Nguyễn family) went on board to accompany us. Since we visited the Tam Nông Bird Sanctuary in the middle of the Rainy Season we found ourselves surrounded by an immense body of water. We could distinguish, here and there, clumps of Cajuput, tufts of grass, water lilies and an occasional bird.

It was not until February or March, in the Dry Season, that the Bird Sanctuary came alive with food sources like shrimps, fish, clams, snails. This is the time for the migratory birds to flock to this place from far away lands to feed and procreate. Among them, in addition to the Eastern Sarus Cranes we could also count other rare water fowls like the Oriental Darter, Lesser Adjutant Stork, Painted Stork, Asian Golden Weaver and numerous other bird species.

In recent days, a recurrence of the H5N1 epidemic threatened to spread to all the four corners of the earth prompting epidemiologists at the World Health Organization (WHO) to caution the public that migratory birds might be its carriers. The H5N1 epidemic held the Mekong Delta under its sway at one time in the past. Though it was subsequently brought under control, another outbreak cannot be ruled out.

Animals and birds were not alone in being endangered. In the plant world, we discovered that of the 130 species of plants growing in the area, the wild rice species known as Oryza rufipogon was also threatened with extinction. In an article about Đồng Tháp Mười, Dr. Trần Ngươn Phiêu mentioned that this special type of rice was another peculiar find in this area. He wrote: "Like the other floating rice species, this wild rice grows tall and rises above the water level. Poor people use small and shallow bottom boats to negotiate their way through the swamp areas where this wild rice grows. They use long bamboo poles to beat the stalks until the grains fall into their boats. Harvesting wild rice in such a way represents a source of income for the poor people who have no fields of their own to till."

In his well researched book about the vegetation of Vietnam (Cây Cỏ Việt Nam 1991, III-2 page 776) Professor Phạm Hoàng Hộ wrote: "Wild rice is of the floating species. Its stem measures 1.5 to 4 meter in length, internodes 10 cm in length, leaf limbs 20cm in length and 1cm in width…it used to grow in deep fields all over the land but most abundantly in Đồng Tháp".

On the other hand, Professor Võ Tòng Xuân added: "The 'ghost' or wild rice Oryza rufipogon (OR) grows in the wild in marshlands and along the canals or ditches of Đồng Tháp

Mười as well as in wetlands of average depth in the provinces of Cần Thơ, Vĩnh Long and Tiền Giang. Another species named Oryza nivara (ON) also grows side by side with the OR in those regions. Their yield is very low: A mere 0.2 to 0.4 ton per hectare. Now that the fields of Đồng Tháp Mười are blanketed with the High Yield Variety / HYV rice, the OR and ON appear to be heading the way of oblivion.". Professor VTX informed us that he has sent specimens of those two wild rice species to the International Rice Research Institute (IRRI) at Banos, 60 kilometers south of Manila for safekeeping. This institute is the largest and oldest international research center on rice in Asia.

In my eyes, the ponds of lotuses or water lilies in the Tam Nông area are placed there by Mother Nature to add to the beauty of the landscape in the Bird Sanctuary.

Moreover it would be unforgivable not to mention an "undesirable" plant that is invading the ecology of the Tam Nông Bird Sanctuary: the "mimosa pigra". A native of tropical South America, this plant was spreading fast in the Bird Reserve wrecking havoc on its ecology and ecological diversity.

According to professor Phạm Hoàng Hộ "Mimosa pigra or pointed Virgin is a sturdy plant of 2 to 3 meter tall. Its leaves also fold up at the touch but at a slower pace than that of the shy Virgin (Mimosa pudica). Along the spine of the leaf grows a vertical thorn of 1.5cm in height separating the leaf into a pair of leaflets. The tips of the petals of the Mimosa pigra look yellow like those of the shy Virgin. Mature seedpods have reddish hairs, 10-12cm x 1.3-1.6cm. They fall off by segments except the two rims. This plant comes from Latin America and grows in the marshlands of Sài Gòn, Trị An, and Mộc Hoá (Cây Cỏ Việt Nam 1991 I-2, page 1029).

In professor Võ Tòng Xuân's view "Mimosa pigra is also named Mai Dương or Ngưu Ma Vương. It poses a headache for the peasants of the wetlands. This plant spreads very fast and proves extremely difficult to eradicate. International studies undertaken to control them have so far proved inconclusive. Does it mean that the national park of Tam Nông Bird Sanctuary, a preserve set up and financed by the International Crane Foundation (ICF) to save the rare and precious Eastern Sarus Cranes, is being suffocated by Mai Dương?"

For this reason; the four nations that border the Lower Mekong: Cambodia, Laos, Thailand and Vietnam; have chosen this motto for the commemoration of the "World Wetlands Day" on February 02, 2004: *"From the mountains to the sea, wetlands at work for us"*.

In the particular case of Vietnam, the Tam Nông Bird Sanctuary was chosen as a test site. Besides the usual celebrations on a festival day like boat racing, soccer games, theater shows…the most noteworthy activity on this occasion was the launching of a campaign to "search and destroy the Mai Dương, Ngưu Ma Vương or the Pointed Virgin plant". It became imperative to sound this alarm to remind the local people that the Mimosa pigra must be viewed as a formidable enemy that must be pursued and destroyed through a sustained campaign in order to safeguard the balance and diversity of the ecology in the Tràm Chim National Park at Tam Nông.

At the time the Bird Sanctuary was designated a national natural preserve, it received an initial allocation of 4 billion đồng from the Vietnamese government. Subsequently, generous donations began to flow in from Denmark, Germany and Japan… to fund the conservation and development projects of the Crane area and buffer zone in the Bird Sanctuary.

In 1995 the International Crane Foundation (ICF) adopted a plan limited to the study of the nesting places of the Eastern Sarus Cranes. Starting in March of 1998 ornithologists introduced the use of electronic tracking rings to expand the scope of the researches to include the total ecological system and activities of this migratory bird. This project which was financed by the Japanese government, also called for the participation of Japanese, American and Vietnamese scientists.

Miss Được, our guide at the Bird Sanctuary, revealed that due to the nefarious effects that succeeded one after another, the number of Eastern Sarus Cranes as well as other rare and precious birds that flocked to the Bird Sanctuary during the Dry Season continued to dwindle over the last few years. This is a disconcerting fact conservationists need to take note of. During the last 20 years the number of Eastern Sarus Cranes that returned to the Bird Sanctuary followed a steady downward curb: from 1,502 in 1988 it dropped to 631 in 1996 then to 154 in 2004 and to a record low of 90 in 2006 (Source VNN).

The reasons leading to this deplorable state of affairs were many: 1) deterioration of the ecological conditions in the Bird Sanctuary caused by the digging of new canals, 2) abnormal rains resulting from the effects of evaporation of large bodies of water stored in the reservoirs of the series of dams being built upstream of the Mekong in Yunnan, 3) pressure from population growth in the surrounding areas evidenced by the construction of numerous local housing projects, 4) infringement on the lands surrounding the buffer zones, 5) need to divert the waters from the Bird Sanctuary, 6) seeping of chemicals from fertilizers used in the rice fields adjoining the Bird Sanctuary...All these factors had a hand in the long term degradation of the preserve.

To make matters worse, a project was being implemented to build a beltway around the Tam Nông Bird Sanctuary to develop "eco tourism". With an ever shrinking land area, it would not be farfetched to conclude that in a not too distant future the days of the rich ecological system of the Tam Nông Bird Sanctuary are inexorably numbered.

Officially hunting is banned in the Bird Sanctuary. However, it is in practice a common occurrence resulting in the killing of many species of rare birds including the cranes.

Conservationists have good reasons to classify the Eastern Sarus Cranes as a flagship species. To protect those cranes means to protect more than 120 other species of birds at the same time. Carrying it a step further, it also involves the conservation of the wholeness of the entire ecological system of the Mekong Delta and the Mekong River...of which the Tam Nông Bird Sanctuary is a living symbol.

On the way to Đồng Tháp Mười one has to pass through the district of Lấp Vò. Several years back, fishermen in the district caught "a giant ray fish" which measured more than 4 meters in length, 2 meters in width and weighed 270 kilograms in the Tiền River. When we inquired, no body seemed to know about it or more precisely have a recollection of it. In the same vein, not many people could imagine that only over thirty years ago, the Mekong Delta was still teeming with fish and shrimps. Nowadays, that food supply had been exhausted and not many people even bothered to ask why. Leaving Thailand aside, the people of Laos and Cambodia (the two nations which cannot be classified as more advanced than Vietnam) seemed to be more concerned about the Mekong and better informed about the mammoth dams spanning the Mekong in Yunnan than the Vietnamese. It is mind boggling to notice that the address for the Vietnam National Mekong Committee is at: "23 Phố Hàng Tre, Hanoi" in the North. A more appropriate location would be the University of Cần Thơ or the University of An Giang in the Mekong Delta.

Over 10,000 years ago - a short time span on the geological

clock - the Mekong Delta still lied submerged on the ocean floor and extended all the way to the Sundra continental shelf. With the passing of time, the pyrite in the Mekong current combined with the iron and sulfur of the seawater to produce deposits that formed an area known as the Mekong Delta we see today. This explains why the low depressions of the Đồng Tháp Mười and Cà Mau Deltas at places are only half a meter above sea level.

Miraculously a new civilization took root and flourished on this new land. In the 1930's, while working on the Ba Thê canal project in the Óc Eo area, district of Thoại Sơn, province of An Giang, workers unearthed an ancient port city. According to some archeologists, nineteen centuries ago there existed in the Mekong Delta a Kingdom called Funan which possessed a highly advanced maritime civilization and a large commercial fleet. This kingdom sat at the crossroad where the Indian culture from the west and the Chinese one from the north met. It was the Indian culture which left the deepest marks as evidenced by the practice of Brahmanism and the Theravada branch of Buddhism in the region. Vestiges of a system of canals serving the dual purpose of irrigation and transportation could still be seen in the Óc Eo area - An undeniable proof that the Funan Society had attained a high level of organization as well as division of labor.

The French archeologist Louis Malleret directed the major excavation works at the Óc Eo site. He maintained that the "Óc Eo Civilization" which existed between the first and seventh century was actually the precursor of the Khmer-Angkor Civilization. Artifacts found at the site included: Roman coins bearing the image of emperor Marcus Aurelius (121-180), Persian coins, statues of Brahman gods and even of Buddha.

Traveling in North Vietnam, where Chinese influence is strong one usually finds statues carved out of wood. As one moves further south Indian influence becomes more pronounced and stone replaces wood as the preferred material used by the sculptors. During the French colonial rule, Louis Mallaret was appointed curator of the Museum of History located in the Saigon's Botanical Garden and Zoo. This institution was reputed for its collection of Funanese artifacts: earthenware, musical instruments, bronze utensils, jewelry made of gold and precious stones displaying intricate workmanship.

So far, nobody has yet come up with a definitive and plausible explanation for the rise and fall of the Óc Eo civilization. The current theory suggests that a catastrophic natural disaster might have brought about the sudden demise of such a resplendent civilization on such a fertile land, Where did the Funanese come from? When did they migrate to this area of wild and unstable swamplands hundreds of years prior to the Vietnamese Southward March? ...Those questions concerning the Kingdom of Funan are still begging for answers. Likewise, the enigma surrounding the civilizations bordering the Mekong River like the jars in the Plain of Jars in Laos and the bronze artifacts at the Ban Chiang site in northeast Thailand remains unsolved. Surely archeologists will find them interesting topics for research in the coming days.

Going into the 7th century, the Mekong Delta was part of the Kingdom of Chenla but still remained sparsely populated by the Khmers. Those people led a contented life in their hamlets and relied on primitive farming techniques for their subsistence. This went on for many centuries until the day they came in contact with the Vietnamese who migrated from the north at the close of the 16th century. At that time Vietnam was ruled by rival "Shoguns" named Trịnh and Nguyễn. The ranks of Vietnamese pioneers continued to swell as the days went by. Though they were not formally organized into a colonizing expeditionary force, their desire to seek a better life in a new land drove them to transform a vast region of swampland into the fertile delta of present day

South Vietnam. Before reaching their final destination, those "pioneers" had to pass through the kingdom of Champa in the central part of Vietnam where they encountered stiff resistance from the local people resulting in years of bloody confrontations. This is somewhat comparable to the situation where the white settlers and American Indians were pitched against each other. With the Khmers it was completely different. These indigenous people were used to a secluded lifestyle. In the face of the Vietnamese influx they instinctively withdrew to the highlands and consequently became a minority in their own land.

Nowadays, these Khmer Kroms number about 900,000 living among twenty million inhabitants in the western region of the Mekong Delta. They are called "Thổ" meaning indigenous people by the Vietnamese. During the *"Mùa Thổ Dậy /* the Uprising Season of the Khmer Krom" they sowed constant fear in the heart of the Vietnamese as they went on a rampage and decapitated the unlucky victims who happened to cross their path.

While most Vietnamese adhere to the Great Vehicle or Mahayama Branch of Buddhism, the vast majority of Khmer Krom practices Theravada Buddhism with an emphasis on self-reliance to attain enlightment through the exclusive worship of the Buddha. The largest conglomerations of Khmer Krom are found in the region of Trà Vinh, Sóc Trang, and Châu Đốc. They live in isolated "sóc" or hamlets and villages organized into "phums" of ten households each. Their simple dwellings with thatch roofs stand in sharp contrast to the nearby imposing and mangificent golden pagodas run by the monks, their spiritual leaders. In the vicinity, one can find stupas which contain the ashes of the cremated deceased. It is for this very reason that in the hamlets inhabited by the Khmer no cemeteries can be found.

Like in Laos and Cambodia, it is a familiar scene in the Mekong Delta where large groups of Khmers live to see the bonzes file out of the pagodas in brilliant yellow robes to start on their morning walk to beg for food.

With the advent of the "Renovation" era, gone is the sight of a monk holding his own bowl. Nowadays, more often than not he is followed in close step by a novice carrying a shining aluminum container with multiple compartments to store the food donated by the believers in one hand while holding on the other an umbrella to protect his teacher from the burning sun. The monk is allowed to eat any kind of food the believers donate be it vegetarian or meat. This practice is frowned upon by the Great Vehicle branch of the North that sticks to a strict vegetarian diet.

CHĂM ISLAM IN CHÂU ĐỐC / CHĂM BHRÂU

The local Vietnamese used to call them "Chà Châu Giang". They live in houses on stilts with wooden walls and brick roofs along the banks of the Hậu River. Actually they are of Chăm origin but on account of their close contacts with the Muslim Malaysians, the Vietnamese mistook them for being Malaysians and called them "Chà".

Turning back the pages of history one can discern two waves of Chăm who immigrated to this area.

In 1755 after he succeeded in repulsing attacks by the Khmers, the court mandarin Nguyễn Cư Trinh submitted to the Nguyễn "Shogun" the "silk worm" strategy proposing the use of the Chăm to hold the Khmer in check. This idea was approved and a number of Chăm who have sought asylum in Cambodia were allowed to return to Vietnam. They were inducted into the "Côn Man" forces and entrusted with the mission to protect the region of Tân Châu, Hồng Ngự, and Châu Giang. In return they were given the right to settle in the land.

When the Chăm threw their support behind a failed uprising led by Lê Văn Khôi against the court in 1833, emperor Minh

Mạng ordered an atrocious massacre of the Chăm throughout Central Vietnam. Those who survived either fled to Cambodia or sought refuge among their compatriots living in Châu Đốc. From Châu Đốc I boarded a motorboat on the Vĩnh Tế Canal to head in the direction of Hà Tiên. Looking back from the canal toward Châu Đốc I could see the verdant Sam Mountain standing tall against the crystal clear sky. This mountain is one of the seven that form the Seven Mountains area. From the distance it resembles a horseshoe crab shell (Limulidae / Sam) with a protruding tail in the form of a small mountain range. Emperor Minh Mạng named it the Vĩnh Tế Mountain. However the local people have the habit of calling the mounts and hills of their region by their shape. Consequently we have names like the Parrot Mountain, the Long Mountain, the Elephant Range, the Cô Tô Mountain, the Bà Om Peak…Thất Sơn is a land rich in myths and dotted with caves and grottos where legendary Monks or Shamans could establish colonies for their disciples and followers.

The craft glided effortlessly on this historical canal that runs straight ahead toward the distant horizon. Fresh water colored red by alluvium flowed in between two rows of green trees. We were not in the high water season but the Hậu River still flowed into the canal bringing with it lumps of blooming purple hyacinths resting amidst their green leaves.

HISTORICAL BACKGROUND

Since the time of the Funan Kingdom (circa 5th century) there already existed a system of canals serving as waterways to connect the ancient capitals to the cities like in the case of Angkor Borei (Phnom Penh), Óc Eo (Long Xuyên), Thị Trấn Trăm Đường (Kiên Giang).

To keep the Southern March going and relentlessly expand the boundaries southward, the Nguyễn emperors found it expedient to adhere to the "silk worm" strategy proposed by Nguyễn Cư Trinh in the preceding century. However this time the conquest and settlement of new lands by the Vietnamese pioneers also went hand in hand with canal digging and road contruction.

Under the reign of emperor Gia Long the first canal named Tam Khê was built. Nevertheless, it was not until the Vĩnh Tế Canal was completed that the Vietnamese inherit from their forefathers a truly monumental construction work. It would be unforgivable not to mention the name of Thoại Ngọc Hầu in any reference to the pacification of the Hậu Giang region and the building of the almost 100 kilometer long Vĩnh Tế Canal.

Researches done by Nguyễn Văn Hầu showed that Thoại Ngọc Hầu was born in Quảng Nam with the given name Nguyễn Văn Thoại. He was intelligent but short tempered. Unfortunately, the rival "shoguns" Trịnh and Nguyễn and later the Nguyễn and Tây Sơn often chose his birthplace as their favorite battleground. The ensuing devastation forced his family to seek refuge on the island Cù Lao Dài on the Cổ Chiên River in the South. He enlisted at a very young age to serve under the banner of "shogun" Nguyễn Ánh. In the beginning, he had to endure long days of hardship and deprivation as well as the perils of warfare. After the dark clouds of hostilities had cleared, he ended up an esteemed court official and keeper of the "pro-consul" seal of Chenla cum defender of the Vĩnh Thanh region extending from the cities of Châu Đốc to Hà Tiên. His reputation as a strict and fair official earned him the love and respect of the military and civilians who served under him. In 1818 upon completion of the Tam Khê canal, the emperor bestowed on him the title "Thoại Hà" and the nearby mountain was renamed "Thoại Sơn" in his honor.

Right afterward, he received the order from the court to take the citizen-soldiers under his command from Gia Định Thành to Châu Đốc to dig a huge canal linking Châu Đốc to Hà Tiên. Knowing that it was a large scale and challenging project emperor Gia Long sent him these comforting words: *"The contruction of this canal is extremely arduous but indispensable for the defense of the country. Its importance cannot be overlooked. You, my subjects, presently have to endure hardship but your sacrifice will benefit countless generations to come".*

This canal built in the new territory started on the left bank of the Hậu River in Châu Đốc and continued on to Hà Tiên where it connected with the Giang Thành River before running into the Gulf of Siam. Right from the beginning Thoại Ngọc Hầu had to mobilize 5,000 Vietnamese citizen-soldiers in addition to a number of Chăm and an additional 5,000 Khmer hired hands to start the work. Very soon afterward a drought followed by a flood and opposition from the labor force brought the whole effort to an abrupt stop.

To clear such a vast wilderness the workers had to rely on sheer human power and primitive selfmade tools like hoes, spades, pestles, and mallets... while measurements were all done by hand. To ensure that the digging was done in a straight line the workers must first clear the reeds and bushes then wait for nightfall to light torches attached to tall poles. A monitor standing on high grounds would flag the workers to position the burning poles in the correct positions for the digging to be done. For that reason there is this lullaby: *"Đèn nào cao bằng đèn Châu Đốc, Gió nào độc bằng gió Gò Công /* What lanterns could be as tall as those in Châu Đốc, what wind could be as lethal as that in Gò Công."

Working round the clock while subsisting merely on rice and salt, the workers could not even fully quench their thirst because water was strictly rationed. Add to that a harsh climate of freezing cold at nights and scorching heat during the days, on top of an inhospitable environment and lack of medical services then we have an unenviable formula for disaster resulting in sicknesses and deaths.

The project had to be interrupted on numerous occasions on account of seemingly unsurmountable obstacles. Not much progress was gained after three years of hard work. Emperor Minh Mạng was left with no other alternative but to order Marshal Lê Văn Duyệt to bring in a reinforcement of 39,000 Vietnamese citizen-soldiers and 16,000 Khmer hired hands. This labor force was organized into three shifts and worked through the night in the deep jungle teaming with mosquitoes, leeches, venomous snakes and wild beasts. Workers or soldiers who wanted to flee could hardly find an escape route. Those who made it to the jungle would face starvation or fall prey to tigers and panthers. Should they choose to swim across the Vàm Nao crocodiles would be laying in wait for them. The Vàm Nao River connects the Tiền to the Hậu Rivers forming the boundary between Châu Đốc and Long Xuyên.

The project lasted five years (1819-1824) under the harsh supervision of "pro-consul" Thoại. He always devoted himself totally to the task on hand and usually achieved the desired goals. Nonetheless his authoritarian and single-minded style of leadership did not endear him to the population and caused high losses of life including those of the soldiers who ably took part in his numerous expeditionary campaigns.

To this day, the elders in the Hậu Giang region still remember and talk about the tribulations their forefathers had to face and endure. Great or small, all monuments or man made wonders be it the Pyramids, the Great Wall of China, Angkor Wat, the Vĩnh Tế canal...always bear a hefty price tag paid for with the lives and miseries of the masses.

The canal project was eventually completed to the great

satisfaction of the entire court in Huế. Thoại Ngọc Hầu's wife was reputed to be an upright person and a devoted as well as supportive wife throughout his years of service to the court. Unfortunately, she passed away two years before the works on the canal ended. In her memory, the emperor gave her name: Vĩnh Tế to the canal and the Sam mountain which runs along its banks.

In appreciation of the Chăm's contribution to the project, the emperor allotted them lands to set up seven villages known as "Puk" in the Chăm language. Nowadays, those who live in those villages are called Chăm Châu Giang.

To honor those who lost their lives while working in the Vĩnh Tế canal project, emperor Minh Mạng decreed that a fleet be organized to retrieve their bones for reburial. They were granted the status of soldiers who gave their life in combat. Thoại Ngọc Hầu presided over the mass burial ceremony to erect a memorial stelae on the Sam Mountain and read in person the "Odes to the Lost Souls of Vĩnh Tế":

> *Trời xanh thẳm mồ hoang lớp lớp*
> *Trăng soi nhòa mấy lớp bia tàn...*

> *The deep blue sky, rows and rows of abandoned tombs*
> *The moon shed her hazy light on the stelae of old...*

The Vietnamese history book, Đại Nam Nhất Thống Chí, noted that in the 17th year of the reign of Minh Mạng, the Emperor ordered the casting of nine gigantic incense burners (Cửu Đỉnh) weighing 4,000 Vietnamese pounds individually. On each was inscribed the memorable deeds of his predecessors. These burners were considered national treasures and displayed in front of the Thế Miếu in the Đại Nội of the old imperial city at Huế. At this place all the Nguyễn emperors from Gia Long, the founder of the dynasty, down were worshiped. Smaller shrines erected on the left and right sides of the courtyard were reserved for the worship of deserving high court officials. Each burner bears a specific name of the royal family: Cao, Nhơn, Chương, Anh, Nghị, Thuần, Tuyên, Dụ, Huyền. The nine burners were arranged in straight rows. The burner called "Cao" bearing Gia Long's name recorded the digging of the Vĩnh Tế Canal. It is placed by itself in the front row. The characters denoting the Vĩnh Tế Canal were engraved on the side of the burner along with its picture at the foot of the Sam River. The whole thing was artistically done to commemorate one of the most significant achievements of the Nguyễn Dysnasty.

This canal of almost 100 kilometers in length runs along the Vietnamese and Cambodian border. In addition to its strategic importance, it also serves as a useful waterway for the movement of goods and people. On top of that, the canal plays a vital ecological role by bringing fresh water from the Mekong to an immense region washing away its salt and aluvium thus redering the land more arable and productive. With the passing of time, an intricate system of canals was developed around the Vĩnh Tế Canal. In total it measures more than 2,000 kilometers long– almost equal to half the length of the main current of the Mekong itself.

Recently, Dutch irrigation experts expressed their admiration for the building of the Vĩnh Tế Canal by the Vietnamese of old, especially for the efficient conduit of freshets from the delta into the gulf of Siam. They also suggested digging a new canal from the Hậu River south of Long Xuyên to Rạch Giá, including another section linking the Tiền and Hậu Rivers similar to the present day Vàm Nao River. An additional advantage of this proposed project is that the waters from these canals will prevent seawater from invading the land bordering the ocean like it is now the case with the city of Rạch Giá.

Like other peoples, the Chăm have an origin, a culture and a history steeped in struggle. Just several hundred years ago the glorious Kingdom of Champa was reduced to a footnote of history. Unrelenting calamities had wrought destruction to everything including the Chăm people...

J. Y. Cousteau once remarked: "If death did not exist, no one can tell how precious life is". I fully agree with him. From the death of a human being, he extrapolates and discusses that of a nation and its civilization. The powerful Kingdom of Champa of the past is nowhere to be found in today's world map.

It was not by accident that I recently reminded my young fellow members of the Friends of the Mekong group that the Mekong River they hold so dear to their heart and show so much concern for, courses through seven countries not six because they omitted the small country of Tibet in their count. Regrettably that nation is facing the abysmal prospect of losing its identity as well as sovereingty.

More than once I have visited the Chăm Islam villages in Châu Đốc Thất Sơn. During the last days of the 20th century, international newspapers repeatedly mentioned a new trend in human conciousness. A seeemingly innocuous but consequential column in an inside page of the New York Times caught my attention. It read: "At the threshold of the 21st century the world will see the emergence of many small new nations arising from the insistence of minorities and even religious groups for self-rule". Recently the French newspaper Le Monde mentioned "The Dreams for Independence in Asia". People began to notice the budding movements for independence of the minority groups and Muslims in Asia. They may be small in numbers but quite active. In his book "Rebels With a Cause" Nicholas L. Kittrie warns of a worldwide political prospect in which "Religious extremism shows a potential to explode in full force. The most ominous source of conflict in the future will come from political-religious extremism." Undeniably religion is a positive force. However, when coupled with politics it could become a "Lethal Duo" resulting in extremism.

One could not help recalling a meeting in San Francisco in preparation for the Conference of the Minority Groups of Indochina a while back. It was tittering on the brink of collapse in the face of determined and uncompromising demands from the representatives of the FULRO (Front Unifié de Lutte des Races Opprimées), a French acronym meaning the United Front for the Struggle of the Oppressed Races. They resolutely declared that the conference could not be held if the Vietnamese members were allowed to attend. Those Vietnamese Americans in question were included in the guest lists on account of the research they did on the history of Southeast Asia at the University of California at Berkeley. In the end the conference went ahead with the participation of an international panel minus the Vietnamese members.

The crux of the argument offered by the protesters was: "The root cause for the collapse of the Kingdom of Champa could be attributed to the Southern March of the Vietnamese which in essence is expansionary as well as aggressive". The more tolerant Chăm researchers offered a very different view: "Throughout history from the 11th to the 19th centuries there existed a constant schism among the Chăm people. It was this internal division which led to the demise of their Kingdom". Ironically, one cannot refute the historical tragedy that the Chăm were also victims of the civil war which was unfolding in neighboring Vietnam. At that time, the rivalry between the Trịnh and Nguyễn "shoguns" threatened to tear that country apart. To ease the constant pressure exerted by the Trịnh "shogun" in the north, the Nguyễn Hoàng "shogun" had no choice but to expand southward at the expense of the Chăm. When Nguyễn Ánh fought against the Tây Sơn, the Kingdom of Chămpa was once again turned into a battleground. Then, during the Lê Văn Khôi uprising against the Huế court, the Chăm got inextricably caught in this political maelstrom and ended up the hapless victims of merciless retributions at the hands of emperor Minh Mạng (1820-1841). One can say that in 1832 the Kingdom of Chămpa was "wiped off the map."

A new leaf has turned for the Chăm people after 1975. Along with over two million Vietnamese, about 25,000 Chăm left Vietnam to seek refuge abroad. Malaysia welcomed them with outstretched arms. The rest resettled in third countries like the United States, France, Australia, Canada… with the largest group going to California. Though the oversea Chăm communities do not represent the majority of the Chăm population, their leaders are graduates of European and American universities. They form a new generation of Chăm who can look beyond the feeling of grief and regret that casts a shadow over their history.

"*Còn đâu nữa những ngày oai hùng cũ*
Khi tháp Chàm ủ rũ dưới màn sương"

"*Where are the glorious days of old*
Now that the mournful Chăm stupas
Are covered by the fog's folds?"

At first the Chăm lived in disparate Chăm communities without kings or leaders. Though speaking the same language they were unable to come to a common understanding with each other. Now that they have grown into a force full of vigor and new ideas, at long last they can muster their full potentials to restore the Chăm civilization. Hopefully, the study of Chăm history and the invigorating sense of solidarity for each other will enable the Chăm communities living in the four corners of the world to eventually achieve their much sought after political unification. Most importantly, they were able to establish a working relationship with and receive support from rich Muslim states like Saudi Arabia, Egypt and nearby Malaysia. With such formidable backings, the idea of restoring a Chăm nation could not be very far from the mind of the militant Chăm leaders.

Using an oar-propelled craft we negotiated our way among the floating houses and fish farms on the Hậu River to berth at the Chăm village called Koh Ka Boaak (Silk Island) across from the provincial city. By a fluke of history, a historical transplant, there are about 12,000 Chăm living in Châu Đốc. The local inhabitants call them "Chà" because like the Malaysians they are followers of the Orthodox branch of Islam. They live in clean and elevated stilt houses in near isolation from their surroundings. The women do not wear veils to cover their faces but use scarves to adorn their heads. They rarely venture out of their homes and are engaged in the handicraft production of silk weaving destined mostly for export to Malaysia. In every Chăm Village one will find a new mosque with tall and imposing minarets. The interiors are spacious and brightly lit, devoid of altars, images or statues. The elders of the village told us that the new mosque was built in 1992 with funds provided by the Overseas Chăm Communities that received active support from Muslim countries particularly Malaysia.

On that day, in the Đa Phước Village rich in historical relics, the elders treated me to a meal in a stilt house decorated with Arab style designs. It was also the first time I was introduced to the tasty Chăm dish named *"tung lamo"*. It was a sausage stuffed with marinated beef, spices, rice and left to ferment under the sun. The sausages smelled delicious while they were being grilled over red burning charcoals. We ate them with fresh vegetables, star fruits and green bananas. The dish was not only exotic but above all quite delectable. That afternoon before bidding farewell to the Đa Phước village I held three-year-old Karem in my arms. The baby's face looked gentle and bright. She belonged to the 21st century Chăm generation, the Globalization era. I asked myself if I were a Chăm who still holds dear to his root what dreams and aspirations would then abide in my heart? Truly the answer to that question was not easy to arrive at!

One thing I am certain of is that baby Karem has to survive to keep the dream alive in an open and tolerant heart. In that way, the griefs of past history could be forgiven and the hatred or doubts of the present neutralized to smooth the way for a harmonious and prosperous life in a clean natural environment. Her generation deserves to inherit such a future. Nevertheless, that promising prospect does not come easily by itself when there still exists a small but very active minority who stubbornly relies on the assistance from outside powers to establish a "self rule" or autonomous nation within "the context of a Vietnam which is fragmenting into pieces."

At this time, I only find it within my power to silently pray that she will not be drawn into bloody adventures and crushed by conflicts motivated by racial or religious hatred. May this thorny road not be hers to walk. May she enjoy as a Chăm the absolute bliss of living in an era dominated by a Culture of Peace.

Bidding farewell to the 20th century also means to forsake the Culture of War and espouse a fundamental transformation in the thoughts and behaviours of each and every man on this planet. Imaginative nonviolence will take the place of oppression. Cultural creativity and constructive dialogues will take over from mutually destructive conflicts. Baby Karem must live and grow to keep alive that dream of a harmonious coexistence between the many enhic groups on this land of destiny which only over eight thousand years ago was the cradle of the civilization of humankind.

I fervently wish that one day, when Vietnam is blessed with a government firmly rooted in the soil of democracy and observant of humanistic values, the Vienamese head of state will step forward to openly apologize to the Chăm people and all the other minorities for the pain and loss our forefathers visited upon them during our Southern March. Such an act does not mean to step back and make a revision of history because it is not in anybody's ability to change the past. It is rather to look ahead into the future so that we can learn from the lessons of the past and prevent history from repeating itself in the form of tragedies under different names and shapes. From its inception the expansion of Vietnam has gone through successive stages in the country's Southern March. Some people claim that there is no need to revisit this 'fait accompli' in our history. However I am convinced that it is imperative that we view it from a standpoint of a new world order where "fairness to the minorities" requires respect for their sacred rights to life, growth and happiness. The tears and hopelessness of the Chăm and Montagnards should be enough to awaken our conscience to the injustice they have suffered and force us to contemplate a future in which all the ethnic groups in Vietnam can march in lockstep toward a common tomorrow.

A VISIT TO THE UNIVERSITY OF AN GIANG – SIX YEAR OLD

We returned to Cao Lãnh to continue with our trip to Long Xuyên, the capital city of An Giang Province where the Óc Eo archeological site of the Funan Kingdom in the 1st to the

6th century is located. I had an appointment with my friend Võ Tòng Xuân at the An Giang University's campus. An unexpected change occurred when my travel companion, Nguyễn Kỳ Hùng, who also went along with me in an eventful trip seven years ago had to return to Saigon for personal reasons. It's a pity that in the coming days I could no longer enjoy the exquisite pictures of the Mekong Delta taken through this artist's lens. Another lonely journey like the one to Laos and Cambodia awaited me in the days ahead.

Being no stranger to Long Xuyên, I returned this time to be astonished at all the changes and developments that had taken place.

In 1970 when professor Đỗ Bá Khê delivered his speech to the first graduating class of the University of Cần Thơ, the city of Long Xuyên could only claim a Teacher Training College consisting of four classes and 260 students. Three decades later, the number of high school graduates in the Mekong Delta soared to 40,000 per year. As a result, the University of Cần Thơ became hopelessly overwhelmed by the situation and the authorization to build the University of An Giang was arrived at in December of 1999. With a budget of over US$ 35 million, actual construction on a 40 hectares lot began in January of 2001, the first year of the 21st century. Though the University of An Giang was totally funded by local sources, it was put under the academic supervision of the Ministry of Education and Central Training.

Following in the footsteps of the University of Cần Thơ which was established in the 1960's, the University of An Giang became the second and also the youngest state institution for higher learning in the Mekong Delta.

The helmsman who so ably steers the university since its conceptual stage is professor Võ Tòng Xuân himself - a familiar and beloved figure to the farmers of the Mekong Delta. He once held the position of vice-rector at the University of Cần Thơ and prior to 1975 was better known as one of the discoverers of the Miracle Rice HYV (High Yield Variety), a rice species with short stalks and very high yield. The introduction of the Miracle Rice into the Mekong Delta was hailed as a trailblazer in the fight against hunger and poverty. The International Rice Research Institute (IRRI) praised it as the Green Revolution in Rice Cultivation. With such leadership it was to nobody's surprise that the University of An Giang was developing along the path designed to combine conventional teaching with applied science to serve the public good. This same concept of R&D (Research and Development) is widely applied at American universities.

Before meeting Võ Tòng Xuân, I took a walk to have a look at the installations: auditoriums, libraries and naturally meeting and conversing with a few students. They were very young, unassuming in manners and simple in their dresses. Their talks were sincere and direct while displaying extreme politeness toward the visitors to their campus. Could this be one of the beauties or charms of the Văn Minh Miệt Vườn / Civilization of the Orchard ? It is safe to assume that they were not the children of the "Big Shots" or "High Cadres". Should such be the case, their parents would have enrolled them at the University of Saigon or paid their way to study at foreign institutions in the West especially in the United States.

These students belonged to a disadvantaged generation. In spite of being born after the war and growing up in the granary of the Mekong Delta, they were educated by an elementary and high school system rated as the most backward in the country due to a penury of classrooms and teachers...In the eyes of the nation's educators this system even lagged behind that of the Central Highlands. Graduating from such an inadequate system, they obviously were ill prepared to enter colleges. Only an intense love for learning could help them bridge the immense gap between the two school levels.

The University of An Giang fits the category of a Community City College on the way of development. Piles of bricks and sand from unfinished construction works scattered around the campus. The two-storied library looked pretty elegant and was considered the symbol of the University. It was neat, well kept and organized in the American way with a whole array of PCs for the students to use. Coeds and male students stood in an orderly line in front of counters to check out or return books. The library's collection of books - either new or in English - was still limited but the students could go on the Internet to obtain the information they needed.

That morning I walked into a large auditorium crowded with students from various departments. From the podium, professor Võ Tòng Xuân was delivering his lecture on the basic topic: "Scientific Methods and Research Stages". Even though I entered from the back, the room was packed and I was not able to find a vacant chair. A male student immediately stood up to offer me his seat. I later found out from him that he was a senior and about to graduate.

The lecture was clear, concise and intended to help the students write their dissertation (a short thesis) to meet the requirement for graduation. The dissertation represents a personal attempt on the part of the student to address the practical issues concerning the economic and social development of the Mekong Delta. Personally I found that the most interesting part of the lecture that morning was about the research on "rice" Võ Tòng Xuân, the agronomist, was pursuing.

After class, Xuân and I met. Though this was our first face-to-face meeting, I have read about him and kept track of his works and career for a while. He was the source of inspiration for one of the "characters" in my previous book about the Mekong, "Cửu Long Cạn Dòng". On the spot we had already something in common to start the conversation with. His demeanor was easy going, devoid of any formalities. Xuân personally prepared tea for us to enjoy in his principal's office that I had the habit of referring to as the rector's office. The room was rather small. The numerous stacks of books lying around the place made it even more so. Among them I saw the first edition of "Cửu Long Cạn Dòng" published by "Văn Nghệ" in California in 2000 - the birth year of the University of An Giang.

At noon on the same day, instead of using a car, I rode a Honda-for-hire with Võ Tòng Xuân to go downtown and have lunch with several of his young colleagues. We enjoyed a hearty meal consisting of local dishes and delicacies of the Mekong Delta like catfish sour soup, fish simmered with brine in an earthen pot, salad with shrimps and lotus roots.

After lunch, Xuân had to go back and take care of his busy schedule. He left it up to me to choose the activities I wish to participate in. One of them was the presentation of a thesis by a lecturer at the University of An Giang before the top level judging committee chaired by Xuân. The thesis on that day embodied statistical data compiled by the candidate. The committee commented on the deficiencies in the methodology used to compile the data and their interpretation. The candidate was given time to defend his work. At the end, the scores were added showing that the candidate only earned 52% of the total and his thesis was rejected. While all this was going on, in another lecture room a US trained Vietnamese American engineer from Florida was making a laptop and power point presentation about an "economy" rice roasting machine he invented. That afternoon, two delegations – one from the University of Southern California – paid a visit to the school. Both of them wanted to meet with professor Võ Tòng Xuân.

Xuân had young colleagues working with him. They were trained in various foreign countries, able and full of enthusiasm. However not one of them was yet ready to fill Xuân's shoes. They joined Xuân and the University of An Giang because they knew that's where the future lies. With their expertise and command of a foreign language they could easily find employment with foreign private companies i.e. from Taiwan or Korea and command much higher salaries. The lady director of the Office of International Relations held a PhD. in education from the University of Southern California (USC). The person responsible for organizing the University's library and website was an engineer who graduated with an MSc. in computer science from an American university on the East coast even though his main duty was to teach Information Science. We were told he had been admitted to a doctoral program at an university in Australia for the following academic year. A reporter named HV who used to work with the Tuổi Trẻ Daily News decided on her own to come and work with the University of An Giang. The author of numerous chronicles and captivating photographs, she was encouraged to further her studies in journalism at Columbia University in New York...

In addition to its indigenous teaching staff the University could also rely on the collaboration of the Voluntary Faculty consisting of foreign visiting professors who volunteered their services. Xuân confided in me that although these educators came to teach gratis, the University always sought to offer them honorarium it deemed proper. An anecdote that the staff here was fond of telling concerned a visiting professor who came by himself but left with his "better half" leaving the University with a reduced staff of one "collateral damage".

The University of Cần Thơ and University of An Giang were

entrusted with the mission to train the manpower as well as talents to meet the needs of the economic and social development of the Mekong Delta. As Vietnam was about to be officially admitted into the World Trade Organization (WTO), the need to "reinforce the ability to cooperate, compete, and integrate with the world market" becomes more pressing than ever.

As things stand now, the An Giang Province in particular and the entire Mekong Delta as well are suffering from a dire shortage of experts at the college and post college levels in various fields, be it in economics or social sciences. There also exists a critical demand for an army of skilled technical workers in the seafood and agricultural produce processing industries, eco-technology and tourism development.

Based on current progression curbs, by the year 2010 the projected student body for a four year training program will reach 10,000 in the fields of teacher training, agriculture, sea food processing industry, eco-technology, information industry, computer science, environment engineering, rural business management…The objective of the academic programs was tailored to meet the practical needs of the various sectors of the economy. The training therefore was designed not merely to train graduates to become civil servants but also to prepare them to perform well at the "address – location" or firms in the private sectors.

It must be admitted that the faculty of the university still remains very wanting. Out of a total number of 600, only 50% hold master degrees and a much smaller percentage has PhDs. From my conversations with the students I learned that Xuân relentlessly urged the young lecturers of the University to go study abroad. He was also constantly seeking out opportunities to help them do so in order to raise the quality as well as quantity of the teaching staff. Moreover, the University was pursuing an active "search and attract" campaign for new "gray matter". A promising and at the same time challenging prospect indeed for such a young University! Performing the duties of university rector was only one of the numerous hats that Xuân wore. On the side, he was simultaneously carrying out these on-going projects: 1) discover a gene for a new species of rice which could adapt to the "sweetened water" caused by the drying up of the Mekong and salt intrusion from the sea 2) Convince the farmers of the Mekong Delta to implement the "Three Less Three More" program. One of the "Three Less" is to reduce the use of insecticide in order to lower the level of toxicity which was nearing a critical point deemed harmful to the ecosystem; 3) set up a "Rice Museum" of the Mekong Delta exhibiting the farming implements our forefathers used to clear this wasteland. The list could go on ad infinitum.

Xuân kept a close watch on the development of the dams of the Yunnan Cascades along with the diversion projects of the Mekong water in Thailand and their combined impacts on the Mekong Delta. As far as he was concerned Vietnam did not have much say on these issues. Facing those "adversities" he was trying his best to turn them into "opportunities" like the development of shrimp farming, sea crabs farming in the "sweetened water" zones to replace rice cultivation and at the same time augment the farmers' income. Another of his pet projects was to study the possibility of applying the technology of rotation watering of the rice plant without a reduction in yield to prepare for the day the Mekong dries up …It seems as if a 24 hour day is just too short for Xuân. Being a Southerner he is unabashedly optimistic seeing that the glass is always half full instead of half empty…

A Vietnamese proverb says *"Tre già măng mọc"* meaning when the bamboo tree becomes old, the shoot will grow to replace it. Xuân is relentless in nurturing the younger generations to take over after him.

"So long! University of An Giang". The next time I come back to the Mekong Delta I look forward to visit the "Rice Museum" Xuân holds so dear to his heart.

POLLUTION ON THE BROWN HIGHWAYS

At the first light of day I boarded the boat at the Ninh Kiều Berth. A fresh breeze ran over the vastness of the Hậu River. Our motorboat roared at full speed against the current so that we could arrive at the peak hours of the two floating markets at Phong Điền and Cái Răng. Once there, we were met by the all too familiar scene of boats of different sizes loaded with fruits or vegetable from the local orchards sailing on the canals and converging on the floating markets to ply their wares to the merchants. The boat owners still hung cauliflowers, cabbages, bananas, and coconut... on high poles to advertise their wares. To my eyes, without any doubt, the place had lost some of its hustle and bustle and signs of prosperity that I saw during my last visit seven years ago. The goods on display were poorer in variety as well as quantity.

In place of a full breakfast, I got by with a cup of hot coffee flavored with condensed milk purchased from a small boat that snaked its way through the maze of the floating market.

By 9 o'clock in the morning, the place was abuzz with the sounds of people talking and boats moving. It got even noisier with the arrival of the vessels ferrying tourists along the riverbanks and heading our way. Oar propelled crafts were becoming a rarity now. Even small dinghies were equipped with gas engines. Large boats and barges bulging with sand and construction materials were powered by diesel engines. Black smoke billowing from their stacks lingered over the water and released a strong smell of burning in the air. No wonder not only in Saigon but also on the ferries sailing the rivers of the Western Region, many a young girls in the Mekong had to wear gauze masks to protect them from the polluted air.

Even if we ignored the toxic chemicals which had completely diluted in the water and no longer were visible, the sight of lumps of dry grass and plastic bags of all colors in various stages of disintegration floating amidst the water lilies was evidence enough to convince us that the Mekong was being used as a sewage system for industrial waste and domestic garbage. This scene was repeated everywhere we went: right on the Saigon river, the waste and trash from a floating restaurant were unceremoniously dumped into the current. It was not uncommon then to see a watercraft suddenly come to a dead stop because its propeller got caught in thrash or waste forcing the steersman to dive into the water to untangle the mess. I saw it at least twice in a half morning boat ride up the Hậu River.

On land as well as along the riverbanks, billboards often appeared pointing to a nearby Cultural Village or Hamlet. Ironically right next to it were also signs of defecation and littering. The people who lived in the vicinity still used that water to bathe, wash vegetables, or cook - in brief the whole thing is unsanitary and unconscionable. As the sun continued to rise in the sky, I could feel the heat of the tropics as my back was getting wet with sweat.

We found refuge from the midday heat at the Phong Điền Fruit Orchards rigth on the riverbank. The owner was an exceptionally robust looking, retired school-teacher in his seventies. A widower, he lived with his son and grand child. One of his children resided in Canada. The event leading to his becoming a widower was heartbreaking. Except for her arthritis, his late wife was quite healthy. To treat her, an incompetent doctor from the North gave her an injection in the spine leading to her untimely death while she was still in her fifties. Stricken by panic, the doctor's wife pleaded with him to forgive her husband and desist from taking him to court. That was what our owner eventually did. It happened 20 years ago and the doctor from Hanoi also had passed away. We found out that our retired teacher was the pioneer who opened the first Fruit Orchard in the region, giving birth to an entirely new industry called "eco tourism" in the Mekong Delta. In his garden, visitors could go fishing at a meandering rivulet, just relax on hammocks strung under the green foliage of fruit trees or stay inside thatch huts and taste the fresh fruits that were in season. The owner took me to his home to show me the family altar which consisted of a table, a cabinet and an almost three hundred years old pair of câu đối (wood panels inscribed with parallel matching verses). Before we took leave, he asked me to write a few words in the guest book. A glance at its pages told me that people from the four corners of the world came here and left words of commendation in their native tongues.

On the way back, I asked the steersman to stop at the Lê Bình Market by the riverbank, not far from the Cái Răng Floating Market. Walking over to the fish section, I found it so small and in no way comparable to its Thai counterpart in Nongkhai. Before my eyes were baskets of small fish: tilapias / anabas; eels; frogs; and basa or Pangasius fish, a catfish native to the Mekong River in Vietnam but sought after by international consumers. Most of the fare displayed was raised on farms. It was quite a disheartening scene.

On this trip, I noticed that restaurant goers worthy of the appelation "connoisseurs" developed a new habit when entering an establishment serving specialty dishes. The first question that came out of their lips was: "Do you serve river or farmed fish?". This phenomenon was only a few years old and seldom failed to surprise foreign visitors. Conventional wisdom dictated that fish caught in the wild taste better than those raised on farms. For the same reason, freerange chickens were preferred to raised ones. The industry of farming aquatic animals be it of the sea or fresh water variety was developed in preparation for the day Mother Earth can no longer adequately provide for the growing demand of her children. Several restaurants have introduced a novelty food: horse meat. Assuredly, it does not come from horses raised in the Mekong Delta but rather imported from Australia, the land from Down Under.

During this trip, thanks to the observance of a strict diet I was luckily spared the common intestinal ailments contracted by tourists. I made it a point to stay away from uncooked vegetable or ice cubes, while sticking to bottled water and unpeeled fruits... (just like I did on my journeys to Yunnan, Laos, Cambodia and Thailand). Throughout my stay in Vietnam, the H5N1 epidemic was raging and prompted me to give up fowl meat as well. The meals my driver and I shared together consisted mainly of hot dishes like sour fish soups, (red snapper cooked with sesbania javanica flowers), catfish simmered with brine, fried small prawns or pork cooked in coconut juice. And how can I forget the special concoction of pergularia buds fried with garlic I ordered that day for the first time that so delighted and surprised my taste buds? The delicacy is hailed as an *"Exotic Dish of the South / Món Lạ Miền Nam"* by the famous Vietnamese writer Vũ Bằng. As for that most delicious and attractively arranged dish of deep-fried puff fish I tasted seven years back on the bank of the River, it had disappeared from the menu.

It is an undisputable fact that the sources for natural sea and fresh water food are being exhausted. This confirmed once more the statement professor Võ Tòng Xuân made a year ago in an interview (10/10/2005) with an RFI reporter named Ánh Nguyệt:

"Generally speaking, the food source coming from the Mekong

is on the decline both in quantity and variety. However, at the present time the fresh water food source comes mostly from farming while that from fishing in nature has greatly diminished. This state of affairs is very different from 1975 when peace was just reestablished. We can safely assert that the harvests of shrimps and fish caught from the rivers were quite abundant then. Nowadays, it is farming that provides the lion's share of the fresh water food supply. Based on the export statistics of Vietnam, seafood harvested from the ocean accounts for half of the exported quantity while the remainder comes from farmed aquatic food source. The catches from the rivers prove to be statistically insignificant. At the present time, river fishing is an activity practiced only by farmers and their families living along the riverbanks. It represents an additional source of food for them – That's all..."

Nowadays, it is quite safe to assert that the flow of the Mekong current is getting weaker at many sections especially during the Dry Season. A case in point: the flow rate recorded for the Mekong at Phnom Penh showed a drop from 2,000 m^3/second to 1,600 m^3/second. That rate will surely be further reduced as the river enters the Mekong Delta. The weaker water flow may account for the apperance of sand banks at certain sections of the river.

The local people told us that a sand bank was being formed in the middle of the current right across from the Hoa Sứ Restaurant built on the bank of the Hậu River. Though it was not yet high enough to be seen above the water level, passing boat must exercise extreme caution if they do not want to run aground. The people simply accepted it as a natural phenomenon. But could it be man caused? No body seemed to care or wanted to think it through.

The inhabitants on the riverbanks appeared to be overtaken

by a new self perpetuating frenzy: they competed to build embankments in front of their houses not to prevent the land from caving in but to enlarge the front area of their properties. An embankment of reinforced cement that the people called "kè" was built in front of the Hoa Sứ Restaurant extending it an extra 5 meters into the current. Who issued the building permits and had the needed money to pay for such large-scale projects if not the "big shots" or "high cadres"? Such blatant practices occured daily and in plain view of the public. Do we need a new law to safeguard and save the river in the face of such abuses?

THE CẦN THƠ BRIDGE AND CONTRACT PACKAGE III FROM CHINA

On September 25, 2004 prime minister Phan Văn Khải attended the ground-breaking ceremony of the Cần Thơ Bridge project spanning the Hậu River. When completed it will be the longest suspended bridge in Southeast Asia. This is one of the two largest projects in the Mekong Delta - the other being the Cà Mau Gas-Electricity-Fertilizer Complex.

The first bridge of its kind, the Mỹ Thuận Bridge strides the Tiền River with a span measuring 1,535 meters. Built in 2000, it connects the two provinces of Vĩnh Long and Tiền Giang.

The expected time for completion of the Cần Thơ Bridge was set for 2008. It would also mark the end to the operation of the barge system serving the cities of Vĩnh Long and Hậu Giang on National Route 1A. The Cần Thơ Bridge is 2.75 kilometers long, 26 meters wide and has four lanes running in both directions. It claims a clearance of 39 meters allowing big ships with 15,000 tons displacements to navigate through. If the access ways at both ends of the bridge were included in the computation, the total length of the construction works would be 15.85 kilometers. The bridge will replace the Cần Thơ Barge

System which ferries a daily load of 20,000 vehicles and 87,000 passengers. Consequently the Cần Thơ Bridge will play a vital role in the economic development of the Mekong Delta and raise the standard of living for its 20 million inhabitants. Moreover, it is expected to act as a catalyst to attract foreign and domestic investments into the macro economic development plan of Tây Đô until the year 2010.

The consortium in charge of the implementation of the project included the following construction companies: Taisei, Kajima, Nippon Steel Co., the China State Construction Engineering Corporation. They worked under the overall supervision of the consulting firm Nippon Koei-Chodai. The whole undertaking bore a price tag of US$ 342.6 million, the highest of its kind in the country. This is also the longest bridge in Vietnam. In the ground breaking ceremony, the Japanese Consul General in Saigon, Mr. Osamu Shiozaki, revealed that since 1992 Japan's ODA (Official Development Assistance) has provided a total of US$ 7.4 billion in aid to Vietnam to build 70 bridges on National Route 1A.

According to the Vietnam News ["vnagency.com.vn" 07/09/2004] the Cần Thơ Bridge will be the third one to span the Lower Mekong - The first two being the Friendship Mittaphap Bridge linking Vientiane and Nongkhai, Thailand; and the Mỹ Thuận Bridge connecting the two provinces of Tiền Giang and Vĩnh Long, Vietnam. However, the author believes that the above information is inaccurate. In his opinion, the Cần Thơ Bridge (2008) would actually be the "fifth" one. The other four are: (1) Mittaphap Bridge (Laos and Thailand 04/1994), (2) Lao-Nippon Bridge/Champassak Bridge (Laos and Thailand 08/2000), (3) the Kompong Cham Japanese Bridge (Cambodia 12/2001), and the Mỹ Thuận Bridge (Vietnam 05/2000).

The progress in the building of the Cần Thơ Bridge is rated as "somewhat slow" leading to the suspicion that its projected completion date of 2008 would not be attained.

The project for the Cần Thơ Bridge called for three contract packages: The construction of the access ways to the bridge from Vĩnh Long will be assumed by local Vietnamese contractors (Package 1: Thăng Long, Cienco 6, Cienco 8) reported the slowest rate of progress, while the works on the bridge proper (Pakage 2: Japanese) and the access ways to the bridge from Cần Thơ (Package 3: Chinese) showed a satisfactory rate of progress. Package 3 is named: "Construction Project Detour QL1 / National Route 1A Cần Thơ Bridge". The China State Construction Engineering Corporation was entrusted with the building of a highway 7,690 meters long, 24.1 meters wide with 4 lanes of circulation and 9 secondary bridges having a total length of 1,165 meters. Intersection no. 3 has a flyover at National Route 91B, a 10-gate toll station and a service area of 21,000 m². Actual work began on 02/25/2005 with an estimated duration of 1,365 days or a projected completion date of 11/21/2008.

The roads leading to the construction sites of the Cần Thơ Bridge were closed to the general public. To reach their giant steel frames and towering cranes that sprang up to the blue sky, I had to use the river route. To my surprise, I found in the middle of the current a small dredging boat securely moored to a recently built foot of the bridge. A woman and her small son were the sole occupants on the boat. Upon close inquiry I learned that her husband was diving under the rushing water of the brown highway to scavenge for discarded steel bars. There was no way to tell how many bars he could retrieve and how much he would earn per day but obviously this is a very perilous new way to make a living.

As in the case of the Mỹ Thuận Barge, the Cần Thơ Barge System will close down in 2008. Then the Mandarin Route will run in one uninterrupted stretch from the northernmost Nam

Quan pass to the southernmost point of Cà Mau. However, from a larger perspective, the Mandarin Route does not stop there, because deep in their heart every Vietnamese believes that it will continue on to the Paracels and Spratlys islands. Seven years ago, I conveyed this very same thought to the composer of the ode cum musical piece "Con Đường Cái Quan / The Mandarin Route". He may no longer remember the conversation we had together at his cozy home in Midway City, California. That night Phạm Duy, the composer, autographed for me a picture of him pouring wine on the tomb of Văn Cao on his first return to Vietnam.

Văn Cao, the friend who was offered a drink in such an unusual way, is in no uncertain term an accomplished artist gifted in many disciplines like poetry, painting, soldiering and music. A proponent of modern Vietnamese music, he composed in 1944 the song "Tiến Quân Ca / The Forward March Song". One year later, the government led by Hồ Chí Minh declared independence from France, and chose that song as the country's National Anthem. When the "Nhân Văn Giai Phẩm" affair unfolded in the late 1950's Văn Cao was implicated in it. The term "Nhân Văn Giai Phẩm" is an amalgamation of the name of the "Nhân Văn" and "Giai Phẩm" periodicals that advocated for the democracy and freedom of expression in art and literature during the peace time that came in the wake of the first Indochina War.

The reactions of the Communist party were swift and merciless. It shut down the independent press, suppressed the movement by arresting its participants, executed some and sent the rest to concentration camps for long periods of internment. Văn Cao was among those unlucky souls. A number of those intellectuals were rehabilitated during the "Renovation" era of the late 1980's. Unfortunately it came too late. They were then too old or sick for any creative work. In the first decade of 2000, the government gave some of them posthumous awards. As for Văn Cao he passed away at the age of 72 heart broken and in abject poverty. Again, at the age of 85, Phạm Duy returned to the homeland to embark with his children on a journey along the Mandarin Route. During this trip he found the inspiration to compose the aforementioned musical piece. At the time of this writing that region in Asia is beset with political uncertainties. As tumultuous events are rumbling from an "East Sea In Turmoil", I wish to remind Phạm Duy of this well known phrase *"tam bách dư niên hậu"* penned by Nguyễn Du, the beloved poet of the Vietnamese people. With those few words the poet wished to express his doubts whether three hundred years hence the people would still remember him. Nevertheless, I for one hold to an unshakable conviction that no matter how long it takes the archipalegos of Paracels / Hoàng Sa and Spratlys / Trường Sa will one day revert to our national patrimony.

THE GENERAL HOSPITAL OF CẦN THƠ THIRTY YEARS AGO

Even though the purported goal of my field trips was to carry out "ecological research", I frequently made observation stops at hospitals and schools during the times I spent in the provinces of An Giang, Hậu Giang, and Tiền Giang. We can conclude that there exists "a common denominator in the condition of public health and education " in the Mekong Delta of which the General Hospital of Cần Thơ was a typical example.

Known as a large hospital in Tây Đô, the facility was nevertheless crowded and old. Three decades after the so-called "liberation day", a lack of upkeep caused the hospital to fall into a state of disrepair and its equipments or machinery were either outdated or no longer in working condition. It was not an exaggeration to compare it to an old bus designed to hold 40 passengers but was instead used to carry hundreds. In another word, on top of being excessively "overloaded" the vehicle was also being driven on a bumpy road. Taking a ride on such a bus surely means to put one's life at risk. However when one falls sick and needs medical care one is left with not many options.

End of August 2006, on a day like any other, the afternoon was drawing to a close yet the outpatient ward was still swarming with patients waiting for their medicine or for their turn to see the doctor. On any single day, it's not unusual for the hospital to accept more than 500 patients and for a doctor to see from 70 to 100. The latters might be very sick and exhausted but somehow there was always that air of resignation that permeated their demeanor. The signs posted in the Emergency Room did not look different from those at any other hospital but its equipment appeared rather rudimentary. A heartrending scene struck me profoundly. The smell of damp earth coming up from the ground filled the air after a sudden downpour of a tropical shower. Family members hurriedly carried a man on a stretcher from the ER to the patient's ward without any protection against the drenching rain.

Up in the patient rooms the situation turned even more tragic when one was confronted with the ratio between patients and hospital beds. Two persons had to share a mat covered metal bed lying head to toe alongside each other. When the need for patient's space became more pressing, two beds would be put side by side to accommodate five instead of four patients. Even then it is still preferable to having to lie on the floor. An overnight stay at the hospital under such conditions would make a healthy person sick. To make matters worse, short cuts in treatments were routinely taken and hospital stays reduced to the minimum to make room for incoming patients. Anywhere you go, be it the waiting area, the examination room, the ER or the recovery ward… this medical institution was operating under a constant threat of being overwhelmed with no sign of relief in sight. By profession I am quite used to the working conditions at hospitals. Nevertheless, I had to admit I was left totally unprepared for the stifling atmosphere of this place and its indescribable "hospital odor" which pointed to a poor and inadequate level of maintenance.

As I walked over to the Hemodialysis Unit, I was greeted by the humming of the outdated equipments that were struggling strenuously to service the fully occupied stations. The head of the unit, a young physician, was sitting at his desk next to a huge stack of files. He introduced me to a middle age colleague who appeared to be a man of few words. Since the tight budget did not allow for the purchase of new equipments he must rely on his ingenuity to fix and keep the existing ones in working order so that the patients could receive their dialysis. No wonder why the head of the unit refered to him as the "irreplaceable person". In Vietnam, the two principal causes leading to terminal renal disease were diabetes and high blood pressure. Those stricken with such a condition have to receive hemodialysis three times a week else their chances to survive were nil. Besides the head physician of the unit, not many people knew about our unsung hero. With more than three decades working in the medical profession, the image of nurses in white uniforms and cheerful, quiet orderlies caring for their indigent patients always arouse in me a sense of hope and admiration.

A common excuse cited to explain away the poor condition of the hospitals and public health system in the country was a penury of funds. To say that the country is still poor amounts to an insult to the intelligence of the listeners. The crux of the problem here is how you set your priorities. The funds to finance construction works were readily available. For proofs, one only needs to point to the imposing and brightly lit public buildings in the Mekong Delta like the Office of the People's Committee of the Province which is in itself a smaller replica of the Independence Palace in Saigon, the Headquarter of the People's Army, of the Security Force and so on...

At the end of 1999, during a visit to the Mekong Delta, this author wrote: "The post offices, banks, hotels were some of the new constructions in the Mekong Delta. Only the schools and hospitals remain backward and in decrepitude during the "Renovation' era." Alas! This is still the case on my return visit to the Mekong Delta seven years later.

Bidding farewell to the General Hospital of Cần Thơ we drove to the district of Ninh Kiều to visit a new hospital under construction at the outskirt of the downtown area. From the outside, the structure looked rather large and modern for a hospital. Right in front stood a big billboard showing the construction plan of the General Hospital of Tây Đô. A motto in bright red letters proclaimed: "Come to Tây Đô – Come to where trust is."

The sick people, doctors and entire personnel of the General Hospital of Cần Thơ were anxiously counting the days toward the completion of the project that called for a general hospital with 700 beds. Actual construction started on 12/19/2004 and the date of operation was scheduled for the beginning of 2006. More precisely February 3 of that year. When that targeted date could not be met it was postponed to August of 2006. Further delays in construction once more caused that date to be moved probably to December of 2006. Unfortunately, based on what we saw of the work progress at the end of August, it would be highly doubtful that this third deadline could be met considering that bare iron pillars and steel frames still lined the outside walls of the structure. The city of An Giang would have to wait until 2010 before it could start building a general hospital similar to the one in Cần Thơ.

An interesting statement on that large board caught our eyes. It announced a policy statement concerning the future activities of the General Hospital of Tây Đô : "treatment on demand with high standard services, courteous staff, conscientious services, clean and fresh ventilated environment." [sic]. "High standard services" here referred to those being offered to the "big shots, high cadres, or the wealthy loaded with money". I wondered what percentage of the hospital's future activities would be devoted for the treatment of the poor who made up 95% of the inhabitants in the Mekong Delta.

The type of health system or hospitals in Saigon geared to the "market economy" has been transplanted to the provinces. It meant that regardless of how small and underequipped a hospital might be, it always operated a "shining island" where special treatment was provided to a minority of privileged and wealthy patients. Their rooms were fully furnished with modern amenities like TVs, refrigerators, private bathrooms and restrooms, and naturally 24/24 air-conditioning. With "high standard" treatments the patients upon request could avail themselves of all kinds of tests, diagnostic machines and imported medicine. Of course, they had to be willing to pay astronomical prices to be admitted into the "shining island".

Personally, I believe that "after having adequately satisfied the basic health and social needs of the majority of the people, it would not be wrong (for the government or public health system) to set up those special units with high standard services". However, it would be heartless if not insensitive for the authorities to give high priority to the establishment of the "shining islands" in its drive toward development.

As if in a flashback, I recalled my trip to Siem Reap to visit Angkor in 2001. On that occasion I went to the Jayavarman VII hospital that was inaugurated by Hun Sen in 1999. The name

Jayavarman VII bears a rich historical connotation because he was the last king of the Khmer-Angkor dynasty in the 12th century. His achievements did not stop at enlarging the borders of his kingdom or building magnificent palaces. To show his concern for the public good, he expanded the road networks, constructed countlesss hospitals and sanitarium for the poor.

The Jayavarman VII was a small but clean and pleasant looking provincial hospital. Somehow in my mind that place remains forever associated with the image of Khmer mothers stepping confidently through its doors with their babies in their arms while the Buddha-like bust of Jayavarman VII kept watch over them in the rising sunrays. Below it a plaque bearing a meaningful message attributed to the monarch himself reads: *"Les souffrances des peuples sont les souffrances des rois /* The sufferings of the peoples are the sufferings of the monarchs.*"*

From the Mekong Delta, this author wishes to convey to the Vietnamese authorities that, in this day and age, this very same message still retains its full meaning of eight centuries ago.

CROSSING THE MỸ THUẬN BRIDGE – REMEMBERING THE MỸ THUẬN BARGE

On this visit to the provinces in the Western Region, on several occasions I had the chance to use these barges: the Cao Lãnh and An Hòa barges to go to Long Xuyên, the Sông Hậu Barge to cross from Vĩnh Long to Cần Thơ, the Rạch Miễu Barge to travel from Mỹ Tho to Bến Tre…One must give high marks to the barge system in the Mekong Delta which operated in an extremely efficient and orderly manner. Thanks to the addition of a number of new barges the "turn around" time was very short. Cars no longer needed to line up in long exasperating lines to wait for their turn to embark. Depending on the width of the river, we only had to wait from 15 to 30 minutes to be ferried across and continue on with our trip.

The memory of the Mỹ Thuận Barge as a cultural feature of the good old days is always alive and well in my mind: Years back, on a barge that took me across the Tiền River during one of its late trips of the day I look at the distance toward the location of the future Mỹ Thuận Bridge before it metamorphosed into an ultra modern one in May, 1999... Seven years have passed since that time, much water has flowed under the bridge and millions of tons of silt have been dumped into the Biển Đông / East Sea.

From Cần Thơ I boarded the Hậu River ferry to go to Vĩnh Long then drove to the province of Tiền Giang. This was the first time for me to drive on the Mỹ Thuận Bridge after its inauguration. One must have endured the hassles of having to spend "whole days waiting for the barges" to fully appreciate the conveniences the bridge has to offer. The bridges spanning the Mekong always possess some kind of magical attraction to me. Whenever the opportunity arises I never fail to take a walk on them. The only exception for me is the Lao-Nippon /Champasak Bridge. It was completed in August, 2000 and sat astride the Mekong in the South of Laos. As for the other bridges: from the Jinhong suspended bridge in Yunnan down to the Mittaphap Friendship Bridge in Vientiane then the Kompong Cham Bridge in Cambodia and now the Mỹ Thuận Bridge on the River Tiền... We have met, got acquainted and became no longer strangers to each other. It must be said that each and every one of them represents an architectural work of art, a jade or diamond bracelet built to adorn the current it embraces...

I think it would be interesting to jot down on this page an observation I found heart warming. Even though my visits with my colleagues in white gowns were mostly unannounced and between complete strangers, they always greeted me with wide open arms, warmth and sympathy. My visit to the General

Hospital of Tiền Giang (Mỹ Tho) brought me the added joy of meeting the coeds I taught Physical Therapy to more than two decades ago. They still looked young and happy in what they were doing. Their patients adoringly called them the "five dragon princesses" in appreciation for the loving care they received from these professionals. It was also uplifting to learn that from Saigon to the provinces, Physical Therapy units were still operating full steam and to good effects in general hospitals as the "third step" of medicine after the "preventive" and "curative" ones.

THE VIỆT ĐAN BARGE AND RẠCH MIỄU BRIDGE
From Mỹ Tho we took the Việt Đan (Vietnamese Denmark) Barge to cross the branches of the Rạch Miễu River then drive straight ahead toward the city of Bến Tre. On the way we passed the Cồn Phụng (Phoenix Island) made famous by the Coconut Monk. The people called him "Ông Đạo Dừa" or the "Coconut Monk" because he subsisted mainly on coconut pulp and milk for years.

Born Nguyễn Thành Nam in 1909 in the city of Bến Tre, he was known under different names and one of them was Cậu Hai / Uncle Hai. He led an extraordinarily colorful life. After he finished his training as a chemical engineer in France, he returned to Vietnam, got married and had a daughter.

At the close of World War II, he unexpectedly left his family to pursue a monastic life. Then in 1963 he built a floating pagoda on a big barge in the symbolic shape of an unified Vietnam minus the Bến Hải River which was at that time a political demarcation line separating the North from the South. By the same token, he expressed his wish for the harmonious coexistence between the two largest religions in the country: Buddhism and Christianism. The floating pagoda was given the Buddhist name: "Con Thuyền Bát Nhã" or the "Prajna Boat", a Sanskrit word signifying the

"Noble Eight Paths" believed to help mankind escape the Sea of Sorrow and attain Nirvana through enlightenment. It was moored at the Phoenix Island on a branch of the Mekong River. His followers clad in brown attires numbered in the thousands. They regarded him as a holy man while some non-believers derided him as a mad shaman.

The emergence of the Monks or Shamans dates back to the days of the Southward March in Vietnam. In those "Wild West" times, they were the products of faith mixed with a large dose of superstition. When human knowledge was at a loss to explain the occurrence of every natural disaster or calamity, a belief in ghosts and supernatutal powers or even groundless prophecies could at the least bring some sort of reassurance and comfort to the bewildered.

In his work "Thần, Người và Đất Việt" the author Tạ Chí Đại Trường wrote: "Each Monk assumes the mantle of a 'pope', a religious leader in the making as long as he demonstrates the ability to assemble a group of followers…He takes on a greater than life image as they attribute to him the undefined common "consciousness" of their time."

In other words, the Monks at times merely acted as a reflection, a crystilization of the hopes and dreams of their contemporaries. As late as the middle of the 20th century, the age of advanced science, the Monks still acted as a pole of attraction to the people eventhough the influence of superstition and belief in supernatural powers have greatly diminished. What prevailed afterward was a religious sense mixed with worldly concerns occasionally intermingled with a touch of political ideology.

The Coconut Monk was truly a typical representative of this new generation of Monks as the Southward March drew to a close.

During the Vietnam War the Coconut Monk gained notoriety

for his conviction that he could end the war and reunify the North and South of Vietnam by peaceful means. To that end, he sent out invitations to leaders of the North and South as well as the world to a "peace conference" on his Phoenix Island. Nobody took him up on the offer. All sides to the conflict looked at him with a suspicious eye.

Of light build and stooped back, he nevertheless possessed an exteremely sharp mind. A huge and ever-present key dangled in front of his belly symbolizing the key of peace. Three times a day he climbed into his watchtower. From there he could look to all the four corners and pray for the peace of the land and the welfare of the people. Though the war might be raging all across the country, the Phoenix Island on the Mekong, between the cities of Mỹ Tho and Bến Tre, remained an Island of Peace, an Oriental Disneyland. At that place, no weapons and curfews existed. While the laughters of children and the sound of prayers or chants were resounding through the air, they were occasionally interrupted by the thumping of artillery shells or explosion of bombs in the distance. Only half a kilometer from the island, scenes of fighting and death still marred the riverbanks of the Mekong.

During the Tết Offensive, the city of Bến Tre was ravaged by the Việt Cộng, as well as the Americans with their proclaimed strategy of "We destroy to save"! Appalled by the devastation, he grew even more convinced that he was divinely entrusted with the mission to bring about peace to the nation. In a desperate effort, the Coconut Monk sent a petition to the Saigon government to let him lead a delegation to Hanoi and arrange for a Peace conference with the assurance that should he fail, he would volunteer to stand on the front line and be shot at by both sides. Nonetheless, the War Government headed by Nguyễn Cao Kỳ resolutely turned down the Coconut Monk's request.

The inevitable happened in April of 1975: the Americans left and South Vietnam fell. The Coconut Monk was immediately arrested by the Communists and imprisoned at the Cần Thơ Jail where he passed away fifteen years later. His followers dispersed to wherever they chose. As for the "Prajna Boat" the local authorities had it towed not to the "Berth of Enlightenment" but to the "Berth of Enjoyment" instead. It was "prostituted" into a floating restaurant run by the city government's Tourism Company for the organization of weddings, meetings, parties including nightly dancing and karaoke sing alongs under the glare of bright lights and to the blare of loud music.

Since 1963, his floating pagoda was known as the "peace island" throughout the fiercest years of the Vietnam War and different tongues from the Tower of Babel have been used to name it. The government of South Vietnam regarded the island as a "den of draft dodgers" because many of the Monk's disciples grew long beards or hairs and refused to serve in the nation's Armed Forces. In the Vietcong's eye it was an "operation base of the CIA" due the presence of American war protesters who joined the sect. Those foreign disciples of the Coconut Monk wore dark brown robes and went barefoot like the rest of the group. As for the American advisers they called it a Vietcong's "R & R / Rest and Recreation area". Clearly at that time, there was no room left for the uncommitted who chose to stay out of this internecine free for all. They would either be treated as deserters and sent to hard labor at the correctional camps in Thất Sơn or thrown into the all-consuming carnage of the hopeless war.

Where is the truth?

The verifiable truth is: the Coconut Monk has passed on to the other world and the Phoenix Island has become a tourist attraction.

Bến Tre, a coastal city in the Mekong Delta, lies in between two branches of the Tiền River. To this day, in the absence of bridges, the only way to get to Bến Tre is by barge. For that reason, the project to build the 2.8 kilometer long Rạch Miễu Bridge linking Tiền Giang and Bến Tre is strategically important in the development of these two cities. Regrettably, this project had created endles controversies and scandals. Its construction started in 2002 with a scheduled completion date of June 2006. Since then it was plagued by regrettable incidents that continued to this day.

Midway into the project the contractors quit claiming shortages of funds and rising prices of construction materials like cement, steel, iron and gas. Coming to their rescue, the government raised the financing of the project from 696 billion Vietnamese đồng (US$ 43.7 million) to 988 billion Vietnamese đồng (US$ 62.1 million) to allow the works to resume. But the story did not end there.

Next came the scandal involving the "extraction" theft of more than 10 tons of steel at the very site of the construction. The mastermind behind it was none other than the assistant manager of the project. He was a 29 years old engineer born after the fall of Saigon in 1975. The security force caught his divers red handed with the tools of the trade like diving suits, modern electric cutters, generators, and an intricate work schedule based on the movements of the tide to avoid detection. Inexplicably, the whole case was dropped two weeks later. According to the rumor mill, the young engineer was then transferred to a construction project in the northern part of the country. It was reported in the newspaper Thanh Niên issue of 4/19/06 that this cover up was so outrageous that it created an uproar forcing the government to reopen the case for further investigation.

However the most serious and disconcerting problem was the poor quality of the construction works disclosed in newspapers' reports. The works were not finished and yet there were pillars or "mố" which already showed signs of cracking or sinking. A typical example: cracks were found in "pillar 58". The problem was "fixed" by pumping anti-absorbent liquid into the cracks then close them with glue! The director of the Rạch Miễu Bridge project defended this "practice" as totally safe and sound meeting high safety standards.

The same director also revealed another earthshaking news. He confessed that initially the Vietnamese government intended to "self plan and self implement" the building of the suspended Rạch Miễu Bridge (the Vietnamese called it the "dây văng / thrown cable" bridge project). When it was finally recognized that the whole endeavor went beyond the technical capabilities of the local engineers and Vietnamese contractors, the government and the Ministry of Communication and Transportation had to turn to more qualified foreign companies (possibly French or Swiss) to do the "suspension" part of the work. [www.bentre.gov.vn]

With so many generals in charge of operation "Rạch Miễu Bridge", it is feared that once this much prayed for structure sees the light of day in a fragile state of health it may not live out its expected lifespan. Who will then be held accountable for the long-term wellbeing of the inhabitants of the two provinces of Bến Tre and Tiền Giang or to a larger degree of the Mekong Delta?

Unlike the case of the Cần Thơ Bridge, this time I could use the land route from the city of Mỹ Tho to get close to the construction teams at the head of the Rạch Miễu Bridge. I arrived at lunchtime and the workers were either milling around or sitting on their Honda motorcycles. They all wore orange uniforms, and safety work helmets. The local people were carrying on with their usual activities near the construction site. I was able to take many lively pictures at the foot of that Rạch Miễu Bridge.

Standing on the Việt Đan Barge heading toward Bến Tre I saw a long row of tall and slender pillars made of reinforced cement that looked like a platoon of soldiers manning their positions across a branch of the Tiền River. The barge was not very far from the Phoenix Island and I was reminded of the film "Platoon" directed by Oliver Stone. In the film a platoon of soldiers was thrown into the battle even though it was ill trained for its assigned mission. Now, similarly this "platoon" of substandard cement pillars was thrown into the raging current of the large body of brown water to face an uncertain future. Nobody could predict with certainty how long it would last at its position. Should anything go awry, the people who had to suffer any long run consequences would be the poor inhabitants of the Mekong Delta.

The Rạch Miễu Bridge could be considered a typical example of a poorly planned, irresponsible and extremely wasteful construction project which was being duplicated all over Vietnam now.

The moment the Việt Đan Barge docked, we went ashore then drove past the Châu Thành District to enter the city of Bến Tre. With a population of about 1,3 million souls it was a rather poor agricultural city compared to the others in the Mekong Delta. In August of 2006, the province was threatened by an outbreak of the H5N1 epidemic that started in the Thạnh Phú and Tân Hưng Districts. The "brackish water / nước lợ" in Bến Tre is not suitable for rice growing leading the people to grow coconut trees instead. Capitalzing on this product, the local entrepreneurs developed the much acclaimed manufacturing of coconut candies and fritters destined for export. Contrary to what many people believe, it is not the Siamese coconut "dừa xiêm" but rather the red one "dừa đỏ" which tastes the best thanks to its sweet milk and aromatic pulp.

Under a burning sun we stopped at a roadside store to quench our thirst with fresh red coconut drinks. The very attractive young lady who tended the place looked like a schoolgirl. With a big smile she split open the coconut fruit with three skilful cuts of the knife. She graciously accepted the payment for the drinks but straightforwardly refused the tip we offered her. All we, the driver and I, could say to the proud lady was we owed her a humble apology. We also bought two red coconuts with the intention of drinking them instead of the bottled water on our return trip.

In lieu of a conclusion for this chapter I have this simple thought: there would be no lasting economic development if it does not march in tandem with development in education and public health.

Mekong Delta,
September 2006

Life on water in the Mekong Delta

Civilization of Jars, water everywhere yet people still show a need for these jars

Mỹ Thuận Bridge near completion

Pagoda on the bank of the Tiền River

Children going barefoot to school in Cà Mau

Timid little boy in Năm Căn

Chăm Islam temple in Châu Đốc

Tam Nông Bird Sanctuary in Đồng Tháp Mười

Back to the floating village

Such means of transportation is not uncommon

East Sea fishing fleet resting at port during the full moon

Construction site of the Cần Thơ Bridge on the Hậu River

MEKONG
THE TALE OF A RIVER

Extinction is forever
Endangered means we still have time
Sea World San Diego

INTRODUCTION

China has built and will continue to build mammoth hydroelectric dams. It will also blast the Mekong's current to widen the waterway and render it navigable for ships with 700 tons displacement to transport Chinese made goods from the river port of Simao to Vientiane.... On top of that, Thailand is considering plans to divert the waters of the Mekong even during the Dry Season. To date, none of those projects has been fully implemented. However, the immediate effects resulting from the existing ones are already being felt by the nations located downstream the river: abnormal flooding during the Rainy Season, diminishing fresh water or intrusion of salt water during the Dry one, and alarming reductions in the quantity as well as variety of fish and shrimps. What can the 18 million inhabitants of the Mekong Delta do to adapt and survive in this *changed environment?*

The above paragraph gives a summary of the article written by Dr. Ngô Thế Vinh, the author of *"Cửu Long Cạn Dòng, Biển Đông Dậy Sóng / The Nine Dragons Drained Dry, East Sea in Turmoil"*. In years past, through numerous articles the author along with the members of the Friends of the Mekong Group had sounded the alarm concerning the catastrophes that may befall the Mekong River and its delta. He also went on several observation trips to the Upper Mekong and did an on site report of the Manwan Dam, the first of the 14 giant hydroelectric dams to be built on the Lancang Jiang (Upper Mekong) in China.

[www.vietecology.org]

AN UNREALIZED DREAM

Since the 1940's, American dam builders have paid considerable attention to the potentials for hydroelectric production of the Mekong. In 1957, in the midst of the cold war, the Mekong River Committee was established under the auspices of the United Nations. It maintained a permanent office in Bangkok and was comprised of four member nations: Cambodia, Laos, Thailand and Vietnam. During the planning stage, in its development projects the United Nations divided the Greater Mekong Subregion (GMS) into two basins:

The Upper Basin encompasses the province of Yunnan in China and the Lower Basin the four nations along the Lower Mekong. The two Basins are separated by the Golden Triangle that borders Laos, Myanmar and Thailand.

The development plan for the Lower Basin of the Mekong represents an ambitious "Great Dream" of the United Nations to improve the lives of all the people who live along the river's current. Even though half of the Mekong's current meanders through Yunnan Province, China at that time was a closed society

which went undetected on the radar screen of the world.
Then the Vietnam War spread to the three countries of Indochina for over thirty years. Although the fighting did not take place in Thailand, this nation nonetheless provided logistical bases to the American war efforts. For this reason the building of large hydroelectric dams like Pa Mong, Sambor, Khemmerat on the main Mekong current and other development projects were put on hold allowing the Mekong to retain her pristine state for some more time.

Thus, the "Great Dream" had changed into a "Missed Dream" in a region still drenched in blood and where peace proved elusive.

IN THE HEART OF THE KILLING FIELDS

Though the Vietnam War ended in 1975, in the neighboring land of Angkor the Khmer Rouge had consolidated their authority and launched their atrocious genocidal campaign. The moribund Mekong Interim Committee was established in 1978 without the participation of Cambodia. During that time, Thailand introduced a plan to divert a significant amount of the Mekong's water to irrigate the Northeastern part of the country which was suffering from prolonged drought. This plan was met with tenacious opposition from Vietnam. As a result, Thailand claimed that the organization no longer remained relevant to the changed political, economic and social conditions of the region and refused to acknowledge its legal authority. Facing such dissension, the Mekong Interim Committee fell into a state of near paralysis.

METAMORPHOSIS AND DEGRADATION

Immediately following the restoration of peace, the six nations in the Greater Mekong Subregion (GMS) turned their focus to the exploitation of the Mekong River. These countries may run along the same river's course but harbor conflicting interests as well as different priorities in their development outlook. Consequently, the creation of a multinational coordinating institution similar to the Mekong River Committee became the first order of the day.

On April 5, 1995 the four original nations of the Mekong River Committee met in Chiang Rai, northern Thailand, to sign "The Agreement on the Cooperation for the Sustainable Development of the Mekong River Basin" and changed its name to the Mekong River Commission. A fundamental modification was introduced into this Agreement: In the past, members of the defunct Mekong River Committee could veto any project they deemed detrimental to the main current of the Mekong. The new by-laws removed that veto power and the language used for the approval of projects were deliberately left vague so that for all practical purpose member countries were only required to inform and consult with each other.

The Mekong River Commission headquartered in Vientiane consisted of three permanent bodies: the Council, the Joint Committee (JC) and the Secretariat. The office of the National Mekong River Commission of Vietnam is located at 23 Hàng Tre Street, Hanoi in the Red River Delta.

It could be said that the Mekong River Commission is a "poor and downgraded version" of the former Mekong River Committee. In contrast to the original ambitious goal of exploiting the Mekong River's potentials for the long-run prosperity of the whole region, the Mekong River Commission only sets for itself much more modest objectives in both scale and scope.

After ten years in operation (1995-2005), the Mekong River Commission was able to show some early achievements like reaching an agreement for information sharing among the four member nations; setting up an "internet website" for the forecasting of flood and monitoring of the current's flow during the dry seasons; reaching in April, 2002 an agreement of historical import on the exchange of hydrological data between China and the Mekong River Commission.

STRANGULATION OF THE LIFE LINE – CHINA BLOCKED THE FLOW OF THE RIVER

The strategic plan for the building of the 14 dams in the Yunnan Cascades dated all the way back to the 1970's. It is tantamount to striking a fatal blow to the lifeline of the river.

Over the last three decades, China has been vigorously exploiting the Lancang Jiang (the Chinese name for the Mekong) with the construction of giant hydroelectric dams blocking the main current of this river. In so doing, it is creating havoc to the integrity of the environment and the source of water, fish, alluvium in the regions located downstream.

At this moment, of the 14 dams in the Yunnan Cascades only two: Manwan (1,500 MW) and Dachaoshan (1,350 MW) were completed while two others: Xiaowan (4,200 MW) and Jinghong (1,350 MW) were under construction. Yet the water of the Mekong had never reached such low levels during the Dry Season.

At several sections, the river practically dried up showing its bare bed. Fishing and agricultural activities were directly affected. All those phenomena could not be singly attributed to "lack" of rainfalls. The fact that the Mekong current dropped to an unusual low in 1993 even though it did not happen during the Dry Season but rather during the time China was diverting the river's waters to fill the Manwan's reservoir, the first hydroelectric dam in Yunnan, speaks volume about this point.

To have enough water to operate the two hydroelectric dams of Manwan and Dachaoshan, China frequently closes their gates causing the water level of the river to dip to its lowest levels. During the month of March of 2004, tourism agencies in Laos had to cancel ten sightseeing tours because several sections of the river were too shallow to navigate. In the North of Thailand, the 38 year old boat skipper at the Chiang Khong berth named Odd Boutha sighed: "If China continues to build dams like this, the Mekong will turn into a stream".

Chainarong Sretthachau, director of the Southeast Asian Rivers Network, opined: "China really has the power to control the current of the Mekong".

Due to its fast growing economy, China now faces the formidable task of maintaining a 5 to 6% annual growth in her electricity production. At the same time, things do not get any easier with the prospect of depleting oil supplies. To tackle the problem, China was pressing ahead with the building of one to two nuclear reactors a year regardless of the consequences (National Geographic, August 2005).

Recently, were it not for the vehement objection of American lawmakers, the Chinese National Offshore Oil Corp. (CNOOC) would have bought Unocal, the second largest US oil company, stock, lock and barrel for the sum of US$ 18.5 billion. Had the deal gone through, China would own a strategic oil source and by the same token dominate the exploitation rights of the oil pockets in the entire East Sea (New York Times, August 3, 2005).

With an unquenchable thirst for energy supplies, it is quite obvious that China will not stop at or slow down for anything in her quest to harness the rich potentials for hydropower the Mekong River has to offer.

Commenting on the Chinese plans to exploit the Mekong, Tyson Roberts, a Ph.D. from Stanford, who studied Mekong fishing since 1970 at the Smithsonian Tropical Research Institute (USA) remarked: "The construction of hydroelectric dams, use of the river as a navigation channel, and heavy commercial shipping will eventually asphyxiate the Mekong River. The exploitation steps China undertook will result in the degradation of the ecology and catastrophic pollution causing the Mekong to die a gradual death as it is the case with the Yangtze and other big rivers of China"

In the case of Cambodia, the plain and simple truth is that her heart, the Tonle Sap Lake, can only keep beating as long as the Tonle Sap River succeeds in alternating the direction of its current. During the Rainy Season the Mekong River must reverse course and flow into the lake. This is of vital importance to the supply of fish and rice cultivation in the Land of Angkor. Unfortunately, there is no assurance that things will remain that way in the future. During a ceremony to release breeding fish into a lake in the eastern part of Cambodia, Prime Minister Hun Sen expressed his satisfaction with the current way the Mekong River was being exploited, particularly in regards to big brother China, when he declared: "There is no cause for concern".

Before boarding the plane to attend the Summit Meeting in Kunming, Mr. Hun Sen publicly voiced his almost unconditional support for China's exploitation plan of the Mekong River in spite of desperate warnings from alarmed expert environmentalists. Outdoing himself, Mr. Hun Sen added: "Critics raised these issues merely to show they pay attention to the environment. At times, they use their objections to impede the cooperation the six countries should offer each other". (Phnom Penh, AFP, 6/29/05)

Due to shortsightedness and consideration for immediate gain, Hun Sen was willing to sacrifice the Mekong River and the Tonle Sap Lake that serve as the lifeline and heart of the Cambodian nation (Prior to his trip, Beijing has extended to Cambodia a US$ 30 million loan in addition to another US$ 70 million fund to be used for the improvement of the national highway system).

Brushing aside all criticism, Beijing confidently walks on the path it had chosen for itself. The second Kunming Summit Meeting of the six nations in the Greater Mekong Subregion was held on the 4th and 5th of July in 2005 under the glare of the light bulbs powered by the Manwan hydroelectric company. On this occasion, Chinese Prime Minister Wen Jiabao delivered this frank statement: "the region should not become overly dependent on China while China principally relies on her own for her development. Despite China's impressive economic growth, we must be sober enough to recognize that China's per capita GDP ranks below the 100th mark in the world due to her huge population. We have all reached a critical development stage." (Beijing, AFP, 07/04/06)

Preservation of the ecology, whenever mentioned during the Summit, only sounded like empty "mottos" in the face of unending construction by China of a series of hydroelectric dams across the main current of the Mekong. Those activities raised considerable criticism on the part of expert environmentalists. They voiced their concern for the detrimental effects that befell the Lower Mekong even though it is still too early to assess fully the extent of the damages.

DRAWING BLOOD FROM THE EARTH – THAILAND DIVERTS THE CURRENT

Very early in the 1990's, Thailand considered two bold plans to divert the waters of the Mekong.

- Project Number One: KONG-CHI-MUN

Since 1992, the Thai government had revealed the existence of a large scale plan requiring a total investment cost of US$ 4 billion to save the Northeastern area of the country from prolonged drought.

Named the Kong-Chi-Mun-Irrigation Project (KCM), it was

poorly planned though generously funded. Its goal is clearly defined with the political slogan "Promote irrigation, continue the Kong-Chi-Mun project for the fertility of Isaan lands". The project called for the use of a 200 kilometer long network of giant aqueducts to redirect the Mekong's waters near Nong Khai to a series of dams sitting astride the Chi and Mun Rivers. The waters will then be used to irrigate the rice fields in those rivers' basins.

Initially, the water diversion was to be carried out during the Rainy Season solely. Subsequently, Thailand decided to do it during the Dry Season as well at a flow rate of 300m^3 per second. (compared to the present flow rate of 1,600m^3/second/Dry season of the Mekong Delta).

Phase I of the KCM project was approved even though a team of Thai experts had maintained that the environmental impact analysis (EIA) was still incomplete and the investment costs too high. The implementation of Phase I of the KCM project brought about at its onset the destruction of flooded forests, rise in the level of salt content in the waters of cultivated areas in the northeastern part of Thailand and direct changes to the way of life of the local inhabitants.

Evidently, the KCM project posed imminent and serious threats to the Mekong River. Hence, early in 1992, the reaction from the Vietnamese government was swift and immediate. It officially launched a protest requesting Thailand to renege on the project because it would aggravate the intrusion of salt water into the Mekong Delta especially during the Dry Season. Even Laos could not refrain from voicing her fear that with the planned water diversion of 300m^3/second, the water level of the Mekong would drop creating grave navigation problems on this "brown highway", the lifeline of the Lao people. Cambodia's Minister of Ecology, Dr. Mak Moreth, also joined in to sound the alarm concerning the ominous effects from the slower flow

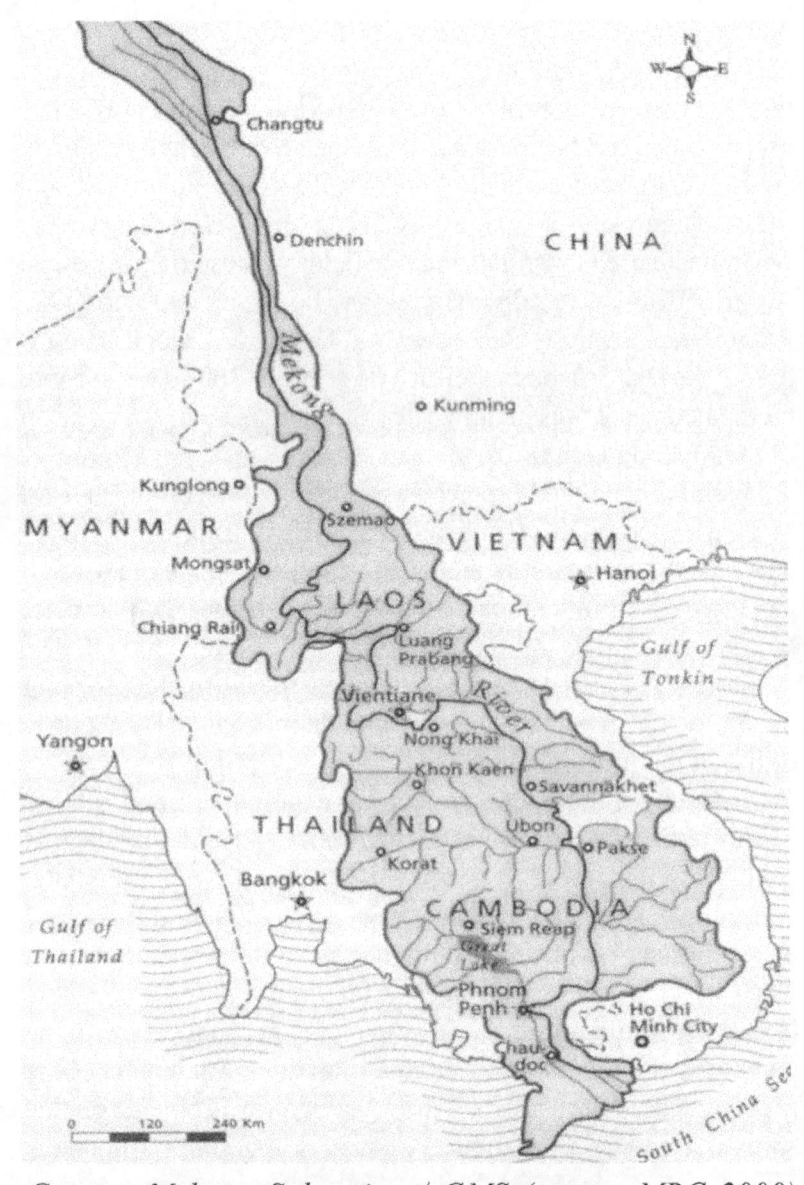

Greater Mekong Subregion / GMS (source MRC 2000)

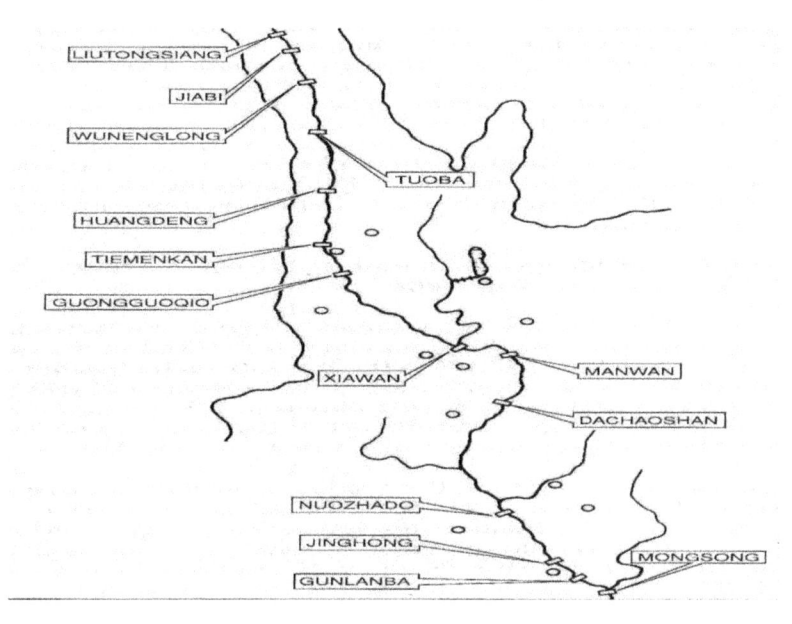

The 14 hydroelectric dams of the Mekong Cascades in Yunnan (source: Yunnan Provincial Government 1995))

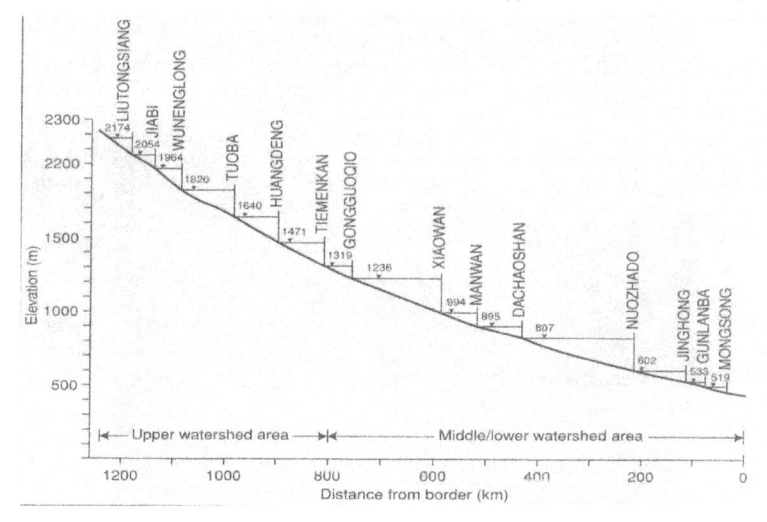

China has built several dams on the upper reaches of the Mekong. NGO organizations have long blamed China for shrinking the Mekong. But China denies responsibility. [AP, April 01, 2010]

Author at Manwan Dam 2002: the first and historic dam in the Mekong Cascades

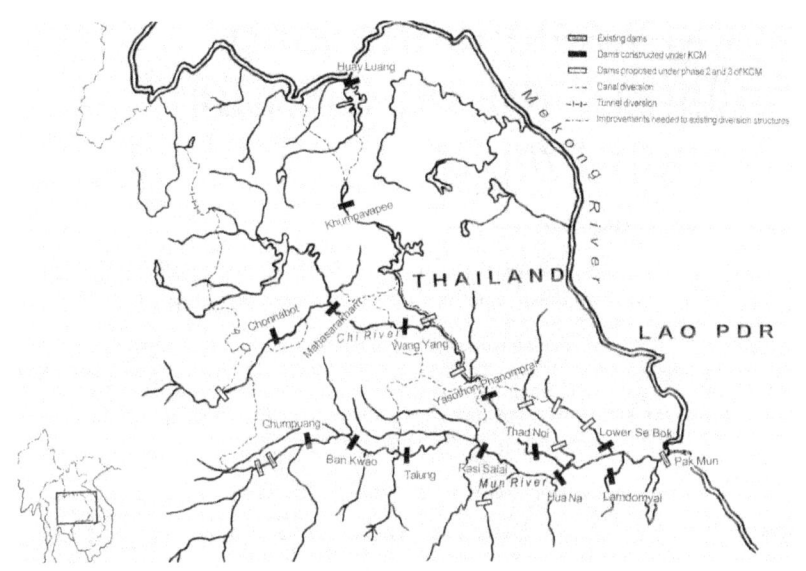

Kong Chi Mun Project (source:Watershed Vol.6 No.3)

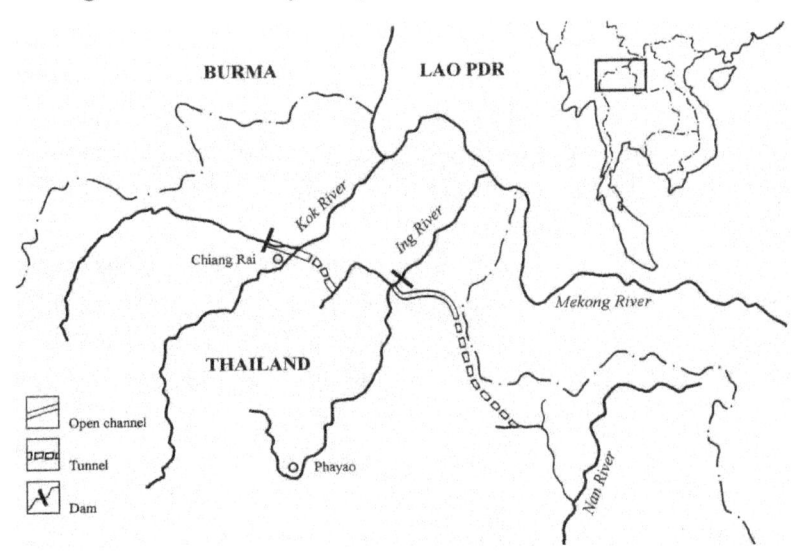

Kok Ing Nan Diversion Project (Watershed Vol.2 No.3)

rate of the Lower Mekong emanating from Thailand's diversion project. Nevertheless, according to the bylaws of the Mekong River Commission, member states are precluded from exercising their veto power leaving Thailand free to proceed with her plan despite the protestations raised by the neighboring nations of Cambodia, Laos, and Vietnam.

Professor Võ Tòng Xuân, Rector of Vietnam's An Giang University, worries that the building of big dams and their huge reservoirs in China coupled with Thailand's large scale water diversion would increase the risk of saltwater intrusion into the rice growing areas of the Mekong Delta. In his opinion: "That will exacerbate conflicts and trans-boundary competition for water supply in the years to come - particularly when the water flow in the Mekong River Basin becomes naturally low. The question we should raise is how to use the Mekong's waters wisely and how to keep the delta green".

- Project Number Two: KOK-ING-NAN

Two years had barely passed before the Thai government announced in 1994 a second big project named Kok-Ing-Nan to divert waters from the Mekong's two major tributaries in the vicinity of Chiang Rai in northern Thailand. The two rivers in question are: Kok and Ing.

The Japan International Cooperation Agency (JICA) provided the fund and human expertise to perform the project's feasibility study that was finished in November of 1999.

One must admit that this is quite an audacious undertaking with an ambitious scope to match. The total cost of the project amounted to US$ 1.5 billion to pay for the construction of mammoth tunnels stretching for a distance of 100 kilometers to channel the waters from the two tributaries of the Mekong named Kok and Ing into the Nan River, an affluent of the Chao Phraya River.

The Phraya River, long a lifeline of the Thai people, is now drying up and suffering from the intrusion of salt water. Waters diverted from the Mekong's two tributaries will be fed into the reservoir of a huge dam named after queen Sirikit that was in constant dire need of water. This water will then be used for dual purposes. First, it will irrigate the immense fields in the Chao Phraya Delta which was suffering from prolonged drought. Secondly, it will satisfy the demand for water of the expanding industrial zones and the 10 million residents of the capital city of Bangkok.

Considering that both the Kok and Ing Rivers lie within the territorial borders of Thailand, this country's government is expected to retain full control over the implementation of this project.

Once the project becomes fully operational, Thailand will be in a position if she so wishes to divert a water mass of 2,200 MCM (Million Cubic Meters) from the Mekong River.

GIVING A HELPING HAND TO THE FORCE OF NATURAL DISASTERS

To block a river's flow by building dams or to divert a river's current in order to tap its water will bring about "man-made disasters" whose impacts could not yet be fully foreseen. Nevertheless, we cannot turn a blind eye to "natural disasters" whose destructive force is amplified many folds with the complicity of human hands.

It is a known fact that the Upper Mekong Basin is the home of numerous volcanoes and frequent earthquakes. In 1996, a magnitude 6 earthquake was registered in the vicinity of the projected site of the Xiaowan Dam which will be also the highest dam on the main current of the Lancang Jiang.

Hiroshi Hori, a renowned Japanese expert on the Mekong, had

worked with the United Nations' Mekong River Committee and also served as Chairman of the Japan International Cooperation Agency (JICA)'s Committee for the Environmental Study on the Mekong River Basin. He authored a book entitled "The Mekong: Environment and Development" (United Nations University Press, Tokyo 2000).

Mr. Hori made the following remark: "The Upper Mekong Basin is located in an earthquake zone. The area near the borders with Myanmar is known for frequent earth crust movements. It is feared that earthquakes will become more prone to occur if dams are built in the Upper Mekong Basin."

In their studies of big dams, geologists noticed that the weight of the gigantic mass of water constantly stored in the dams' reservoirs could create an imbalance in the topography causing faults to appear in the earth layers underneath the bottom of the dams. This in turn may bring about a rupture in the dams' structure resulting in a phenomenon called reservoir-triggered seismicity.

If an earthquake ever happened within the Yunnan Cascades, the damages would be amplified manifolds because the houses and installations in the neighboring areas are not built to meet earthquake proof standards.

Due to his vanity, greed and shortsightedness man has become impervious to the dangers posed by natural disasters. Besides, he also loses control of his science and technology. In the event of a Reservoir Triggered "Big Flood", who would be able to predict accurately the number of cities and the tens of thousands of souls that would be lost in the countries downstream the river?

The safety of the dams built in an unstable geological setting surely does not rank as a top priority in the mind of the project engineers of the Great Han when they designed the series of 14 dams in the Yunnan Cascades.

THE COLLATERAL DAMAGES OF DEVELOPMENT
In April of 2001 a project named "Navigation Channel Improvement Project on the Upper Mekong River" was signed by the four countries of China, Laos, Myanmar, and Thailand. Its main purpose was to facilitate the use of cargo ships with 500 to 700 ton displacements to transport Chinese made surplus goods from the river port of Simao, Yunnan to the Thai cities of Chiang Khong and Chiang Sean then further south to Luang Prabang and the capital city of Vientiane in Laos. On their return trip, those ships will bring back minerals and raw materials to satisfy China's industrial development needs that were growing by leaps and bounds.

The two countries of Cambodia and Vietnam that lie downstream were totally ignored in the process even though they were destined to suffer from the direct and lasting effects of those actions.

According to plan, 21 sections of the Mekong River from Yunnan to Laos where rapids and islets were found will be made wider and deeper with the use of dynamites. Hundreds of tons of rock will be pulverized then used to fill deep cavities in the riverbed by a fleet of backhoe boats. The many species of fish that live in these cavities will be deprived of their natural habitat. People and fishermen in Laos and Northeast Thailand believed the giant Mekong catfish, Plabeuk or Pangasianodon gigas, that live in deep pools during the dry season will be severely threatened with extinction. Meanwhile, fishermen will also lose their fishing grounds during that period.

Right from the start, it is recognized that the reconfiguration of the Mekong's rapids with dynamites will bring about grave imbalances for the region's hydrology. The current flow will course faster and more turbulently causing the riverbanks to cave in and the destruction of the crops planted along the river's path. The nefarious impacts wrought upon the ecology and the lives of the people of Laos, Myanmar, and Thailand will be instantaneous. Not to mention the chain reaction effects that will alter the way of life of the people in Cambodia and Vietnam who live further down the river.

It is noteworthy to recall that Hanoi and Phnom Penh failed to voice their objection against this project. Surprisingly enough, it was left to the small organizations of Burmese indigenous peoples who live without any freedom under the Burmese military junta to do so. They fought for the right to exist of their two far away neighbors by insisting that "The plan to widen the Mekong must receive the approval of all the nations the river runs though including Cambodia and Vietnam."

When will the people of Cambodia and Vietnam be given the right to be fully informed of - or better still - consulted on the ominous potential disasters that are hovering over their heads?

A MATTER OF SURVIVAL

The pressing question one must confront is: What should the 18 million inhabitants of the Mekong Delta do, now or in the days ahead, to adapt and survive in that situation?

Professor Võ Tòng Xuân, Rector of the University of An Giang, is a well known figure prior to 1975 for being the inventor of the Miracle Rice HYV (High Yield Variety), a rice species with short stalks and exceptionally high yields.

During an interview in December, 2004 with an RFI reporter named Ánh Nguyệt, professor Võ Tòng Xuân was asked about the critical issue concerning the increasing scarcity of fresh water and encroaching salt water in the Mekong Delta that took place following the relentless construction of the huge dams in Yunnan, China and the diversion of the Mekong's water by

Thailand. He responded that prior to 1975, the year Vietnam was reunified, the Mekong Delta's aquatic food products were quite abundant. Unfortunately the situation had changed. Currently, the harvests of shrimps and fish showed a reduction in both quantity and variety. The fish caught from the rivers became negligible to the point where it was only looked upon as an adequate source of protein to the families of the poor local farmers. As for the export of fish and shrimp, the lion's share came not from natural sources but rather from basa fish and shrimps raised in "sweetened water" farms. The remainder was made up with fish caught from the East Sea.

Professor Xuân continued on:

"The peasants of the Mekong Delta possess the ability to adapt quickly. They could change their farming method overnight: abandoning completely the cultivation of traditional rice and switch to the Miracle High Yield variety in order to overcome the problems posed by flood and drought. In areas threatened by salt and "brackish water / nước lợ", instead of growing rice people could plant other kinds of tree or go into raising shrimps that could survive in "brackish water". Then we must not forget seawater crabs farming which is much in vogue nowadays. The farmers can use seawater to raise seafood with a higher return than in the case of rice cultivation. At the present time, the Rice Institute of the Mekong Delta is mobilizing its pool of biological know-how to isolate the "genes" which are compatible to salinity in order to cross breed species of high-yield rice and come up with a variety which can grow in water containing a milder level of salinity than pure salt water. Furthermore, Vietnam is working hand in hand with the MEREM Group (Mekong Resources Economic Management) financed by Japan to study the changes in marine environment and the varied ecology of the Mekong. The knowledge thus acquired will allow it to advise the governments in the region on safer utilizations of water resources." With the above optimistic assessments and expectations in mind, professor Võ Tòng Xuân also asserted that any protestation launched by Vietnam would only fall on deaf ears. China or Thailand will carry on with their plans to exploit the Mekong.

THE CHALLENGES OF THE 21ST CENTURY

At the threshold of the 21st century, high technologies driven by greed could easily allow man to kill a river or entirely annihilate the rich but equally very fragile ecology of this planet.

Though the six nations bordering the Mekong are driven by the same urgent need to exploit the Mekong in their drive toward development, they operate under different political, social and cultural circumstances. Conflicts of interest and disagreements are bound to arise when they all depend on the same waterway whose resources are in no way limitless.

On one hand, it would practically be easy for those nations to agree on a number of general principles like *"to achieve the sustainable development, for social and economic development consistent with the needs for environmental protection and maintenance of ecological balance, cooperation and mutual benefits, basin wide management and equitable use."* On the other, as the saying goes "the devil is in the details". An ocean size gap separates principles from actual facts. Faced with different set of circumstances, different countries will arrive at different interpretations of those principles and adopt different courses of action to deal with different actual facts.

Who will be in charge of ensuring a "minimum flow" of the Mekong to prevent seawater of the East Sea from encroaching further inland deep inside the Mekong Delta during the Dry Season? Likewise, how can one make certain that the current will be strong enough to allow the Tonle Sap River to reverse course and flow into the Tonle Sap Lake during the Rainy Season so that the "heart" of Cambodia will keep on beating? So far, nobody is able to offer a plausible solution to those predicaments.

In a not too distant future, the Mekong - that Danube of the East - will turn into a dead river so that hydroelectricity could be generated. It will also be reduced to a waterway used for transportation purpose - or worse - as a sewage line to dump industrial waste from factories in Yunnan.

Turning our eyes to Vietnam, the image of a Mekong Delta over half a century ago with rice fields stretching to the far horizon and fish or shrimps teeming in the streams has become now a thing of the past. It's enough to bring tears to one's eyes. During a recent return visit, all that I could see is a more impoverished Mekong Delta heading the way of continual decline. One hundred years from now, will there still be a Mekong Delta and a Văn Minh Miệt Vườn / Civilization of Orchard ?

Mekong Delta - California
11/ 11/ 2005 – 03/ 01/ 2008

254 MEKONG THE OCCLUDING RIVER

In Lieu of Epilogue
THE MEKONG AND MISSISSIPPI SISTER-RIVER PARTNERSHIP
Similarities and Differences

"At the time of printing, we were informed of this heartening development that we would like to share with the readers in order to show that major efforts are being made to save the Mekong after all"

*

Much attention was given to the meeting on 7/23/2009 between the American Secretary of State Hillary Clinton and her counterparts from the four nations of the Lower Mekong region: Cambodia, Laos, Thailand and Vietnam. They met in a sideline meeting to the ASEAN conference held in Phuket, Thailand. For the first time, the U.S. and the countries of that region sat together to discuss about cooperation covering various areas.

The meeting took place in extraordinary circumstances with

China showing complete disregard to the objections from the scientific communities as it pressed on with the construction of the series of hydroelectric dams over the Upper Mekong. This country was also setting the stage to put into operation the Xiaowan Dam, the fourth dam which is many times larger than the existing Manwan, Jinghong and Dachaoshan Dams. In view of China's behavior and her tendency to consider the Mekong as her personal property, the news about the upcoming partnership between the commissions of the two rivers following the meeting of the five foreign ministers from the U.S., Cambodia, Laos, Thailand and Vietnam is greeted as a positive step which can usher in a brighter era to the gloomy prospects of the Lower Mekong.

On the occasion of the "partnership" between the two rivers; Ngô Thế Vinh, the author who devoted his works and researches in the later years to the Mekong, has completed an analysis of the similarities and differences between those two large rivers as well as the prospects for future cooperation.

A MEETING WITHOUT ANTECEDENT
Last July (7/23/2009) on the occasion of the ASEAN conference, responding to the request from the United States, the foreign ministers from five countries met in a sideline meeting in Phuket, South Thailand. The participants included Mrs. Hillary Rodham Clinton of the U.S. and her counterparts from the four countries in the Lower Mekong Basin: Cambodia, Laos Thailand, and Vietnam. Representing Vietnam was Mr. Phạm Gia Khiêm, Deputy Prime Minister and Minister of Foreign Affairs. An unprecedented declaration was issued covering the issues of common concern especially in the areas of Environment, Health, Education, and Infrastructure Development in the

region.

The American Secretary of State stressed the importance her country holds toward the Lower Mekong Basin and each of the countries in question. At the same time, she also reconfirmed the commitment of the United States to work toward the peace and prosperity of the ASEAN region as a whole. The four foreign ministers of Cambodia, Laos, Thailand, and Vietnam welcomed the closer cooperation of the United States with the four countries of the Lower Mekong in the areas of mutual concern in order to secure a lasting development for the region.

The foreign ministers reviewed the common efforts underway and agreed to open up new areas for cooperation. They particularly applauded the initiative "The Mekong River Commission and Mississippi River Commission Sister-River Partnership" which allowed for the sharing of technical experience and know-how in areas such as the following: adaptation to climate change, coping with floods and droughts, development and impact evaluation of hydroelectricity, management of water resources, and provision for food safety.

The foreign ministers also agreed to let the group of experts carry on with their detailed discussions on each of the areas of cooperation and monitor the ensuing results.

A fact sheet was also issued by the American Department of State. In the year 2009, the United States will provide assistance to the Lower Mekong Basin in the areas that still remain deficient: Environment, Health and Education.

1/ Environment: The U.S will spend more than $7 million in 2009 on environmental programs in the Mekong Region. Programs in this area include: Development of "Forecast Mekong", a predictive modeling tool to illustrate the impact *of climate change and other challenges to the sustainable development of the Mekong River Basin. An agreement between the Mekong River Commission and the Mississippi River Commission to pursue a "sister-river" partnership to improve the management of trans-boundary water resources. Support for projects that promote the sustainable use of forest and water resources, preserve the tremendous biodiversity of the Mekong Basin, and increase access to safe drinking water. The US is seeking Congressional approval for an additional $15 million in 2010 for assistance related to improving food security in the Mekong Countries.*

2/ Health: US assistance to the Mekong countries in the health field will total over $138 million in 2009, and focus on the following areas:HIV/AIDS – working in partnership with Mekong countries, ongoing US assistance has contributed to the 50% reduction in HIV/AIDS infection rate in Cambodia, and provide treatment and prevention services to over 2 million people across the region. Pandemic influenza – the US has provided $95 million since 2006 to support ongoing programs in Mekong countries to prepare for, and respond to threats from outbreaks of pandemic influenza. Malaria and tuberculosis - US assistance support the tracking, identification and treatment of multi-drug resistant malaria and TB in Mekong region. Plans to hold a "US-Mekong Conference on Integrated Approaches to Infectious Disease" in the next 6-9 months.

3/ Education: U.S assistance in the area of education for 2009 totals $16 million, including: support for more than 500 student and scholarly exchanges with the Mekong countries each year through the Fulbright Program and other educational programs. Support for increasing basic education enrollment and expanding broadband Internet *connectivity in rural communities. Plans to hold a "US-Mekong Forum on the Internet, Education and Development" to promote best practices and regional collaboration on the use of Internet connectivity to foster development.(1)*

For a start, the total amount of fund involved is not sizeable in itself. However, it conveys a vital commitment signaling the reengagement of the United States in Southeast Asia at a time when China is exerting worrisome pressure on the region, especially on Vietnam. Once Vietnam becomes overwhelmed and under control, a Domino effect will inevitably occur causing the remaining countries in the Mekong River Basin to successively fall to Chinese expansionism.

THE TWO RIVERS ENTERING A SISTER-RIVER PARTNERSHIP

On July 29, 2009, a preliminary meeting between the Mekong and Mississippi Commissions was held in Vientiane, the capital of Laos, immediately following the meeting at the ministerial level between the American Secretary of State and the four foreign ministers of the countries of the Lower Mekong Basin. The Commissions expressed their intention to cooperate on the issues pertaining to the use of water resources in the two basins as well as exchange technical cooperation and know-how to determine the optimal way to adapt to climate change as it affects the ecology of the two rivers. The two Commissions also commit themselves to work together to promote a sustained policy for hydroelectric development, cope with floods and droughts, coordinate the utilization of water resources, address the issue of food safety, and improve the navigation of inland waterways as well as expand riverine trade. (2)

Mr. Michael J Walsh, President of the Mississippi River Commission, remarked: "While the Mekong and Mississippi Rivers are experiencing challenges, their respective Commissions also have considerable institutional and professional expertise in dealing with these challenges. Both organizations will profit from a closer partnership and the sharing of best practices..."

Mr. Jeremy Bird, CEO of the Mekong River Commission Secretariat, commented: "The Mekong River Commission and the Mississippi River Commission are very similar in terms of their principles and mandates, Both organizations strive to sustainably manage water resources against challenges related to climate change, extreme floods, hydropower development, increasing demand for water, improving navigation and trade, and involving people in the basin more on decisions that affect their lives. Both organizations are therefore well-placed to benefit each other through technical exchanges and learn how to best manage their respective complex trans-boundary rivers." The two Commissions are working in tandem to reach a common future action plan.

THE HISTORY OF THE TWO COMMISSIONS

- The Mississippi River Commission: was established more than 130 years ago on 06-28-1879. It was entrusted by the U.S. Congress with the duty to improve the navigation on the waterways, expand commerce and trade, and prevent destructive floods on the Mississippi. With its headquarter located in Vicksburg in the state of Mississippi, the Commission is responsible to advise, monitor and report on the improvement programs of the Mississippi in order to consult with the Government, Congress and Armed Forces on issues pertaining to a basin that covers 41% of the area of the United States. (4) The president of the Mississippi River Commission, Mr. Michael J. Walsh, has a very interesting background. He graduated from the Polytechnic Institute in New York with a bachelor's degree in civil engineering and a master's degree in construction management from the University of Florida. He returned from the Iraq war with the rank of Brigadier General of the US Army corps of engineers. Since February 20, 2008 he served as Commander of the Mississippi Valley Division and President of the Mississippi River Commission. Mr. Walsh manages a construction program with a budget of US$ 7,5 billion encompassing a basin that comprises 10 states reaching all the way to the Gulf of Mexico. He also serves as Commander of Task Force Hope, in support of the FEMA / Federal Emergency Management Agency's response to the devastating Katrina Hurricane in 2005. To this day the region has not fully recovered from it.

- The Mekong River Commission: is a relatively young inter-government organization that consists of four nations: Cambodia, Laos, Thailand, and Vietnam. Established in 1995, it is a reincarnation of the 1957 Mekong River Committee. Its mission is to cooperate in the development of the Mekong River Basin in the areas of: fishery, agriculture, sustained development of hydroelectricity, maintenance of the navigation of the waterways, prevention of floods and preservation of the Mekong River Eco-system. One must also add to that list: management of the impacts of climate change like unusual big floods and prolonged droughts including rises in the sea level. The Commission has the duty to provide advices, facilitate and expand communication between governments, private organizations and civil socicties in order to cope with the existing challenges.(5)

Mr. Jeremy Bird, a leader who is a newcomer to the scene, was appointed CEO of the Mekong River Commission Secretariat in March, 2008 with a three year term at a time when the prestige of the institution was at its rock bottom. Mr. Bird, a British national, is a Chartered Engineer with postgraduate qualification in water law and policy and has over 25 years of international experience in the field of water resource management. In addition to 15 years working with the Mekong River Commission on the area of water exploitation, he is an old-time member of the of the United Nations Environment Programme (UNEP) and World Commission Dams (WCD). It is important to note that Mr. Bird's long time association with the WCD provides him with an exhaustive understanding about the extents of the threats posed by the big hydroelectric dams to the entire eco-system and the life of the communities that live along the river's banks.

THE GEOGRAPHY OF TWO RIVERS

1/ Countries: (a) Mekong runs through 7 countries: Tibet, China, Myanmar, Thailand, Laos, Cambodia, Vietnam; (b) Mississippi runs through one country /10 states

2/ Length: (a) Mekong: 4,880 km; (b) Mississippi: 3,734 km

3/ Basin: (a) Mekong: 795,000 km^2; (b) Mississippi: 2,981,076 km^2

4/ Source: (a) Mekong: Mount Guozongmucha, Tibet Qinghai; (b) Mississippi: Lake Itasca, Minnesota

5/ Mouth: (a) Mekong: Mekong River Delta, Eastern Sea;

(b) Mississippi: Louisiana / Gulf of Mexico
6/ Elevation: (a) Mekong: 5,224 m; (b) Mississippi: 450 m
7/ Average Discharge: (a) Mekong: 16,000 m^3/sec; (b) Mississippi: 12,743 m^3/sec

In fact, the Mississippi is part of the "Missouri-Mississippi" river system, the largest in North America. Its total length comes to 6,300 km and has an average discharge of 16,200 m^3/sec. It ranks fourth in length after the Nile/ Egypt, Amazon / Brazil and Yangtze / China.

SIMILARITIES AND DIFFERENCES

The similarities are apparent. On the other hand, one can point to striking differences between the two rivers. For example, the Mekong's elevation is 12 times higher than that of the Mississippi. This indicates that the Mekong possesses an extremely rich potential for hydroelectricity generation that is unavailable to the Mississippi. Presently, there are only four dams built on the main Mekong current. In dimensions and height, the Xiaowan dam records a height of 293m. The existing 40 dams that were mostly built in the 1930's on the Mississippi do not have anything to match that figure. In addition, the Mekong's ecology system ranks second only to that of the Amazon. What is unique in the world: only the Mekong can flow in both directions when during the high season, its tributary, the Tonle Sap River, reverses its course and runs into the Tonle Sap lake. This is considered a wonder in the world.

On the other hand, while the Mekong has the misfortune of meandering through many countries, the Mississippi only flows within the boundaries of the United States and bears the name "misi-ziibi", meaning "the Great River", given to it by the Ojibwe Indian tribe. The people living along its banks speak only one common language: English, and possess a high level of consciousness for the ecology. As for the Mekong, it courses through seven countries – with Tibet now being reduced to an autonomous region of China. Consequently it is called by different names: Dza Chu / Tibet, Lancang Jiang / China, Mae Nam Khong / Laos and Thailand, Tonle Thom / Cambodia, and Cửu Long / Vietnam. The people who live along its current hail from various ethnic groups, speak different languages and belong to diverse cultures. But, perhaps the most significant difference is that the Mekong has yet to run through a "land weathered by Freedom and Democracy". The Mekong continues to be exploited and abused even under the motto "to destroy in the name of construction". Meanwhile, the voice raised by the communities living along its current continues to be ignored.

The Mississippi has entered the literature of America and the world. It served as the set for the works written by Mark Twain (1835-1910) like "Life on the Mississippi" and for William Faulkner (Nobel prize 1949) like "the Bear", one of his three most popular short stories. Moreover, it is the inspiration for "Moon River", the theme song of the 1961 film "Breakfast at Tiffany's" played by Audrey Hepburn.

There is not yet a literary work about the Mekong which is significant enough to be considered of a world-class category, besides the travelogue "Voyage dans les Royaumes de Siam, de Cambodge, de Laos et Autres Parties Centrales de l'Indochine" (1883) written by the French explorer Henri Mouhot (1826-1861), this French author was credited for the "rediscovery" of the Angkor Wat with its vibrant Khmer culture of the 13th century. The Angkor Wat is always regarded as a "wonder" of the Mekong. One must also note the diaries written by the French members of the "Expédition du Mékong 1866-1868" like Francis Garnier and Doudart de Lagrée as they were exploring for a trade route with China.

GETTING READY FOR ACTION
With a fresh breath of vigor and opportunity knocking at the door, one wonders whether Vietnam's Mekong Commission is ready to join this new era. It would be unacceptable if its personnel operates like ordinary government employees. On the contrary, they must possess a high dose of "gray matter" including an ability to foresee far into the future as well as a heart devoted to the survival of the Mekong. They need a vision to project hundreds of years into the future and it is not too early now to think of investing into the training and improvement for the next generation of experts. As planned, each year 500 Fulbright scholarships will be allocated to the four countries of the Lower Mekong. If this number is divided equally among them, Vietnam will be awarded 125 recipients. A small number of them will be experts in their field while the lion's share of them will consist of Vietnamese students who graduated from local universities. They are chosen to study or do researches in the United States for a period of one year or longer.

It is useful to recall that the Fulbright program started more than 60 years ago - in 1946. It is sponsored by the U.S. Department of State. To this date, 183,000 students and scholars from more than 150 nations have participated in this program. The criteria used in the selection of the recipients are: "outstanding scholarship and ability to lead". Besides fulfilling the requirements of the study program, attending classes and doing researches; the participants are also given opportunities to exchange their ideas and work together in the search for solutions to international problems. On a practical note, in the particular case of Vietnam this would be to find solutions to settle regional conflicts. The ideal place to recruit the participants to this program is nowhere else but the universities of Cần Thơ and An Giang whose student bodies are born and nurtured by the alluvia and the perfumed rice stalks of the Mekong River. It should be recognized that the number of scholarships is still modest in view of the requirements of the tasks to be accomplished in the future. There should be a ten-fold increase in the number of Fulbright scholarships per year. The government must put forward an appropriate investment project in this area.

Recently, when referring to the "river being strangulated" by the series of hydroelectric dams built in China, many authors of newspaper articles in Vietnam, mentioned the slogan "we have to save ourselves". Yes but how? One cannot fail to pay attention to the proposals from a professor holding a doctorate degree to build dams to contain fresh water or keep in check the encroachment of sea water in the Mekong Delta (6). This is a commendable effort on the professor's part that will require decades of implementation not to mention the "extremely high cost and low feasibility levels" because the Mekong Delta is still a relatively young and unstable land.

A 'THINK TANK' FROM THE CẦN THƠ UNIVERSITY
It is evident that there is no way to prevent China from implementing her gigantic and ambitious electrification plan. Likewise, under the tremendous pressure exerted by the conglomerate of dam builders, the eleven dams planned for the Lower Mekong will without fail be constructed in successive steps. However, at a certain point "the drawbacks and safety risks of each dam-building project must be made

known to be monitored and rectified".

The time has never been more urgent and critical for the University of Cần Thơ and its Mekong River Department to assume their role of "intellectual lighthouse". It is our hope that the future main center dealing with the issues pertaining to the Mekong River will be located not at the Mekong River Commission in Vientiane but rather at the University of Cần Thơ. The University will serve as a "think tank" of international stature where researches as well as training courses will be conducted to provide the needed "gray matter" to the entire region.

This is the proposal the author would like to submit in this article. It is the same proposal that the author has expounded seven years back including the concrete steps for implementation (7). At that time we called for the building of a specialized library containing all the books and materials pertaining to the subject matter of the Mekong. As of today, to take into account the new situation, the Mississippi should be added as the second subject matter.

Moreover, we propose the establishment of a teaching staff which consists of the university's regular academic body working hand in hand with experts from the Mekong River Commission and also those from the Mississippi River Commission.(2) One should not forget the international expert advisors from the United Nations Environment Programme (UNEP), the World Commission Dams (WCD), and the International Rivers Network (IRN)…They should be invited to teach at the Mekong River Department as visiting professors. The materials used in their lectures will provide invaluable information gathered from actual work experience.

Candidates to the program will come from a select group of students fluent in a foreign language and meeting the

Fulbright criteria for selection: "outstanding scholarship and ability to lead". Scholarships offered by the University should not be limited to Vietnamese students but should also be extended to those from the countries adjoining the Mekong's current like Thailand; Laos; Cambodia; Yunnan, China; and Myanmar. The fund for training will come from the government's budget. The academic program aims at the training of experts in ecology. Hand in hand with theoretical teachings, students will be given the opportunity to face real world situations through fieldtrips at the dams and important sections on the River. Furthermore, the students will spend a period working as interns at the Mekong River and Mississippi River Commissions. To graduate they must complete a small thesis on the conservation of the Mekong River's ecology.

With such an academic baggage and a sense of mutual dependency as well as responsibility, this group of international students will represent a valuable source of "gray matter" to the Mekong River Commission and the governments in the region that are suffering from a severe penury of trained personnel. This young and dynamic group of experts will form a common core ushering in a new era of stable cooperation for the seven countries along the Mekong current. (7)
The University of Cần Thơ in the Mekong Delta will be the site hosting international conferences and workshops about the Mekong. Looking forward to the year 2010 when Vietnam will assume the chairmanship of ASEAN, it will then have the responsibility to organize and chair many important conferences throughout the year including the meeting of the foreign ministers of the ASEAN countries. Could there be a better time than this to organize a second "Phuket style" sideline meeting in the Mekong Delta itself, the place which

is now becoming the most unforgiving "ecology battlefield" resulting from self-destructive exploitations by the gigantic hydroelectric dams in the Upper Mekong in China. On a more practical note, 2010 would also be an opportune time to review the achievements of the first year of cooperation between the Mekong River and Mississippi River Commissions.

As for the government, it is imperative that a network of "attachés for ecology" be established at its embassies and consulates in the countries of the region: the Vietnamese Consulate in Kunming, Yunnan and the four Vietnamese embassies in Cambodia, Laos, Myanmar and Thailand. They will act as eyes and ears, human observation posts for the Mekong River Department and the Ministry for the Protection of the Ecology.

This must be considered a long-term investment of great import to the "Spirit of the Mekong" that affects all the cooperation and development plans of the region. Naturally, there is a high but well justified price to be paid if one wishes to save the Mekong and the preservation of life in the Mekong Delta for future generations. We should remind ourselves of this mantra from Sea World San Diego: "Extinction is forever, Endangered means we still have time".

NGÔ THẾ VINH, M.D.
California, 09-09-2009

References:
1/ US– Lower Mekong Countries Meeting: Press Release, US Department of State, July 23, 2009.
2/ USA – Mekong Basin Cooperation follows ASEAN Meeting, Vientiane, Laos PDR, July 30, 2009, www.

mrcmekong.org.
3/ Changing Currents: Navigating The Mekong's Past, Present and Future_Watershed, Vol. 12 No 3, November 2008.
4/ Mississippi River_http://en.wikipedia.org/wiki/ Mississippi River.
5/ Mekong River_http://en.wikipedia.org/wiki/Mekong River.
6/ Trung Quốc khai thác Sông Mekong và nguy cơ giết chết Đồng Bằng Sông Cửu Long_htpp://vietnamweek.net 06/21/2009
7/ Cần Thơ University, Mekong Delta and the Mekong River _Ngô Thế Vinh_ Đi Tới Magazine, Montréal, Canada, No. 59 & 60, Jul-Aug, 2002

ADVANCE TESTIMONIALS FOR: "MEKONG - THE OCCLUDING RIVER"

Aviva Imhof
Witoon Permpongsacharoen
Michael Walsh
Phạm Phan Long
Nguyễn Đức Hiệp
Trần Ngươn Phiêu
Võ Tòng Xuân
Lê Xuân Khoa
Ánh Nguyệt
Nguyễn Xuân Hoàng
Phan Nhật Nam
Hoàng Khởi Phong
Đặng Văn Chất
Phạm Phú Minh

AVIVA IMHOF, *Campaigns Director, International Rivers, Berkeley, California.*
"Dr. Vinh's love of the Mekong River and the life it supports comes through on every page of this book. Part travelogue, part history, part autobiography, Dr. Vinh weaves a compelling story about his travels through the countries sharing the Mekong River and gives the reader a frightening picture of what dam construction in China is doing, and could do, to his beloved river."

WITOON PERMPONGSACHAROEN, *Publisher Watershed, People's Forum on Ecology, TERRA*
It's really great to know that someone tries to do something on his/her capacity to protect the Mekong. It's really true that the Mekong and her people are facing a serious situation "prosperity or destruction"? We need more people like you working to "Save the Mekong for our future generations" by helping to "Stop destructive developments for the Mekong's sustainability."

MICHAEL WALSH, *President Mississippi River Commission*
Thank you for your book "Mekong - The Occluding River." As you know the Mississippi River Commission signed a letter of

intent with the Mekong River Commission in July 2009. We are exploring ways to communicate lessons learned and river science. A current thought is to try to facilitate a link between river research centers and universities in both countries. These centers help provide people a view of the past, the current state of the watershed, and some thoughts and ideas on how to manage for the future.

We are currently developing stronger relationships with these river research centers in the United States and plan to encourage them to have exchange scientists from the Mekong and to the Mekong. I have enclosed a 200-year Vision the Mississippi River Commission signed on August 20, 2009. Please provide a feedback on this "working" vision. We applaud your great work.

PHẠM PHAN LONG, PE, *Chairman , Viet Ecology Foundation*

Dr. Ngô Thế Vinh seems to find himself in the midst of one big battle after another through every phase of his life. As a medical doctor, he is destined to be engaged in the fight to save lives and care for his patients one at a time. However, his intellectual sensibility has forced him to be deeply involved with the wider issues in the life of the people he treats.

His conscience and courage take him on daring investigative missions in order to write and expose the plight of the Thượng, the minority groups in Central Vietnam, and the American involvement in the corruption of the Saigon government during the Vietnam War.

In the last 15 years, Dr. Vinh has intensely focused his attention on the Lancang-Mekong countries. This combat physician took notes of the beneficial economic progress but also took on the governments and destructive developments in the region. Page after page, "Mekong - the Occluding River - The River's Tale", becomes his current combat operating theater.

To write this book, Dr. Vinh investigated and traveled to the most forbidding reaches: from the high mountains in Yunnan to the dam reservoirs in Laos, to mystic Cambodia and the seasonally inundated Mekong Delta in Vietnam because he wanted to learn first hand of the changes that were occurring in the life of the people on the ground. Readers will benefit greatly from his travel diary, the wealth of facts concerning the cultural and historical backgrounds, and the richness of his observations and perspectives.

Dr. Vinh seeks to protect the cultural heritage and livelihood of the 65 million Chinese, Burmese, Laotian, Thai, Cambodian and Vietnamese fishermen and farmers living along the banks of this mighty river as well as the future of their children. Dr. Vinh personifies the courage of an independent Vietnamese writer and a Vietnamese-American intellectual of our time.

Dr. NGUYỄN ĐỨC HIỆP, *Ph.D. from the University of Sydney in biomedical engineering, senior scientist for the Department of Environment and Climate Change, NSW, Australia*

This is an excellent book on the Mekong River, its ecology, the threat posed by dams and the economic, social, historical context of its influences on the lives of the people who lived in the basin of this great river and many of its tributaries.

The Mekong River has its source in Tibet. It flows through China, Myanmar, Laos, Thailand, Cambodia and finally reaches Vietnam where it forms a fertile delta before it meets the sea. Dr. Ngô Thế Vinh gives us a panorama of cultural diversities of the people who live along the river and its tributaries and their tumultuous histories. This book combines the author's wide knowledge, his attachment to the river and the people with his personal observation and experiences in an interesting journey through Yunnan (China), Laos, Thailand, Cambodia and Vietnam. More than just a focus solely on the environment and hydrological aspects of the river, Dr. Vinh also paints a human dimension brush which gives us an essential background to understand this river and its entwining connection to the economic, social and cultural history of the region. And hence we can see a grim future for the people in Laos, Thailand, Cambodia and Vietnam caused by the construction of many giant dams on the upper reaches of the river in Yunnan. Some of these dams have already been in operation and their effects are deleterious to the river system: bank erosion, loss of livelihood due to lack of fish and lack of water during the Dry Season, some species in danger of extinction, salinity penetration from sea water in the Mekong delta…

I thoroughly enjoyed reading this book from the beginning to the end and learned many things from it as I did with another great book on the Mekong by Dr. Milton Osborne. However, in the end the book makes me think and deeply concern about the future of the Mekong River. The future will be worse when more new dams will be put into operation. There is an urgent need for an awareness of the environmental damages caused by these dams and deforestation in the Mekong basin and actions to be taken to mitigate or prevent the looming disaster. The first step is for China to cooperate, consult and be transparent to the MRC countries in its plan and operation of the dams as the author has pointed out. And this is what we can only hope for China to do the right thing.

Dr. TRẦN NGƯƠN PHIÊU, *former Minister of the Department of Social Services of the Republic of Vietnam, author of "Phan Văn Hùm – A Biography"*

Born in the Southern part of Vietnam, during the summer vacations of my student years, I enjoyed rowing a small boat stacked with a jar of rice, a coal stove, and condiments like salted fish, salt, sugar...to visit the villages in the region. All that it took was a straw mat to help me sleep comfortably through the night and bring me warmth and protection against mosquitoes or flies. Memories of the rice fields, orchards and the Mekong River are indelibly carved in the heart and mind of the young men of the South like me.

Later in life, I had the honor of befriending Ngô Thế Vinh, a comrade in arms, a colleague and at the same time an author. Though not a native of the South, he is emotionally attached to this river that uncharacteristically has two currents and nine estuaries. His literary career took a new turn when he used his pen to write about this life-giving river in the southern delta. With his book: "Cửu Long Cạn Dòng, Biển Đông Dậy Sóng / The Nine Dragons Drained Dry, East Sea in Turmoil", he was first among the Friends of the Mekong Group to awaken public opinion to this immediate issue which undoubtedly will remain to be so for many decades to come.

...For millenniums, China has exerted considerable influence on the thoughts and way of life of its neighbors' intelligentsia. However, with its relentless drive toward material gains and economic development coupled with its efforts to sinicize Tibet, the Uyghurs and other minorities this country is now facing increasing protestation from the world community. The natural resources we inherit from our forebears are limited. More than two thousands years ago, Lao Tzu, this great man of China, preached that we should learn to live in harmony with nature. Nowadays, in addition to the four hydroelectric dams it already built, China insists on the construction of fourteen more on the Upper Mekong regardless of the damaging impacts they may inflict on the ecosystem and the livelihood of the people living downstream.

Ngô Thế Vinh authored "Mekong, The Occluding River" in an apparent attempt to sound the alarm on the dangers facing the Mekong and the East Sea. Those two areas will undoubtedly play a crucial role in the political future of Southeast Asia.

Prof. VÕ TÒNG XUÂN
Rector Emeritus, An Giang University, Vietnam
The Man Who Shouts"SOS" For The Mekong

Dr. Ngô Thế Vinh is deeply interested in measures that protect the eco-system of the Mekong and the Mekong Delta. He has collected a wealth of precious data concerning the more than 4,000 kilometer long Mekong current flowing from Tibet to the East Sea. Many of his articles written with a heart felt style have been published to provide readers in Vietnam as well as overseas with useful information concerning not only the early construction stages of the dams in the Mekong Cascades of Yunnan but also about the calamities that the 14 dams in this Cascades may wreak on that river's ecology affecting the tens of millions of people who inhabit its banks. Dr. Vinh is fully aware of the extremely ominous prospects the ecology of the Mekong Delta is facing due to the construction of gigantic hydroelectric dams upstream the river like the Xiaowan Dam, the world tallest, which has been recently completed. Therefore, in his articles he never tires of drawing the attention of the Vietnamese as well as international public opinion to this issue. To add urgency to it, he recently authored a travelogue named "Mekong Dòng Sông Nghẽn Mạch / Mekong - The Occluding River" to record his experience during his travels along the Mekong's current. Dr. Vinh does not live in Vietnam. Nevertheless his heart and mind are inextricably anchored to the bed of his river.

Prof. LÊ XUÂN KHOA
President emeritus, Southeast Asia Resource Action Center
Former Adjunct Professor, SAIS, Johns Hopkins University

Dr. Ngô Thế Vinh is not only a medical doctor who cares for his patients, he is also an ecologist deeply committed to the welfare of the people at large. While continuing his medical career, he has never lost his interest in environmental issues with a special concern over the future of the Mekong River. In his 650-page book Cửu Long Cạn Dòng, Biển Đông Dậy Sóng / The Nine Dragons Drained Dry, East Sea in Turmoil published in 2000, he already alarmed the world of the disastrous consequences of the gigantic hydroelectric dams being built in the Upper Mekong by China. The lives of tens of millions of people in Burma, Thailand, Laos, Cambodia and Vietnam who make their living in the basin of this river will be seriously affected. To further his research, Dr. Vinh made several fact-finding trips to China and four countries in the Lower Mekong and, in 2007, finished another book entitled Mekong, Dòng Sông Nghẽn Mạch / Mekong, the Occluding River, an English version, is expected to be in circulation in July, 2010.

Dr. Vinh's foresight in his first book and the findings in his second book concur with important observations by renowned international experts. As he wrote in the Foreword, "Destructive exploitations of the Mekong have brought about a chain of reaction of harmful phenomena such as ecological devastation, depletion of natural resources, and environmental pollution. All those disastrous outcomes are taking place sooner and at a more alarming rate than expected."

Political leaders in the U.S. and Southeast Asia are well aware of this grave situation and are trying to work with China towards effective ways to protect the environment, the culture and livelihood of some sixty millions people in the affected areas.

A group of non-governmental organizations representing North American citizens with roots in Southeast Asia, in a letter to the 2010 ASEAN Summit to be convened in Hanoi on April 8, 2010, addressed the Mekong issue, emphasizing that: "The four large hydroelectric dams already built and operated by China have caused adverse impacts along the 2500 km river valley in Myanmar, Laos, Thailand, Cambodia and Vietnam. Yet there seems to be little determination as to the causes and how to bring about transnational environmental and economic justice. We urge you to lead and partake in efforts to engage China and riparian countries to arrive at a comprehensive impacts mitigation that is just for the affected people."

The voice of the Southeast Asian people has been raised. To this effect, Dr. Ngô Thế Vinh has made no small contribution.

ÁNH NGUYỆT, *former RFI Reporter*
Mekong - The Occluding River
From Prediction to Realization

Never before news media in Southeast Asia and environmental organizations have given such vigorous coverage of the Mekong being drained dry or received such extraordinary support from their Western colleagues. Almost daily, we are being bombarded with reports about the catastrophic impacts resulting from the

280 MEKONG THE OCCLUDING RIVER

Mekong's water reaching record low levels, the salinization of the Mekong Delta, and the accumulative effects that incessantly reshape the lives of the tens of millions of inhabitants in the countries bordering that river's banks.

A noteworthy point: until recently, in Vietnam, any mention of the arrogant behaviour of China concerning the exploitation of the Mekong has been looked upon as sensitive if not taboo in the public forum. However, nowadays, Vietnamese newspapers have begun to forcefully and openly confront this issue. On the other hand, Ngô Thế Vinh, the author, had addressed this very issue since the first decade of this millennium: first in his book "Cửu Long Cạn Dòng, Biển Đông Dậy Sóng /The Nine Dragons Drained Dry, East Sea in Turmoil" and subsequently in his writings about his field trips along the Mekong beginning in Yunnan then continuing southward to Laos, Thailand, Cambodia, and the Mekong Delta. Early on, Ngô Thế Vinh set foot in the Manwan hydroelectric dam. Very soon afterward he saw with his own eyes the sections where the Mekong bared its bed in Laos and the dwindling population of fish and shrimps in the Tonle Sap Lake as well as in the Southern part of Vietnam. All those events were summarised in the Vietnamese version of his book, "Mekong Dòng Sông Nghẽn Mạch / Mekong-The Occluding River", which was initially published in March, 2007 to be followed by a second edition along with an audio book at the end of the same year. The book has raised heated debates or even invited attempts to refute any Chinese responsibility for the nefarious impacts that may result from that country's plan to construct a series of dams in the Cascade of Yunnan.

We are in the year 2010, the English version of the "Mekong Dòng Sông Nghẽn Mạch / Mekong-The Occluding River" will soon reach the bookstores at the time the Mekong is drying up and its ecosystem gradually degraded. Those geological phenomena are no longer predictions but have become undisputed facts that sadly verify Ngô Thế Vinh's forewarnings. He is an author who lives with his time and yet sees well ahead of it.

NGUYỄN XUÂN HOÀNG, *author of*
"The Nonconformist"
Reading "The Tale of a River" by Ngô Thế Vinh
The book "The Tale of a River" I have in front of me is a captivating and fascinating travelogue written by Ngô Thế Vinh. Captivating and fascinating not only because it is full of informative news supported by research materials, statistics, real persons and real events but also because it is written by a pen imbued with love of humanity, of life, and of country.

Ngô Thế Vinh's beloved Mekong has overwhelmed me with her powerful current leaving me totally defenseless. For many days, I have read the book or listened, again and again, to the audio book read by Ánh Nguyệt with her southern accent.

This is the work of Ngô Thế Vinh depicting his travels to the source of the Mekong in Yunnan, then onward to Laos, Thailand, Cambodia and all the way to the Mekong Delta. The author paints a tragic picture of the gradual degradation of this river that is and continues to be worsening at a faster rate than anticipated by many. The cause of all this could be attributed to the hydroelectric dams in the colossal Cascades in Yunnan which are blocking the flow of the Mekong's main current.

Ngô Thế Vinh wrote about a character who will continue to leave a deep impact on the readers: Prof. Võ Tòng Xuân, a person who is identified intimately with the southern part of the country; its rice stalks, river, rice bowl and hard working people. In addition, this professor also occupies an irreplaceable place in the hearts of the Mekong Delta farmers. A real person in life, he appears however like a personage that comes straight out from a novel. From the "The Green Belt" to the "Mekong - The Occluding River" Ngô Thế Vinh not only manages to keep intact his humanism and cultured literary style but succeeds to accomplish extraordinary feats.

Looking for the first time at Ngô Thế Vinh's book title "The Tale of a River" I was instantly reminded of Hermann Hesse's "The Tale of a River" that Phùng Khánh and Phùng Thăng translated into Vietnamese from the story of Siddhartha of the Weg nach Innen. It's not my intention here to compare the two literary works. Ngô Thế Vinh's "The Tale of a River" is somewhat different. It tells me that even though my heart is "occluding", not only is this world still worth living in, it also awakens me to this realization.

PHAN NHẬT NAM, *author of "On The War Trails"*
It is time for the river to dry and the stone to be worn out
As one reads "Mekong - the Occluding River"
The writer is left with no other recourse than his prophetic vision. Ngô Thế Vinh wrote *"Cửu Long Cạn Dòng, Biển Đông Dậy Sóng / The Nine Dragons Drained Dry, East Sea in Turmoil"* in the later part of the 20th century.

Nowadays, the threat of Chinese hegemony no longer needs to be imposed through the hooves of the horses or at the points of the lances like during the feudal dynasties. Neither is it necessary to use the "human waves" tactic of the Korean War in the first half of the 20th century or more recently the Sino-Vietnamese border conflict in 1979. Instead, the Chinese threat these days is found in the massive quantities of goods labeled "made in China' which are flooding the daily life of the world population. Meanwhile, as the system of hydroelectric dams in Yunnan has gone into operating mode, the diversion of massive quantities of water of this sacred river has begun in the Upper Mekong in preparation for the generation of electricity. The river will also be used as a waterway to reach South Asia. The inevitable consequence is: the Mekong current will no longer be able to maintain a minimum flow during the Dry Season to prevent salt water of the East Sea from encroaching into the Mekong Delta. Worst of all, this life line of the people of Southeast Asia will be turned into a drainpipe to transport the waste from the industrial zones of Yunnan. When that time comes, the Pla Beuks will surely become extinct and the 100 million people living in the Lower Mekong will also suffer.

HOÀNG KHỞI PHONG, *author of*
"Men of One Hundred Yesteryears"
Ngô Thế Vinh the Pulse Taker of the Rivers

I cannot tell what motivated Ngô Thế Vinh, to show such deep concern for the Mekong Delta. The only thing I know was in 1999, with his voluminous work named "Cửu Long Cạn Dòng, Biển Đông Dậy Sóng / The Nine Dragons Drained Dry, East Sea in Turmoil" he voiced his misgivings about the well-being of the Mekong. More than ten years have passed, supposedly his distress signals have so far failed to reach his homeland, he issued an even more passionate call in his next work: "Mekong - The Occluding River". In order to see and hear for himself to write this book, the author traveled several times to the very source of the Mekong. In order to personally observe the dams upstream in Yunnan, he trod his way to the foot of the Manwan Dam whose existence some local people do not even know of or are forbidden to go near. Those dams are and will continue to be hot or sensitive issues for China. Water from the river's current is being diverted into gigantic reservoirs. Consequently, downstream, the area of the Tonle Sap Lake dwindles while in the Mekong Delta, the sea water level at times stands higher than that of the river allowing sea water to flow inland and causing the eco-system of that region to become contaminated by salt.

As early as seven years ago, he had the foresight to call for the establishment of a Department of the Mekong at the University of Cần Thơ. Just recently, in the 08/30/2009 issue of the publication "Tuổi Trẻ Weekend" he renewed that call with his article *"There is a need for a Department of the Mekong at the University of Cần Thơ."*

In my eyes, Ngô Thế Vinh, the writer, is not merely a medical doctor who cares for his patients. More than that, he is a *"pulse taker of rivers"* exploring for ways to mobilize public opinion to rally to the protection of the rivers' natural flow. A case in point is the Mekong that represents the "life line" of over 60 million souls who inhabit her banks. At this very moment, sections of this river are occluding on account of historical circumstances and narrow considerations aiming only for short-term gains.

Prof. ĐẶNG VĂN CHẤT
UCLA and Charles Drew University, Los Angeles, California
Editor, The Vietnamese Mayflowers of 1975

"The Nine Dragons Drained Dry / East Sea in Turmoil" published in 2000, is a well-researched yet prophetic book about the Mekong River. A decade has passed. The impacts of poorly planned and uncoordinated exploitation of the Mekong River are becoming more and more obvious. A physician, a writer, and most importantly a humanist, Dr. Ngô Thế Vinh is sounding again the call for a socially and ecologically responsible management of the resources of the life-giving river. I find in "Mekong - the Occluding River" a skillfully penned book by Dr. Ngô Thế Vinh for all of us to share and enjoy.

PHẠM PHÚ MINH, *former editor 21st Century Magazine, author of "Hanoi in My Eye"*
In May, 2009, I had the opportunity to sail on the Mekong in the Golden Triangle Area. Throughout that journey, looking at the vast and unfamiliar landscapes, the person who was constantly in my thought was Dr. Ngô Thế Vinh. The simple reason was: before I came to this place to have a look at the Mekong's turbulent current, I have read many of his travelogues and studies about this river that stretches from Yunnan all the way to the southern delta in Vietnam.
I came to know Ngô Thế Vinh, not as a childhood friend, but rather through the relationship between a magazine editor and its contributor over the past fifteen years or so. Each time I decided to publish one of his articles or studies, I could tell the depth of his concern for the vicissitudes the Mekong has gone through during the last several decades and their effects on the people and country of Vietnam. He nurtures a profound love for his people and fatherland. This love expresses itself not merely as felt emotions, but also through his intellect, **deliberations,** steady influence which commands international credence, and books published at regular intervals. He did all this for the sole purpose of saving his river and at the same time sparing the livelihood of the Vietnamese living in the Mekong Delta in the face of the selfish behavior of China as this country continues to build a series of dams upstream mindless of the enormous damages it visits upon the countries lying downstream - especially Vietnam.
 When the reactions from the governments downstream turned muted, the voice raised by Ngô Thế Vinh and the "Friends of the Mekong Group" offers the most significant, objective

forum because it is free of any self-serving regional interests. When 21ˢᵗ Century Magazine (Thế Kỷ 21) made public their views, I feel myself totally immersed in the common chorus of intellectuals and people who are fully aware of their responsibility toward their country. In particular, together, we came to an understanding of the workings of today's world in regards to the interactions between large and small nations, between small nations themselves, and moving beyond that, of the unpredictable nature of global climate changes.

During the time we worked with each other, we were fellow travelers walking in close step on the same road. Vinh, myself, all members of the "Friends of the Mekong Group", the Mekong Delta with the Tiền and Hậu Rivers and its gentle inhabitants - we are all inextricably fused into a common body to undergo helplessly the unending agony of watching a man-made disaster unfolding before our eyes. At this time, "Mekong – the Occluding River" has joined the rank of publications, written articles, and research data that appeared in the past on this topic. Together, they represent a relentless, impassioned effort to uphold the right to exist of the ecology and of the human species. Moreover, they will remain a tribute to the struggle of the human mind and soul against the calamities emanating from greed and selfishness.

INDEX

A

ACV / Air Cushion Vehicle 107
Across-the-bridge noodle 11
Adubjadej Bhumibol 53, 89
AK47 & M16 75, 150, 165
Albright, Madeleine 53
Americanization 41, 88
An Giang University iv, 196, 246, 277
Angkor Borei 184
Angkor Dance 165
Ánh Nguyệt / RFI iv, 206, 250, 271, 279, 281
Anlong Gong 136
Anlong Kngah 136
AP / Associated Press 148
APL / Anti Personal Landmines 147
Apsara 114, 165
Aral Lake 146
ASEAN Conference 255, 256
Aurelius, Marcus 180
Attachés for ecology 269

B

Babui 75 mamburao 254
Bach at the pagoda 125
Bách Khoa magazine 108, 109, 115
Baguette bread & coffee 70
Bai minority 28
Bamboo curtain 41
Ban Chiang 95, 96, 97, 181
Ban Koum Dam xiii
Ban Phanom 102
Bangladesh 148
Banna airport 32
Bassac River 129, 132, 133, 136
Bay of Bengal 148
Bellwood, Peter 97
Biển Đông / East Sea iv, v, x, 1, 2, 11, 39, 86, 148, 212, 218, 232, 234, 238, 251, 252, 276, 277, 278, 280, 282, 283, 284
Biosphere Reserve 118, 119, 121
Bird, Jeremy 260, 262
Bird sanctuary 117, 118, 121, 122, 123, 171, 172, 173, 174, 176, 177, 178, 179, 230

Bon Om Tuk / Water & Moon
Festival 129, 159
BOOT / Build Own Operate
Transfer 68
Bow fish 28
Brackish water / nước lợ
225, 251
Brahmanism 180
Brezhnev, Leonid 80
Bronze age 61, 95
Bronze drum 80
Brown highway / xa lộ nâu
156, 203, 210, 241

C

Cà Mau Gas-Electricity-
Fertilizer Complex 208
Cái Răng floating market
205
Cambodge Soir 131
Cần Thơ Bridge xi, 171,
208
Cần Thơ University 266,
270
Cao Xuân Huy 108
Cây Cỏ Việt Nam / Phạm
Hoàng Hộ 175, 176
CCP / Cambodian People's
Party 153
Centre for Southeast Asian
Studies 35

Chà Châu Giang 183
Chainarong Sretthachau 238
Chakri Sirindhorn 65, 90
Chăm Bhrâu 183
Chăm Islam 109, 132, 156,
157, 158, 159, 166, 183, 190,
230
Chao Phraya River 144, 246,
247
Chenla 181, 185
Chennault, Claire 7
Chevasson, Louis 114, 115
China Telecom & China
Mobile 13
Chinese expansionism 259
Chruoy Changvar bridge
132, 159
Clinton, Hillary 255, 256
CNOOC / Chinese National
Offshore Oil Corp 238
Cô Tô Mountain 184
Cổ Chiên River 185
Coconut Monk / Ông Đạo
Dừa 219, 220, 221, 222
Collateral damage 200, 249
Common denominator 89,
212
Con Đường Cái Quan / The
Madarin Route 211
Cormorant 27, 28, 30, 31, 48
Cousteau, J.Y. 190
Cù lao Rồng, Phụng, Quy,

Thới Sơn 58
Cultural village 204
Culture of Peace 194
Culture of War 194
Cửu Long Cạn Dòng, Biển
Đông Dậy Sóng / Nine
Dragons Drained Dry, East
Sea in Turmoil v, x, 1, 234,
276, 278, 280, 282, 283, 284

D

Dachaosan Dam xiii, 81,
237
Dali San Ta 27, 47
Dang Xiao Ping 10, 41
Danube of the East 32, 253
Dây Văng 224
De Lagrée, Doudart 29, 53,
83, 84, 265
DEA / Drug Enforcement
Agency 110
Deforestation 65, 71, 146,
275
Dian Lake 39
Dith Pran 133
Dohamide / Đỗ Hải Minh
108, 109
Domino effect 259
Don Sahong Dam xiii
Dong Feng 13, 21
Dòng Sông Nghẽn Mạch /

Mekong - The Occluding
River iii, v, vii, x, 1, 81, 271,
272, 274, 277, 278, 279, 280,
282, 283, 284, 286
Diversion project 202, 245,
246
Dreams for Independence in
Asia 190
Dry Season 16, 55, 56, 57,
81, 93, 118, 122, 174, 178,
207, 233, 237, 241, 249, 252,
275, 283
Dừa Xiêm / Siamese coconut
225

Đ

Đại Nam Nhất Thống Chí
188
Đặng Văn Chất v, 271, 284
Đỗ Bá Khê 196

E

Earthquake 67, 247, 248
East is Red 15
East Sea / Biển Đông iv, v,
x, 1, 2, 11, 39, 86, 148, 212,
218, 232, 234, 238, 251, 252,
276, 277, 278, 280, 282, 283,
284
Eastern Sarus crane 173,

174, 177, 178, 179
Eco-casino 62
Eco tourism 178, 205
École Francaise d' Extrême Orient 114
Ecology battlefield 269
EDL / Électricité du Laos 67, 68
EIA / Environmental Impact Analysis 241
Environmental Research Station for the Tonle Sap Biosphere 118
Erhai Lake 27, 28, 29, 30, 48
Exotic Dish of the South / Món Lạ Miền Nam 206
Expansionist policy / invasion 140, 141

F

Fairness to the minorities 195
Fait accompli 135, 195
Fall, Bernard 73, 76
Fatal ecological threshold 144
Faulkner, William 264
FCCC / Foreign Correspondents' Club of Cambodia 126, 127, 128, 129, 167
FEER / Far Eastern Economic Review 20, 140
FEMA / Federal Emergency Management Agency 261
Fontereau, Alex De 80
Forecast Mekong 257
Fourth Party Congress 76
French Indochina 64, 112, 115
Friendship Bridge 59, 99, 132, 218
Fulbright scholarship 265, 266
FULRO / Front Unifié de Lutte des Races Opprimées 191
Funan 180, 181, 184, 195
FUNCINPEC / Front Uni National pour un Cambodge Indépendant Neutre Pacifique et Coopératif 153

G

Garnier, Francis 29, 30, 53, 85, 265
General hospital of Cần Thơ 212, 215
General hospital of Tây Đô 215, 216
General hospital of Tiền

Giang 219
Gia Long 157, 185, 186, 189
Global warming 148
Globalization 41, 72, 88, 194
GMS / Greater Mekong Subregion 234, 235, 242
Golden Triangle 38, 107, 234, 285
Gongguoqiao Dam xiii
Green Revolution 197
Greene, Graham 54

H

H5N1 175, 206, 225
Hải Vân pass / Col des Nuages 76
Hainan island incident 11
Haji Yusuf 158
Hamilton-Merritt, Jane 70
Hậu River ferry 218
Hepburn, Audrey 264
Hesse, Hermann 282
High-tech mogul 88
Hill of Poisonous Medicine 161
Hiroshi Hori 247
Historic dam / Manwan 15, 50, 244
Historic hatred 141
Hitchcock, Alfred 122

HIV/AIDS 79, 258
HIV epidemic 111, 145, 158
Hồ Chí Minh 91, 211
Hoàng Khởi Phong v, 108, 271, 283
Hoàng Văn Hoan 91
Hợp Lưu magazine 127, 128
Horticultural Exhibition 18
Houay Ho Dam 68
Hui / Han Islam 18, 19, 26
Hun Sen 111, 123, 125, 137, 138, 151, 152, 153, 154, 158, 162, 216, 239
Hứa Bảo Liên 9
HYV / High Yield Variety Rice / Lúa Thần Nông 176, 197, 250

I

ICF / International Crane Foundation 173, 177
Ieng Sary 138
Imhof, Aviva iii, 271, 272
Industrial zone 39, 142, 143, 145, 151, 247, 283
Intellectual lighthouse 267
Internet 28, 53, 56, 72, 127, 128, 198, 236, 258, 259
Intrusion of salt water 2, 233, 241, 247
IRN / International Rivers

Network   iii, 267, 272
Irrawady dolphin   37, 107
IRRI / International Research Rice Institute   176, 197
Isan Plateau   87, 93
IUCN / International Union for Conservation of Nature   173

J

Jadavpur University   148
January seventh 1979 / Independence Day vs Victory Day over Genocidal regime   138
Jayavarman VII   105, 123, 124, 125, 174, 216, 217
Jiang Zemin   11
JICA / Japan International Cooperation Agency   246, 248
Jinghong Bridge   33, 49
Jinghong Dam   xiii, 32, 34, 37, 81

K

Kang Kek Ieu / Comrade Deuch   161
Kantha Bopha hospital I, II   124
Katmandu of Yunnan   27
Katrina Hurricane   261
Kaysone Phomvihane   73, 74
KCM / Kong Chi Mun   240, 241
Khamsay   52
Khánh Trường   x, 127, 128
Khmer bodies Viet souls   140
Khmer Krom   111, 139, 182
Khmer Rouge   106, 112, 124, 126, 130, 132, 133, 137, 138, 140, 141, 146, 150, 154, 157, 158, 160, 161, 162, 165, 235
Khone waterfall   107, 120
Killing Fields   xi, 105, 106, 125, 132, 138, 144, 155, 235
Kingdom of Champa   111, 156, 182, 190, 191
Kittrie, Nicolas   190
KNP / Khmer National Party   153
Koh Ka Boaak / Silk Island   193
Kok-Ing-Nan   246
Kompong Cham Bridge   151, 152, 170, 209, 218
Kompong Chhnang   130, 144, 145, 147, 149, 153, 156, 163
Kunming Summit Meeting   240
Kuwait of Southeast Asia   3,

51, 69
Kyoto Protocol   148

L

Land of Two Rivers / Tigris & Euphrates   96
Lang Biang Plateau   8
Lancang Jiang   10, 142, 234, 237, 247, 264
Lancang Mekong Mainstream Dams 2010   xiii
Langlois, Walter   114
Lao-Nippon bridge   209, 218
Lao Lum, Lao Theung, Lao Soung   61
Laos_PDR.com   xi, 51, 72
Lao Tzu   276
Lấp Vò district   179
Lat Sua Dam   xiii
Lê Khả Phiêu   20
Lê Văn Duyệt   187
Lê Văn Khôi   183, 192
Lê Xuân Khoa   iii, 271, 278
Liberation day   212
Lima Site 6   71
Liusha River   32
Lon Nol   105, 106, 140, 151, 160
Luang Prabang Dam   xiii
Lycée Sisowath   161

M

Mae Nam Khong / Mekong River   53, 55, 85, 264
Mahosot hospital   78, 79
Mai Thảo   128
Mak Moreth   241
Malacca, straits of   2
Mallalieu, Mark   135
Malleret, Louis   180
Malraux, André   113, 114, 115
Manwan Dam   viii, xi, xiii, 5, 8, 12, 15, 16, 17, 18, 19, 22, 23, 24, 25, 26, 27, 30, 34, 43, 50, 56, 81, 234, 237, 240, 244, 256, 280, 283
Mao Tse Tung   10, 45, 80
Market economy   216
McCarthy, James   90
Mekong / Yunnan Cascades   2, 3, 17, 35, 50, 56, 58, 123, 148, 202, 237, 243, 244, 248, 277, 281
Mekong Interim Committee   235
Mekong River Committee   234, 236, 248, 261
Mekong River Commission / MRC   236, 237, 246, 257, 258, 260, 261, 262, 267, 268, 273

MEREM Group 251
Michelangelo, Buonarroti 115, 116
Mika Toyota 35, 36, 38
Minh Mạng 140, 156, 157, 184, 187, 188, 192
Mini kingdom of Thailand / Xishuangbanna 31
Ministry of Cults and Religious Affairs 158
Misi-ziibi / Great River 263
Mississippi River Commission / MRC iii, 257, 258, 260, 261, 267, 268, 269, 272, 273
Mississippi Valley Division 261
Mittaphap Bridge 86, 87, 94, 97, 98, 151, 209
Mona Lisa 116
Monivong Bridge 132, 133, 136
Mongsong Dam xiii
Monsoon 97, 124, 173
Moon River 264
Mouhot, Henri 81, 82, 83, 84, 93, 102, 116, 117, 264
Mounds of Skulls and Rivers of Bloods 162, 169
Mùa Thổ Dậy / Uprising Season of the Khmer Krom 139, 182
Multi-drug resistance malaria and TB 258
Muslim mosque 18, 132, 158
Mỹ Thuận Barge 210, 217
Mỹ Thuận Bridge xi, 171, 217, 218

N

9/11 Attacks 109, 111, 113, 158
Na Bon village 62, 63, 67
Naga casino 160
Nam Dong Dam 68
Nam Khan River 83, 117
Nam Leuk Dam 68
Nam Ngum Dam xiii, 60, 61, 62, 63, 64, 67, 68, 69, 94, 103, 160
Nam Theun Hinboun Dam 68
Nam Tiến / Vietnamese Southward March 111, 112, 141, 181, 220
Nam Xong River 71
Nanzhao 27
National Route 1A 171, 208, 209, 210
New Moore Island 148
New York Times 133, 190, 238

Ngô Quyền 63
Ngô Thế Vinh iii, iv, v, viii, 234, 256, 269, 270, 272, 273, 274, 276, 277, 278, 279, 280, 281, 282, 283, 284, 285, 286,
Người Việt Daily News 97
Nguyễn Cao Kỳ 221
Nguyễn Cư Trinh 183, 185
Nguyễn Du 212
Nguyễn Đức Hiệp vi, 271, 274
Nguyễn Hiến Lê 115
Nguyễn Kỳ Hùng 109, 196
Nguyễn Tường Bách and I 9
Nguyễn Tường Bách / Viễn Sơn 8, 9, 10
Nguyễn Tường Lân / Thạch Lam 8
Nguyễn Tường Long / Hoàng Đạo 8, 10
Nguyễn Tường Tam / Nhất Linh 7, 10
Nguyễn Văn Hầu 185
Nguyễn Xuân Hoàng iv, 271, 281
Nguyễn Xuân Nhựt x
Nhân Văn Giai Phẩm 211
Nine Gigantic Incense Burners / Cửu Đỉnh 188, 189
Nixon, Richard 41
Nobel Peace Prize 125

Noble Eight Path 220
Nuozhadu Dam xiii

O

Óc Eo 180, 181, 184, 195
ODA / Official Development Assistance 209
Old Royal Route 72, 75, 76
Olympic Stadium 160, 163, 168
Open Door policy 10, 24, 59
Opium tour Sex tour 79, 103
Orchard Civilization / Văn Minh Miệt Vườn 58, 148, 197, 253
Oryza nivara / ON 176
Oryza rufipogon / OR 175
Osamu Shiozaki 209
Osborne, Milton 115, 275
Ottawa Convention 147

P

Pailin 137, 162
Pak Beng Dam xiii
Pak Chom Dam xiii
Pak Lay Dam xiii
Pak Ou 84, 85, 86, 104
Pandemic influenza 258
Pantouxai 100
Paracels & Spratlys

archipelagoes 13, 37, 148, 211, 212
Pathet Lao 52, 56, 63, 74
Pavie, Auguste 84
Permpongsacharoen, Witoon iii, 271 272
Petro China 13
Phạm Duy 211, 212
Phạm Gia Khiêm 256
Phạm Hoàng Hộ 175, 176
Phạm Phan Long iii, 271, 273
Phạm Phú Minh v, 271, 285
Phan Bội Châu 91
Phan Nhật Nam v, 271, 282
Phan Văn Khải 208
Phnom Penh Post 131, 134, 136, 158
Phoenix Island / Cồn Phụng 219, 220, 221, 222, 225
Phong Điền floating market 203, 204
Phong Hóa, Ngày Nay 7
Phrathat Klang Nam 93
Phuket, Thailand 255, 256
Phuket style 268
Phùng Khánh and Phùng Thăng 282
Phùng Trung Ngân 173
Pimay festival 57, 77, 85
Pla Beuk 30, 37, 65, 90, 92, 93, 97, 107, 283

Pla Beuk fish festival 30
Plain of Cà Mau / Đồng Cà Mau 172
Plain of Jars 66, 97, 181
Plain of Reeds / Đồng Tháp Mười 122, 171, 172, 173, 174, 175, 176, 179, 180, 230
Pochentong international Airport 127, 163
Pol Pot 105, 106, 126, 132, 138, 151, 154, 157, 162
Police blotter 131
Polo, Marco 29, 38, 39
Prajna Boat / Thuyền Bát Nhã 219, 222
Prek Toal 118, 119, 121, 123, 163, 167
Prosperity or destruction 272

Q

Quatre Bras / Chatomuk 129, 144, 159, 163
Quing dynasty 11
Quốc ngữ / Romanized Alphabet of Vietnam 8

R

R&D / Research and Development 197

Rạch Miễu Bridge 219, 223, 224, 225
Ramadan 159, 166
Rainforest 34, 61, 145, 146
Rainy season 52, 55, 57, 81, 93, 118, 129, 142, 152, 159, 173, 174, 233, 239, 241, 253
Rebels With a Cause 190
Red River 39, 40, 63, 236
Rénovateur, Le 51, 74
Renovation / Đổi Mới 5, 51, 55, 183, 211, 215
Reservoir-triggered seismicity 248
Rice museum 202
Richner, Beat 123, 124, 125
River of Time 133
RWB / Reporters Without Borders 109

S

S-21 161
Sam Mountain 184, 188
Sambor Dam xiii
Sanakham Dam xiii
Savang Vathana 60
Schanberg, Sydney 133
Schweitzer, Albert 125
Sea World San Diego 233, 269
Search and Destroy 62, 177
Second class citizen 62, 92, 137
Selabam Dam 68
Settathirat Hospital 78
Sexet Dam 68
Shanghai Bridge and Road Construction Company 33
Shawcross, William 146
Shilin 12, 15
Siem Reap Air 164
Sihanouk, Norodom 105, 106, 119, 123, 124, 125, 138, 143, 169
Sinicization 41, 47
Sister-River Partnership xi, 255, 257, 258, 259
Six Clicks City 70, 73
Southern Silk Road 29, 38
Souvanouvong/ Red Prince 52, 74
Spirit of the Mekong 3, 269
STOL / Short Takeoff and Landing 71
Stone, Oliver 225
Sugar palm tree 116, 152, 154, 160, 163
Stung Treng Dam xiii, 156
Sugata Hazra 148
Surin Buriram 154
Sưu dân / hired hand 62, 141, 186, 187
Swain, John 133

Swan, Peter 136
Swamplands 181

T

Tạ Chí Đại Trường 220
Tam Nông Bird Sanctuary 172, 173, 174, 176, 177, 178, 179, 230
Tam Ting Tam Phum / Pak Ou 85
Tây Ba Lô / Western backpackers 55, 64, 71, 79, 81, 84
Tây Sơn 185, 192
Tea-Horse Road 38
TCNP / Tràm Chim National Park 174
TERRA / Towards Ecological Recovery and Regional Alliance iii, 272
Thái Vĩnh Khiêm x
Thaksin Shinawatra 88
That Inhang festival 77
That Luong 60, 77, 101
Thất Sơn / Seven Mountains 184, 190, 222
Thế Kỷ 21 Magazine / 21st Century Magazine v, 109, 286
Theravada 154, 180, 182
Theroux, Paul 76
Thị Trấn Trăm Đường 184
Think tank 266, 267
Thoại Ngọc Hầu 141, 157, 185, 186, 188
Three Less Three More / Ba Giảm Ba Tăng 202
Tibet 1, 5, 13, 21, 38, 86, 107, 190, 262, 264, 274, 276, 277
Tiến Quân Ca / The Forward March Song 211
Tonle Thom River 155, 264
Tonle Sap Lake xiii
Totalitarian state 5, 20, 24
Tour route 32, 42
Trần Đức Lương 111, 134
Trần Huy Bích 6
Trần Ngươn Phiêu iv, 172, 175, 271, 276
Transnational Migration of the Ethnic Minority Akai 35
Trash of Capitalism 63
Trịnh and Nguyễn Shoguns 181, 185, 191
TRT / Thai Rak Thai Party 88
Trương Khánh Tạo 6, 7
Trương Minh Giảng 141
Tú Xương 58, 59
Tuol Sleng / Museum of Genocidal Crime 130, 150, 160, 161, 162, 163, 169

Twain, Mark 264
Tyson, Robert 238

V

Vàm Nao River 187, 189
Văn Cao 211
Vân Đài 80
Vang Pao 52, 70
Vientiane Times 51
Việt Đan barge 219, 224, 225
Vietcong's R & R 222
Viet Ecology Foundation iii, 273
Vietecology.org 234
Vietnam National Mekong Committee 179
Vietnamese Cambodia
Victory monument 132, 137, 138, 139, 169
Vietnamese Islam Association 109
Vĩnh Tế Canal 157, 184, 185, 187, 188, 189
Võ Tòng Xuân iv, 175, 176, 196, 197, 198, 199, 200, 206, 246, 250, 252, 271, 277, 281
Vũ Bằng 206

U

Udon Thani 33, 93, 95
UNDP/ United Nations Development Plan 135
UNEP/ United Nations Environment Programme 262, 267
UNESCO / United Nations Educational, Scientific, and Cutural Organization 77, 80, 95, 119, 121
Uyghurs 276
Upper Mekong 2, 5, 10, 12, 65, 129, 234, 247, 248, 249, 256, 269, 277, 278, 282
USAID / U.S. Agency for International Development 73

W

Walsh, Michael iii, 260, 261, 271, 272
Wat Botum Vaddei 154
Wat Phou festival 77
Water diversion 16, 241, 246
Watershed iii, 245, 270, 272, 273
Wattay International airport 54, 86
WCD / World Commission Dams 262, 267
Wen Jiabao 240

White, Joyce   97
White-winged ducks   123
WHO / World Health Organization   175
Wild West of Southeast Asia   132
World Heritage Site   77, 80, 95
World Horti-Expo Garden   40
World's Red Book   174
World Water Day (03/22/1999)   5
World Wetlands Day (02/20/2004)   171, 177
WTO / World Tourism Organization   77
WTO / World Trade Organization   201
WWF / World Wild Life Fund   173

X

X generation   94, 158
Xayabouri Dam   xiii
Xi'er River   28, 30
Xiaowan Dam   xiii, 81, 237, 247, 256, 263, 277
Xishuangbanna   31, 32, 35, 37

Y

Yangtze River   97, 239, 263
Year Zero   106, 155
Yi minority   14, 32
Yunnan Manwan Power Generating Co.Ltd   23
Yunnan-Myanmar Freeway   38
Yunnan University   9, 10, 45
Yuon   139, 157

CPSIA information can be obtained
at www.ICGtesting.com
Printed in the USA
LVHW041918310820
664662LV00004B/645